THE LAND OF ISRAEL :
CROSS-ROADS OF CIVILIZATIONS

*Fragment of a cultic stand from the 10th century B.C.
found in the City of David, Jerusalem.*

ORIENTALIA LOVANIENSIA
ANALECTA
————19————

THE LAND OF ISRAEL:
CROSS-ROADS OF CIVILIZATIONS

Proceedings of the Conference held in Brussels
from the 3th to the 5th of December 1984
to mark the
Twenty-Fifth Anniversary of the Institute of Archaeology
Queen Elisabeth of Belgium
at the Hebrew University of Jerusalem

In Memory of Prof. Y. Yadin and Prof. Ch. Perelman

EDITED

BY

E. LIPIŃSKI

Published under the auspices
of the Belgian National Fund for Scientific Research,
the 'Ministère de l'Éducation Nationale', the 'Ministerie van Onderwijs',
and the 'Commissariaat-Generaal voor de Internationale Culturele Samenwerking',
with the assistance of the 'Caisse Générale d'Épargne et de Retraite/
Algemene Spaar- en Lijfrentekas' and the 'Banque Nationale de Belgique/
Nationale Bank van België'

UITGEVERIJ PEETERS
LEUVEN
1985

© by Departement Oriëntalistiek
Orientalia Lovaniensia Analecta
Blijde Inkomststraat 21, B-3000 Leuven/Louvain (Belgium)

D/1985/0602/28

ISBN 90-6831-031-3

Printed in Belgium by Orientaliste, Leuven

CONTENTS

INTRODUCTION

In 1984 the Hebrew University of Jerusalem celebrated the 25th anniversary of its Institute of Archaeology, named after Queen Elisabeth of Belgium. The Belgian Friends of the Hebrew University, who founded this Institute and continue to sponsor its publications, decided to commemorate this event by organizing a Belgian-Israeli symposium on an archaeological and historical topic. H. E. Mr Joseph Hadass, the Israeli Ambassador to Belgium, Mr Daniël Coens and Mr André Bertouille, Ministers of National Education, Mr Philippe Moureaux, Minister-President of the Executive of the French-speaking Community, and Mr Karel Poma, Vice-President of the Flemish Executive and Regional Minister of Culture, conferred their high patronage upon this undertaking. The subject chosen for this colloquium was «The Land of Israel : Cross-Roads of Civilizations».

The opening ceremony was held in the building of the Royal Academies, on the 3rd of December 1984. On this occasion, the events leading to the founding of the Institute were recalled, its importance for archaeological, biblical and judaic studies was stressed, and the purpose of the symposium was outlined. The welcoming address and the introduction to the symposium itself were given by the editor of these proceedings. In their turn, Mr J. Hadass, the Israeli Ambassador to Belgium, Mr A. Bertouille, Minister of Education, Prof. B. Mazar, Past President of the Hebrew University, Prof. Y. Shiloh, Head of the Institute of Archaeology Queen Elisabeth of Belgium, and Prof. R. Vander Elst, President of the Belgian Friends of the Hebrew University, addressed the audience and stressed the importance of the symposium as means of expressing the friendship between Belgium and Israel and of demonstrating the scientific and cultural cooperation between the two countries.

The four sessions of the symposium were held at the University Foundation, on the 4th and on the 5th of December. The chairmanship was held by Prof. H. de Meulenaere, Chief Keeper of the Royal Museums of Arts and History, Prof. P. Bonenfant, Prof. J.R. Mertens, and Mr J. Aviram, Honorary Secretary of the Israel Exploration Society, who also held the closing speech.

The topic chosen for the symposium dealt with the Land of Israel from the third millennium B.C. to Hellenistic times. As the title indicates, the symposium had set itself the task of drawing attention to the great variety of cultures which had characterized the Land of the Bible throughout its history and its territory. Hence, the lecturers aimed at bringing to light the multiple and different cultural aspects of the various civilizations which had met and mixed in that country. However, primary written sources referring to the period dealt with are scarse and often fragmentary, above all with regards to more ancient times, while more recent historiographical texts often have a clearly assigned aim which at times «blurs» historical facts. Consequently, archaeological finds are particularly important for the period under consideration, and they play a major role in the reconstruction of the Land of Israel's historical past. This is why a close cooperation between archaeologists, epigraphists and historians is necessary. This need was taken into consideration by the programme of the symposium, which also aimed at encouraging a fruitful exchange of points of view between scholars of various disciplines.

The most ancient period in the history of the Land of Israel, known at the time as Canaan, dates back to the third millennium B.C. Although it is difficult to separate this protohistoric period from the prehistoric one, which immediately preceded it, the Early Bronze Age constitutes a new stage in the evolution of the history of Canaan. Archaeological finds have revealed a high level of urban civilization, traces of which were found at Ai, Arad, Beth-Shean, Beth-Yerah, Tel Yarmouth, and on several other sites. Prof. A. Ben-Tor examined the Canaanite glyptics of this period comparing it to the art of neighbouring countries. It is needless to say, in fact, that the Canaanite urban civilization of the time was an integral part of the contemporary culture of Western Asia, of which Canaan was only a province. This common cultural background, which does not preclude a great variety of regional features, appears even more clearly during the Middle Bronze Age, which goes from the twenty-first to the sixteenth centuries B.C. The recent archaeological finds at Emar, the important harbour city on the Middle Euphrates, gave Prof. A. Finet the opportunity of studying the relationship between this city situated at the junction of important trade routes and the kingdom of Mari, on the one side, and the land of Canaan, on the other.

The end of the Late Bronze Age is characterized by a period of transition marked by the arrival of the Philistines, one of the «Sea Peoples», who contributed to the political destabilization and to the fall of the Syrian and Anatolian states. Threatened by the same invaders, Egypt not only stood against them, but succeeded in obliging the Philistines to settle along the coastal strip in the South of Canaan. Prof.

C. Vandersleyen presented the Egyptian records on the Philistines, while Prof. T. Dothan drew attention to the Philistine and Egyptian settlements in Canaan, basing herself on the archaeological data collected during recent excavations. It was approximately during this same period that the Israelite, Edomite, Moabite, and Ammonite tribes began to penetrate into the cultivated parts of the country, and to settle amid the Cannanite city-states. The origins and prehistory of the tribes of Israel, however, do not seem to be identical with those of the kindred populations who gave origin to the tribe of Judah. Basing himself mainly on biblical sources, Prof. E. Lipiński outlined the contrasts which existed between ancient Israel and Judah, in spite of undeniable analogies. These contrasts were due to different cultural and institutional elements and, partly at least, also to a different geopolitical situation. Up to David's times, in fact, the city-state of Jerusalem separated the Israelite tribes of the North from the clans which gave rise to the tribe of Judah in the South. The recent excavations in the City of David have brought to light both the traces of the ancient Canaanite Jerusalem and those of the capital of David, Solomon and the kings of Judah. Prof. Y. Shiloh presented the important results of these archaeological excavations he personally leads.

Archaeological finds drive us, at times, to conclusions which contrast with biblical texts. Though the specific case of Jerusalem raises no major problem, matters change when we deal with determined biblical accounts concerning the more ancient phases of the Israelite conquest of Canaan, as it is narrated in the first chapters of the book of Joshua. Prof. A. Schoors discussed the always topical problem of the interpretation of archaeological finds in the light of biblical texts of which, sometimes, only the grammatical sense is accepted by all the scholars.

If the Land of Israel was, during the third and second millennia B.C., a meeting point of civilizations which originated mainly from Egypt and Mesopotamia, the emergence of new centres of political power and of cultural expansion was characteristic, instead, of the first millennium B.C. The Persian Achaemenian Empire played a decisive part in the history of the East Mediterranean basin since the sixth century B.C. Prof. P. Salmon dealt with the relationship existing between Persia and Egypt during the period ranging from the sixth to the fourth centuries B.C. In the circumstances, the Land of Israel was not only a country of transit, but also a source of manpower, as well as an important reservoir of military and economic potential. The harbour of Dor, on the Mediterranean coast, played an important role in this respect. Prof. E. Stern, who leads the excavations at Tel Dor, stressed the importance of this city whose archaeological levels dating from the Israelite and the Phoenician periods were brought to light during the most recent seasons of work.

It is generally admitted that the history of the Ancient Near East comes to its end with the fall of the Persian Empire and the advent of Alexander the Great who, in a certain sense, personifies the surge of Western influences and ways of life in the Middle East. However, the process of culture and of thought cannot be made to fit exactly into rigid chronological patterns, and the Hellenistic times in Judah were characterized by a period of resistance set up by the Eastern civilization against Western influence. The latter is symbolized in Jerusalem by the citadel called Akra of the Syrians and built by the Seleucides in the City of David. Prof. L. Dequeker's lecture dealt with the localization and the historical meaning of this important Seleucid stronghold.

The editor of these proceedings wishes to express his thanks to all the lecturers and contributors to these proceedings for their efficient cooperation. His grateful acknowledgement goes to the various authorities and institutions, without whose generous aid the organization of the symposium and the publication of its proceedings would not have been possible: the Belgian National Fund for Scientific Research, the 'Ministère de l'Éducation Nationale', the 'Ministerie van Onderwijs', the 'Commissariaat-Generaal voor de Internationale Culturele Samenwerking', the 'Commissariat Général aux Relations Internationales de la Communauté Française', the 'Algemene Spaar- en Lijfrentekas/Caisse Générale d'Épargne et de Retraite', the 'Nationale Bank van België/ Banque Nationale de Belgique'. The editor wishes to thank also the printer-publisher Mr E. Peeters and his staff, who have done their best to produce in a short time a high quality volume. Finally, his thanks are due to those who assisted him benevolently in preparing the typescripts for publication, correcting the proofs, and compiling the indices.

By common wish of all the participants to the symposium, these proceedings are dedicated to the memory of two great scholars: Prof. Y. Yadin and Prof. Ch. Perelman, who both passed away in 1984 and who, during their lifetime, not only dedicated their energy to found and develop the Institute of Archaeology, but also conceived the idea of organizing this symposium to celebrate the 25th anniversary of its foundation. To them can indeed be applied the words of the Wisdom of Solomon 7,30: *If day gives place to night, against wisdom no evil can prevail.*

E. LIPIŃSKI

ABBREVIATIONS

AAAS	=	*Annales archéologiques arabes syriennes.*
AJA	=	*American Journal of Archaeology.*
ANET	=	J.B. PRITCHARD (ed.), *Ancient Near Eastern Texts relating to the Old Testament*, 3rd ed., Princeton 1969.
AOAT	=	Alter Orient und Altes Testament. Veröffentlichungen zur Kultur und Geschichte des Alten Orients und des Alten Testaments.
ARM(T)	=	*Archives royales de Mari.* (Transcrites et traduites).
BA	=	*Biblical Archaeologist.*
BASOR	=	*Bulletin of the American Schools of Oriental Research.*
BZAW	=	Beihefte zur Zeitschrift für die alttestamentliche Wissenschaft.
CAH I-II	=	*The Cambridge Ancient History* I-II, 3rd ed., Cambridge 1970-75.
CdÉ	=	*Chronique d'Égypte.*
CHJ I	=	W.D. DAVIES-L. FINKELSTEIN (ed.), *The Cambridge History of Judaism I. Introduction. The Persian Period*, Cambridge 1984.
DBS	=	*Dictionnaire de la Bible. Supplément.*
FGH	=	F. JACOBY, *Fragmente der griechischen Historiker.*
FHG	=	C. MÜLLER, *Fragmenta Historicorum Graecorum.*
IEJ	=	*Israel Exploration Journal.*
IG	=	*Inscriptiones Graecae.*
JARCE	=	*Journal of the American Research Center in Egypt.*
JBL	=	*Journal of Biblical Literature.*
JCS	=	*Journal of Cuneiform Studies.*
JJS	=	*Journal of Jewish Studies.*
JNES	=	*Journal of Near Eastern Studies.*
JSS	=	*Journal of Semitic Studies.*
LÄ	=	W. HELCK-E. OTTO (ed.), *Lexikon der Ägyptologie.*
MIFAO	=	Mémoires de l'Institut français d'archéologie orientale.
MVÄG	=	*Mitteilungen der vorderasiatisch(-ägyptischen) Gesellschaft.*
PEFQSt	=	*Palestine Exploration Fund. Quarterly Statement.*
PEQ	=	*Palestine Exploration Quarterly.*
PJ	=	*Palästinajahrbuch des deutschen evangelischen Instituts für Altertumswissenschaft des Heiligen Landes zu Jerusalem.*
RA	=	*Revue d'assyriologie et d'archéologie orientale.*
RB	=	*Revue biblique.*
RLA	=	*Reallexikon der Assyriologie und vorderasiatischen Archäologie.*
SAOC	=	Studies in Ancient Oriental Civilization.
SEL	=	*Studi epigrafici e linguistici sul Vicino Oriente antico.*
SMS	=	Syro-Mesopotamian Studies.
ThWAT	=	J. BOTTERWECK-H. RINGGREN-H.-J. FABRY (ed.), *Theologisches Wörterbuch zum Alten Testament.*

UF	=	*Ugarit-Forschungen.*
VT	=	*Vetus Testamentum.*
Wb	=	A. ERMAN-H. GRAPOW, *Wörterbuch der ägyptischen Sprache,* Leipzig 1925-63.
ZÄS	=	*Zeitschrift für ägyptische Sprache und Altertumskunde.*
ZAW	=	*Zeitschrift für die alttestamentliche Wissenschaft.*
ZDPV	=	*Zeitschrift des deutschen Palästina-Vereins.*

GLYPTIC ART OF EARLY BRONZE AGE PALESTINE
AND ITS FOREIGN RELATIONS*

AMNON BEN-TOR

Unlike the other periods discussed in this symposium, the Early Bronze Age in Palestine is a prehistoric period in which writing was still unknown. We must therefore resort to mute evidence, that of archaeological artifacts, in order to deal with two problems which are important issues in every period, but especially so in a pre-literary period such as ours:

a) What are the cultural borders of Palestine? These borders are not necessarily identical with its political borders; indeed, in a system of City States, the term «political borders» may not be relevant. The question is therefore: Does the eastern Mediterranean coast or the Levant, which includes modern Israel, Lebanon and Syria, constitute one cultural unit?

Here one must of course take into account the time factor: we are dealing with a long period of approximately one thousand years — from the end of the fourth to the end of the third millennium B.C. It is therefore possible that during part of that long period we may witness a greater degree of cultural uniformity in the region, while during another part there may be a division into several smaller cultural units.

b) The second problem is related to our answer to the first one: it should already be stated that in our opinion the Levant does *not* constitute one homogeneous cultural unit. It may perhaps appear, and often be treated as such, mainly because of the apparent cultural uniformity of the two great political centers bordering it on the north and south, Mesopotamia and Egypt, of which at least the former is also far from being culturally homogeneous. The third unit which is crystallizing in recent years, taking its place between the two mentioned above, is that of Ebla. However, this too cannot fill the gap; it does not extend politically or culturally even over the whole of modern Syria, let alone Israel and Lebanon. Our second question is therefore: What is the degree of contact between the cultural subunits of the region, and to

* The figures were drawn by Mika Sarig of the Institute of Archaeology, the Hebrew University, Jerusalem, at a scale of 1:1. The photographs are the work of Z. Radovan, Jerusalem.

what extent can we discern changes in the intensity of those contacts along the above-mentioned time-axis, from the end of the fourth to the end of the third millennium B.C.

A detailed treatment of these two problems is clearly impractical in a single lecture. Its scope is actually the entire archaeology of the region during the period under discussion. We shall therefore limit ourselves, geographically as well as archaeologically.

— Rather than discussing the entire Levant, we shall focus mainly on its southern part, the area of modern Israel, and, as we shall soon see, on its northern part only.

— Rather than discussing the entire archaeological assemblage, architecture, ceramics, etc., we shall limit ourselves to the main sphere of art expression of Early Bronze Age Palestine — that of glyptic art, the carving of stamp and cylinder seals (fig. 1).

Our question should therefore be rephrased as follows: In what way is the glyptic art of Palestine in the third millennium B.C. original, and what — if anything — does it owe to its relations with its neighbours?

Early Bronze I

The cylinder seal was invented in the fourth millennium B.C., somewhere in the region of southern Mesopotamia or Elam, and spread shortly afterwards over the entire ancient Near East[1]. It is difficult at present to be specific about the origin of the second type of seal, the stamp seal, which was perhaps invented independently in several places. Thus, while the appearance of the cylinder seal in the Levant represents in itself an influence from the Mesopotamian cultural sphere, this is not necessarily the case with regard to the stamp seal.

The earliest instance of the use of the stamp seal to impress clay vessels is probably that of the burial-jars of the Eneolithic cemetery of Byblos[2]. Here, rather large stamp seals were impressed in most cases on the joint between the handle and the body of the jar. It is here that we can place the beginning of three phenomena that will have a long subsequent history and are indicative and characteristic of the Levant:

a) The use of the seal to decorate clay vessels, in contrast to its use in Mesopotamia, where its function was to authenticate documents legally or to indicate ownership.

[1] H. FRANKFORT, *Cylinder Seals*, London 1939, p. 1-4.
[2] M. DUNAND, *Byblia Grammata*, Beyrouth 1945, p. 23-58.

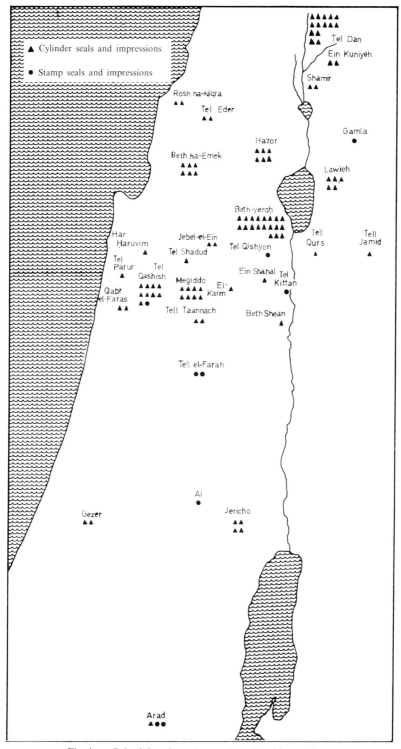

Fig. 1. — Palestinian sites where seals and seal impressions
from the third millennium B.C. have been found.

Fig. 2. — Megiddo Stage V jar with cylinder seal impressions.

b) The manufacture of the seal from a perishable material — wood, which resulted in their rather quick decay; the vast majority of seals is therefore known to us only through their impressions.

c) The carving of the seals in wood resulted in extremely flat and schematic execution of the motifs with few details. Even figurative motifs thus often appear to the unexperienced eye as bordering on the abstract.

The group of Byblian seal impressions is so far unique. One may, however, note a dissemination of the idea southward to Palestine where we find, slightly later, two close parallels to the Byblian material, one cylinder seal impression from Megiddo Stage V (figs. 2-4) and impressions of two stamp seals on a somewhat later jar (EB I/II) from Tell

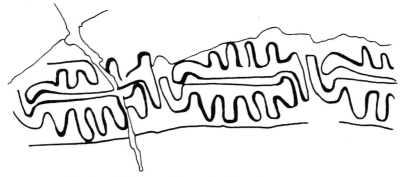

Fig. 3. — Cylinder seal impression from Megiddo Stage V.

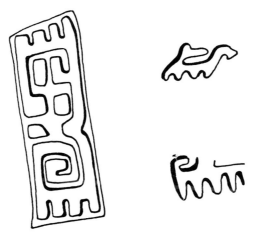

Fig. 4. — Seal impressions from Byblos.

el-Far'ah North (fig. 5)[3]. The resemblance apparent in the motifs, as well as in the flat schematic execution, between the Byblian and Palestinian material is striking. Of special interest is the snake, which appears alternatively with the long horned quadruped on the Tell el-Far'ah jar: this pair is not known at Byblos, but it finds close parallels in North Syria, all the way to Tepe Gawra, and even as far away as Elam (figs. 6-7). How this pair of snake and horned quadruped reached Palestine, directly from the north or from the south via Egypt, is difficult to say.

[3] R.M. ENGBERG-G.M. SHIPTON, in *PEFQSt* 1934, p. 90-93, pl. 6:2-3; R. DE VAUX-M.A. STÈVE, in *RB* 55 (1948) p. 551-552, fig. 3.

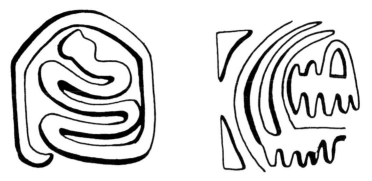

Fig. 5. — Stamp seals impressions from Tell el-Far'ah (N).

Figs. 6-7. — Stamp seals impressions from Tepe Gawra and Tepe Giyan.

Figs. 8-10. — The Gamla stamp seal.

An indication in favour of the Syrian connection is a stone button stamp seal recently discovered at Gamla on the Golan heights, dated, on stylistic grounds, to the late fourth-early third millennium B.C.[4]. A snake and horned quadruped, as well as a figure of a human being with raised arms — a motif to which we shall return later — are portrayed on the Gamla seal (figs. 8-10). This undoubtedly Syrian seal represents the

---

[4] A full discussion of this seal appeared in *Eretz-Israel* 18, Jerusalem 1985, p. 90-93.

southernmost occurrence of this type of seal known so far. These stamp seals, known in large numbers in northern Syria and the ʿAmuq, were never popular in Palestine: the above-mentioned Gamla seal and another one of the gabled type from Tel Qishyon (fig. 11) [5], also a Syrian import,

Fig. 11. — The Tel Qishyon seal.

Figs. 12-13. — The Tel Qashish stamp seal.

[5] C. ARNON-R. AMIRAN, in *Eretz-Israel* 15, Jerusalem 1981, p. 212, pl. 37:3.

are the only examples of this type known so far from Palestine. The local Palestinian variant of stamp seal was the large, rectangular handled type like those found at Tel Kittan in the Jordan valley and Tel Qashish in the Jezreel valley (figs. 12-13). A case for a possible connection with Egypt may be argued on the basis of the unique clay cylinder seal from Gezer (fig. 14). This seal, which I have discussed at length elsewhere[6], should be dated on stylistic grounds to late EB I- early EB II, a period of close relations between Egypt and Palestine. This undoubtedly locally made seal reveals a mixture of Egyptian and local motifs: the shrine is of the Egyptian type, and so are the symbols of the goddess *Neith* and other elements. However, the sacrificed animal portrayed upside-down inside the shrine clearly belongs to the above-mentioned Byblos-Megiddo-Tell el-Far'ah group.

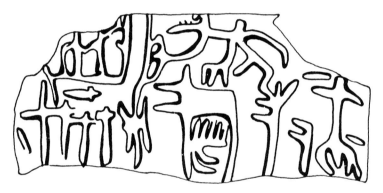

Fig. 14. — The Gezer cylinder seal.

The remainder of the Egyptian glyptic material known from Palestine includes several dozen impressions on bullae discovered in the Egyptian way station of 'En Besor[7] and a cylinder seal discovered in the Sharon plain (fig. 15). In contrast to the above-mentioned Gezer seal, which is of local manufacture though inspired by Egyptian motifs, the 'En Besor and Sharon plain seals are Egyptian artifacts belonging to Egyptian rulers or merchants stationed in southern Palestine, depending on how one tends to interpret the nature of relations between the two countries during the period of the First Egyptian dynasty. The Egyptian seals and

---

[6] A. BEN-TOR, in *Eretz-Israel* 13, Jerusalem 1977, p. 82-85 (in Hebrew); ID., *Cylinder Seals of Third Millennium Palestine* (*BASOR*, Suppl. 22), Cambridge Mass. 1978, p. 11, 83-87. Only this second work will be quoted below.

[7] A.R. SCHULMAN, in *'Atiqot*, English Ser., 11 (1976), p. 16-26; 14 (1980), p. 17-33.

Fig. 15. — The cylinder seal from the Sharon plain and its impression.

impressions disappear as suddenly as they appeared, and had no lasting influence on the local artists. This conclusion is strengthened by the material unearthed at the site of Arad; this important Early Bronze Age Palestinian city maintained close relations with Egypt at the time. Those relations were, however, of an exclusively economic nature. The three seals[8], one cylinder and two stamp seals uncovered at the site, have no relation whatever to contemporary Egyptian art and owe their inspiration to the North, perhaps even as far as the Byblian school of glyptic art. The North rather than the South therefore seems most likely as the source of influence for the above-mentioned Megiddo and Tell el-Far'ah material.

At this point, a step forward has been taken in the glyptic art of Palestine, a step that has so far no parallels elsewhere. At Byblos, the most important center of Syrian glyptic art at the time, the seal type following the above-mentioned stamp seal impressions of Eneolithic Byblos (= Byblos II) consists of the cylinder seals and impressions attributed to the «First Urban Settlement» (= Byblos IV)[9].

The seal impressions of Megiddo Stage V should be viewed as an intermediate phase: the Megiddo impressions portraying a file of animals, or animals in a *tête-bêche* arrangement (figs. 16-19)[10], seemingly represent a transitional stage between those of Byblos II and those of Byblos IV (fig. 20). The absence of such impressions from the glyptic sequence of Byblos is striking and in the present state of knowledge difficult to explain.

Early Bronze II

Little is known about the artistic achievements of the Palestinian seal carvers during the mature EB II period.

---

[8] P. BECK, in R. AMIRAN, *Early Arad*, Jerusalem 1978, p. 53-54, pl. 116: 1-3.

[9] M. DUNAND, *op. cit.* (n. 2), p. 59-70.

[10] R.M. ENGBERG-G.M. SHIPTON, *Notes on the Chalcolithic and Early Bronze Age Pottery of Megiddo* (SAOC 10), Chicago 1934, p. 31-39, figs. 10-11.

Figs. 16-17. — A Megiddo Stage V seal impression.

At Byblos, this is the peak of the manufacture of wooden cylinder seals, attributed to the «First Urban Settlement». The date of their first appearance as well as the duration of their manufacture are somewhat problematic: they should most probably be attributed to mature EB II, but some were perhaps still produced, with certain changes of style, slightly later. Be that as it may, this group, known to us mainly through impressions on jars but also including three ivory seals, is so far restricted in Lebanon to Byblos and is practically unknown from any other site in Syria-Lebanon. A possible exception may be a couple of impressions from central Syria, from the Hama-Ebla region, to which we shall return.

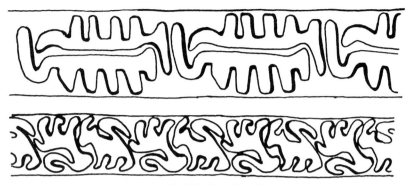

Figs. 18-19. — Megiddo Stage V seals impressions.

Fig. 20. — A Byblos IV seal impression.

Figs. 21-22. — Seal impressions from Jericho.

In Palestine the following occurrences of this type of seal should be noted: three impressions belonging to the same vessel, from Jericho (figs. 21-22), two impressions from Hazor (figs. 23-25), one from Tel Dan, and two ivory seals, one discovered at Beth Shean (fig. 26) and one

A. BEN-TOR

Figs. 23-25. — Seal impressions from Hazor.

Fig. 26. — Ivory seal from Beth Shean and its impression.

in the collections of the École Biblique in Jerusalem[11], of unknown provenience. The resemblance of the Jericho and Hazor material to the Byblian seals and impressions is so close (fig. 27) that one should conclude either that the impressed vessels were imported from Byblos, or that they were locally impressed by imported seals. The École Biblique seal is clearly imported from Byblos, while the origin of the Dan

a) Hazor   c) Jericho   e) Jericho

b) Byblos   d) Byblos   f) Byblos

g) Hazor   h) Byblos

i) École Biblique   j) Byblos

Fig. 27.

[11] P. AMIET, in *RB* 62 (1955), p. 407-408, pl. V: 1.

impression is doubtful. The Beth Shean seal, however, was probably
manufactured locally by an artist who copied Byblian seals: its execution
is substantially inferior to that typical of the seals and impressions
discovered in Byblos.

Early Bronze III

The picture becomes more complex when one reaches EB III.
Palestinian glyptic art attains a climax; the great majority of finds
belongs to that period. The Palestinian seal impressions of the period
can be divided into two groups:

a) *Seals with Geometric Motifs*

The largest number of seal impressions discovered so far in Palestine
belongs to this category[12]: the motifs are rather varied, including
designs such as net, rhomboids, herring-bone, ladder, concentric circles,
spirals, etc. At times one of these is the sole motif depicted on the seal,
while on others a combination of these motifs appears on the same seal
(figs. 28-31).

The center of production of this type of seal must have been located
somewhere in northern Palestine, where most of the impressions were
found.

Impressions of cylinder seals bearing geometric motifs were known
prior to the Ebla excavations mainly from one site in Syria — Hama[13].
For the first time in the long history of contacts in the realm of glyptic
art, Byblos is entirely out of the picture. However, the resemblance
between the geometric Hama seal impressions and the Palestinian ones is
confined to the mere fact that wooden cylinder seals are used to impress
clay vessels. The vessels themselves, as well as the motifs of the seals,
their arrangement and execution, are completely different in the Syrian
seals from those of their Palestinian counterparts. It appears therefore
that these Syrian seals represent a phenomenon characteristic of central
Syria, which may have had extensions to the north as far as Tarsus, but
which was entirely unrelated to what was happening in Palestine at the
time. Two geometric seal impressions from the ʿAmuq do show a

---

[12] A. BEN-TOR, *op. cit.* (n. 6), p. 4-8, 47-52.
[13] H. INGHOLT, *Rapport préliminaire sur sept campagnes de fouilles à Hama en Syrie
(1932-1938)*, Copenhagen 1940, p. 42, pl. XIV: 6 and XV: 1-2.

Figs. 28-29. — Seal impression from Hazor.

resemblance to the Palestinian material, and are so far an isolated find in that region[14].

The glyptic material recently unearthed in Ebla broadens the scope of our discussion[15]. Once again we witness the characteristically central Syrian nature of these objects as regards both the types of impressed vessels and the motifs, which show a close relationship to those previously known from Hama. This resemblance is so marked that it has been shown that one of the Ebla impressions and one of those from Hama were made by the same seal[16]! However, we now find for the first time in the Ebla material one or two impressions that show a close resemblance, in motifs, arrangement and execution, to the Palestinian

[14] R.J. and L.S. BRAIDWOOD, *Excavations in the Plain of Antioch* I (OIP 61), Chicago 1960, p. 296, figs. 235: 7, 236.

[15] S. MAZZONI, in *Akkadica* 37 (1984), p. 18-40.

[16] H. INGHOLT, *op. cit.* (n. 13), pl. XV: 1; S. MAZZONI, *art. cit.* (n. 15), fig. 9.

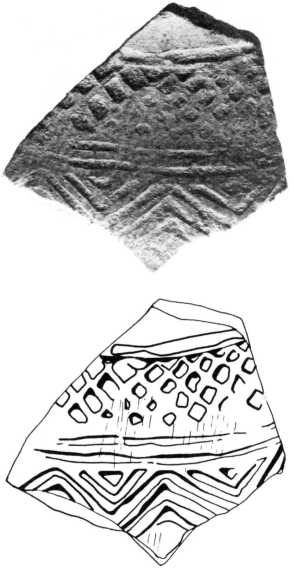

Figs. 30-31. — Seal impression from Tel Dan.

types[17]. It should however be noted that the Syrian impressions, dating from EB IV (= MB I), are somewhat later than the Palestinian ones, which are clearly dateable to EB III.

[17] S. MAZZONI, *art. cit.* (n. 15), fig. 13.

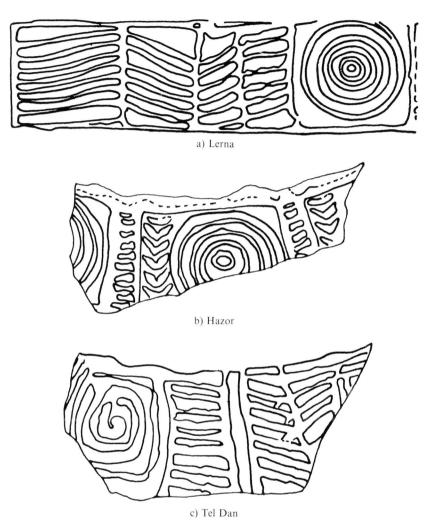

a) Lerna

b) Hazor

c) Tel Dan

Fig. 32. — Seal impressions from Lerna, Hazor and Tel Dan.

A greater degree of similarity exists between the Palestinian geometric cylinder seal impressions and those found in the Argolid, especially those from Lerna[18]. In some cases the seal impressions are so close that the similarity is most probably not accidental (figs. 32-33). However, the absence of comparative material from between the two extremes of Greece and Palestine, especially from sites along the coast of Lebanon-

[18] M.C. HEATH, in *Hesperia* 27 (1958), p. 81-120; 38 (1969), p. 500-521; M. HEATH-WIENCKE, in *Hesperia* 39 (1970), p. 94-110; A. BEN-TOR, *op. cit.* (n. 6), p. 67-69.

a) Tel Qashish

b) Lerna

c) Lerna

Fig. 33. — Seal impressions from Tel Qashish and Lerna.

Syria, causes a severe difficulty in explaining the suggested contact between the glyptic art of Palestine and contemporary Greece. However, one should be cautious in assigning significance to the «silence» of sites in such cases; one should note, for example, that even at such a central site in Palestine as Megiddo, not one seal impression of the type under discussion has been found, while several such impressions are known from Tel Qashish, a small village site a few kilometers to the North.

Some of the EB IV seal impressions bearing figurative motifs, found at Ebla[19], have a certain affinity with the Byblian seals of the «First Urban Settlement» (i.e. EB II). It has been noted that due to stratigraphical difficulties, it is difficult to determine the life span of these seals at Byblos. The Ebla finds indicate some degree of contact between central Syria and the coast, and — more significantly for our subject — one may possibly conclude that the use (and maybe even manufacture) of this type of seal continued at Byblos into EB III-IV. This may perhaps offer an explanation of the impressed jar, undoubtedly originating from somewhere along the coast of Syria/Lebanon, discovered in the Giza cemetery, in an archaeological context of the Fifth Dynasty[20].

b) *Seals with Cult Scenes*[21]

By virtue of the cult scene portrayed on them, these are undoubtedly the most interesting among the early seals of Palestine. Due to the absolute absence of contemporary written documents, it is difficult to determine the exact nature of the cult depicted on these seals. Yet, by common sense and inference, it seems that the scenes portray a cultic dance, related to a fertility cult of the flocks and/or of agriculture. Such a cult was practised throughout the entire region (and beyond), taking its own particular form in different places. The basic components of the scene are the horned quadruped, a well-known fertility symbol, dancing people and a cultic structure. The earliest occurrence of this type of scene in Palestine is on the above-mentioned cylinder seal from Gezer, of late EB I- early EB II date. We are so far unaware of such scenes on later EB II seals; however, the Arad cult stela clearly indicates that fertility rites of this kind were practised in Palestine during that period[22]. At any rate, in EB III we have at our disposal several impressions of

---

[19] S. MAZZONI, *art. cit.* (n. 15), figs. 5, 7, 8, 11.

[20] G.A. REISNER, *A History of the Giza Necropolis* II, Cambridge 1955, p. 75, fig. 98, pl. 53: a-b; A. BEN-TOR, *op. cit.* (n. 6), p. 79.

[21] A. BEN-TOR, *op. cit.* (n. 6), p. 11-13, 57-62, 79-88; ID., in *Levant* 9 (1977), p. 90-100.

[22] R. AMIRAN, in *IEJ* 22 (1972), p. 86-88.

Figs. 34-35. — Seal impression from Rosh ha-Niqra.

cylinder seals from Palestine depicting fertility cult scenes (figs. 34-40), in which people, sometimes disguised as horned animals, are dancing in the vicinity of a structure, most probably representing a shrine.

As with the geometric seals, those cult scene seals represent a group typical of northern Palestine and their distribution is restricted to this region. Nevertheless, this type of seals reveals a certain similarity — whether as a result of direct contact or owing to similarity of subject — to some Syrian seal impressions.

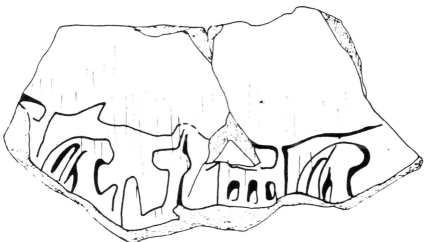

Figs. 36-37. — Seal impression from Tel Dan.

Again our attention is drawn first to central Syria, where a fairly close parallel is known from Hama (fig. 41)[23]. One of the Ebla seal impressions may also belong to this family. One should note again that the Hama/Ebla seals are of EB IV (= MB I), while the Palestinian ones belong to the slightly earlier EB III. One of the Ebla impressions is related to one of the few Byblian impressions which can be clearly dated to late EB III-early EB IV: in both seal impressions one may discern the

[23] H. INGHOLT, *op. cit.* (n. 13), p. 42, pl. XIV: 3.

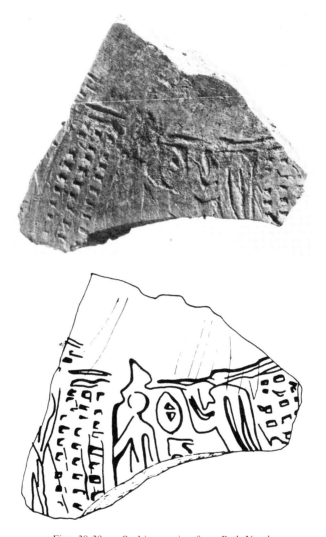

Figs. 38-39. — Seal impression from Beth Yerah.

motif of a human figure with raised arms[24], which forms an integral part of the assemblage of motifs of which the cult scenes are composed.

One may pursue the occurrence of such cult scenes, on which a worshipper disguised as a horned animal is frequently shown dancing in front of a shrine, in the glyptic art of Mesopotamia at Tepe Gawra, Ur

---

[24] S. MAZZONI, *art. cit.* (n. 15), fig. 5; M. DUNAND, *Fouilles de Byblos* II, Paris 1954, p. 201, fig. 209.

Fig. 40. — Seal impression from 'Ein Kuniyeh.

Fig. 41. — Seal impression from Hama.

and even as far away as Elam[25]. The question of whether there was any connection between these and the above-mentioned scenes in Syria-Palestine must remain open for the time being.

Another group of cult scenes on cylinder seals typical of and restricted to northern Syria is the type called by Amiet «Rituel de Haute Syrie»[26]. This group of seal impressions, of which not one example is so far known from outside that region, is the north Syrian counterpart of the fertility cult scene seals of northern Palestine.

[25] A. BEN-TOR, op. cit. (n. 6), p. 79-83.
[26] P. AMIET, La glyptique mésopotamienne archaïque, Paris 1981, p. 167-168, pl. 102: 1351-1354.

Summary

— The practice of impressing cylinder and, to a lesser extent, stamp seals on clay vessels, for whatever purpose, should be regarded as a Syro-Palestinian custom. Seal impressions on pottery discovered in recent years in Mesopotamian sites, on the trade route from South-West Iran to Syria, and in such places as Abu-Dabi and Susa, should most probably be explained as owing to Western inspiration or trade.

— Due to its geographical position as a buffer between Mesopotamia and Palestine, Syrian glyptic art finds are much more numerous as well as varied than those known from Palestine. Seals imported from Mesopotamia, local imitations of such seals and seals inspired by Mesopotamian motifs are completely absent from Palestine, while all three such types are well known from Syria, where they constitute the majority of finds in the realm of glyptic art. Import, imitation and inspiration of Mesopotamian motifs are a typical aspect of the art of Syria beginning as early as the Jemdet Nasr period, through the Early Dynastic to the Akkad and to some extent also the Ur III period.

The impact of the Mesopotamian influence diminishes as one moves further to the south and west of Syria, yet it is still manifest even in sites as far removed (geographically and culturally) from Mesopotamia as Byblos on the Lebanese coast. This phenomenon is entirely absent from the glyptic art of contemporary Palestine. As far as glyptic art is concerned, Palestine constitutes one geographical and cultural unit; the entire phenomenon is confined to the northern part of the country, in the region including the Jezreel valley and north of it (fig. 1). Sporadic finds such as those made at Jericho, a site related to the north via the Jordan valley, or Arad whose art is also clearly northern, fit well into this picture.

— The large wooden stamp seals impressed on the Eneolithic jars at Byblos represent the beginnings of the glyptic art typical of Syria-Lebanon proper, sharing very little with contemporary Mesopotamian glyptics. The southern extension of the Byblian school is represented in Palestine by one impression from Megiddo and two from Tell el-Far'ah North. The latter two perhaps combine Byblian influence on one hand with that of north-east Syria (Tepe Gawra and through it with Elam?) on the other. Other indications for a connection with northern Syria may be found in the Gamla, Kittan and Qishyon stamp seals. The tradition of the Byblian group is carried one step further in Palestine by the rest of the Megiddo Stage V seal impressions.

— Byblos clearly takes the lead again in EB II with the seals attributed to the «First Urban Settlement». These seals were exported to Palestine and imitated there. The connection between the glyptic art of Palestine and that of Byblos, which originated in the previous period, is maintained in EB II. It is as yet unclear whether Byblian influence reached central Syria during the period in question. From the material unearthed so far the answer seems to be negative; however, the new material of EB IV Ebla may possibly forebode surprises.

— The geometric cylinder seals of EB III Palestine constitute a closed and homogeneous group. If there were any connections with northern regions, they were with central Syria and not with Byblos. The same is true for the seals portraying cult scenes, which from a northern Palestinian group on one hand and a northern Syrian group on the other. In between, some seals of central Syria (Hama) may indicate a possible connection with Palestine while others (Ebla) may point out a connection with Byblos.

Connections between central Syria and Palestine during the period under discussion are indicated by other archeological finds such as Khirbet Kerak Ware in EB III and Caliciform Ware in EB IV. It should be pointed out, however, that the network of Palestine's northern connections during these periods is rather complex[2]: relations with central Syria did not replace the relations with the coastal region, including Byblos, but were an addition to them. These relations are perhaps not apparent with regard to glyptic art finds, but are clearly evident in the light of the comparative study of other aspects of the material culture, including various pottery groups other than Khirbet Kerak Ware, such as metallic ware, carved bone handles, crescentic axes and other finds. All are clearly indicative of the cultural relations during this period between Palestine and the coastal region of Syria-Lebanon.

Amnon BEN-TOR
Institute of Archaeology
The Hebrew University
Jerusalem, Israel

LE PORT D'EMAR SUR L'EUPHRATE,
ENTRE LE ROYAUME DE MARI
ET LE PAYS DE CANAAN[1]

A. FINET

Le Royaume de Mari qui s'étend le long du Moyen-Euphrate est déjà prospère vers la moitié du IIIe millénaire comme l'attestent les documents d'Ebla et le confirment les fouilles récentes. Mais, jusqu'à présent, c'est surtout la capitale du XVIIIe siècle, dont l'éclat nous est pour ainsi dire familier à cause des milliers de tablettes cunéiformes qui l'évoquent et le restituent, que nous connaissons le mieux. Pourtant l'apogée n'a pas duré trois quarts de siècle. Se sont alors succédé sur le trône de Yaḫdun-Lim, au règne éclatant, un certain Sūmu-Yamam dont nous savons peu de choses sinon qu'il a dû céder la place au conquérant assyrien Šamši-Adad, représenté à Mari par son fils cadet Yasmaḫ-Addu, puis enfin Zimri-Lim qui, après un long exil, a reconquis pour une quinzaine d'années le royaume et la capitale de son père Yaḫdun-Lim. Vers 1760 Ḫammurabi de Babylone abattait son compétiteur à l'hégémonie et ruinait pour toujours la ville de Mari.

La Mésopotamie est un pays que la nature n'a pas favorisé; elle est dépourvue de bois de construction, de métal et de pierre. À cet égard la région de Mari est un peu moins démunie puisque les falaises calcaires des rives de l'Euphrate l'approvisionnent en pierres de médiocre qualité mais convenables pour les fondations ou soubassements des bâtiments de prestige. Trop friables, elles sont impropres à la mouture du grain. La vallée cultivable est fertile et bien irriguée, mais elle n'est pas très large et ne permet pas une culture céréalière suffisante pour la population. Le plateau steppique ne peut servir que de pâture au petit bétail, et en hiver seulement. Il faut donc que le royaume de Mari fasse venir d'ailleurs les biens dont il est dépourvu ou mal pourvu. Il s'agit de pierres de meules, de bois de charpente ou d'ébénisterie, de métal, de céréales, de légumes,

---

[1] Sur Emar/Imar, voir notamment W.W. HALLO, *The Road to Emar*, dans *JCS* 18 (1964), p. 57-88; H. KLENGEL, *Geschichte Syriens* I, Berlin 1965, p. 275-279; J. MARGUERON, *Quatre campagnes de fouilles à Emar (1972-74). Un bilan provisoire*, dans *Syria* 52 (1975), p. 53-85; M. HELTZER, *Imar*, dans *RLA* V, Berlin-New York 1976-80, p. 65-66.

et — pour les repas d'apparat — de vin, car le royaume de Mari n'est pas propice à la viticulture[2].

Des gens d'Emar venaient régulièrement à Mari. Un texte nous les montre participant à une distribution de viande, avec entre autres des ressortissants de Babylone, de Karkémiš, de Ḥaṣôr et de Haute-Mésopotamie[3]. Des gens d'Emar apportent au palais de Mari des fèves et des pois[4]. D'Emar vient aussi de la fine farine et de la laine[5]. Des gens d'Emar reçoivent des vêtements, un mouton[6]. Leurs marchands vendent des bois aromatiques ou du vin[7].

Ces marchandises sont essentiellement importées du Nord et de l'Ouest, et elles sont le plus souvent acheminées par la voie fluviale, bien qu'il existe aussi un trafic caravanier au départ de Qatna vers Mari, notamment via Palmyre[8]. L'Euphrate est aussi la route principale des marchandises à destination de la Babylonie[9].

Il ne faut cependant pas s'imaginer que par la voie fluviale ou par la voie terrestre le trafic était à sens unique : du Nord-Ouest vers le Sud-Est. Nous savons que Mari était un important marché de l'étain qui y arrivait de l'Elam et d'Ešnunna et qui était redistribué vers Alep, Qatna, Ḥaṣôr, Byblos, Ugarit et même vers Chypre[10]. Il est probable que des bateaux de bitume remontaient l'Euphrate, de la région de Mari au moins jusqu'à Emar[11].

---

[2] Il ne l'est pas aujourd'hui; mais il est possible que la vigne ait été cultivée et du vin fabriqué autrefois dans le district de Terqa situé le long de l'Euphrate, à quelque 70 km en amont de Mari. Voir les remarques de J.-M. DURAND, *ARMT* XXI, p. 104-105 et n. 1-2.

[3] *ARMT* XII, 747,1-9.

[4] *ARMT* XII, 263,24-25.

[5] *ARMT* XI, 14,4-5 (farine *samīdum*); pour la laine, voir S 143, 80 et O. ROUAULT, *Iraq* 39 (1977), p. 148, et *ARMT* XVIII, p. 122.

[6] *ARMT* XXIII, 449,66-68; 258,3.

[7] *ARMT* XXIII, 523; XXI, 210.

[8] La localité d'Alaḫtum était peut-être une oasis disputée entre Alep et Mari, jouant également un rôle d'étape dans ce trafic. Voir B. LAFONT dans *RA* 78 (1984), p. 16. Sur la route du désert, voir G. DOSSIN, *Le royame de Qatna au XVIII siècle avant notre ère*, dans *Recueil Georges Dossin* (Akkadica. Suppl. 1), Louvain 1983, p. 323.

[9] Voir A. FINET, *L'Euphrate, route commerciale de la Mésopotamie*, dans *AAAS* 19 (1969), p. 37-48.

[10] Voir G. DOSSIN, *La route de l'étain en Mésopotamie au temps de Zimri-Lim*, dans *RA* 64 (1970), p. 97-106. L'auteur identifie Layiš — écrit *i-na La*-PI-*ši-im*[ki], A. 1270, 21 — à la biblique Dan, au Nord de Ḥaṣôr; cette hypothèse est acceptée par A. MALAMAT dans *IEJ* 21 (1971), p. 35. Elle est tenue pour peu vraisemblable par P. VILLARD dans *ARMT* XXIII, Paris 1984, p. 466, n. 25; la localité apparaît sous l'orthographe *La-ya-aš* en *ARMT* XXIII, 535, IV, 27.

[11] Voir *ARM* XIV, 27,13-22.

Ainsi se sont développés deux grands ports commerciaux sur
l'Euphrate: Karkémiš au Nord, à la frontière actuelle turco-syrienne,
Emar (ou Imar suivant l'orthographe des documents de Mari) dans la
grande boucle de l'Euphrate, là où le fleuve est le plus proche de la
Méditerranée et de Ḥalab, l'actuelle Alep, la grande métropole du pays
de Yamḥad.

Karkémiš, débouché des produits anatoliens, était la capitale d'un état
indépendant en relations amicales avec le royaume de Mari au temps
des Archives. Les marchandises qui y étaient embarquées vers le Sud
passaient nécessairement par le port d'Emar, à 150 km en aval, compte
tenu des méandres du fleuve. Emar était en outre le point de rupture
de charge pour les produits qui provenaient de la région d'Alep et de
Canaan. C'est là qu'on déchargeait les ânes pour charger les bateaux.
C'est là que des armateurs louaient leurs vaisseaux[12]. C'est là que
des commerçants proposaient leurs marchandises, que se concluaient
d'importants marchés. C'est là sans doute que se côtoyaient diverses
nationalités, réparties vraisemblablement en associations commerciales
groupées en autant de *kârû*, pour reprendre le terme akkadien qui les
désigne. Emar est la clé du pays d'Ebirtum, la région à l'Ouest de la
grande boucle de l'Euphrate — que ce terme géographique soit à tenir
pour un nom propre ou pour un nom commun[13]. La ville devait être
cosmopolite, très peuplée et animée, assez différente de l'Emar hittite
que les fouilles de J. Margueron ont récemment dégagée et qui est
postérieure de cinq siècles à celle que les Archives de Mari nous font
connaître[14]. Il n'empêche que la ville d'Emar restait une importante
métropole de l'Ouest mésopotamien puisqu'une tablette d'époque
médio-babylonienne, c'est-à-dire cassite, la mentionne comme étape
d'un itinéraire imaginaire dont l'aboutissement est Ḥaṣôr[15].

Pour ce qui est du port du XVIIIᵉ siècle, auquel d'ailleurs rêvait peut-
être encore le scribe géographe qui a composé l'itinéraire en question,
rien n'en subsiste aujourd'hui. Le site exact de l'Emar des Archives de

[12] Cf. *ARMT* XIII, 35, 13-21, quelle que soit l'interprétation adoptée (différente dans
A.L. OPPENHEIM, *Letters from Mesopotamia*, Chicago 1967, n° 37, p. 98-99, ou dans
J.-M. DURAND, *M.A.R.I.* 2 [1983], p. 160-163).

[13] Références dans *ARMT* XVI/I, p. 10. On y célébrait un dieu Abba (*ibid.*, p. 253).

[14] Voir J. MARGUERON, *Emar. Une ville sur l'Euphrate*, dans *Archéologia* 176
(1983), p. 20-36. Sur ses relations avec Ugarit, la côte méditerranéenne et Chypre, voir
D. ARNAUD, dans *Syria* 59 (1982), p. 105-107.

[15] A.L. OPPENHEIM, *The Interpretation of Dreams in the Ancient Near East* (Transactions of the American Philosophical Society, n.s., 46/3), Philadelphia 1956, p. 259-260,
268.

Mari n'a pas été retrouvé. Les installations portuaires et la ville basse sont à présent englouties dans le lac Assad. Peut-être d'ailleurs avaient-elles déjà disparu depuis longtemps avant la construction du barrage; la situation d'Emar dans la grande boucle de l'Euphrate l'exposait particulièrement aux caprices du fleuve et à ses crues. Peut-on espérer déceler un jour les vestiges d'une éventuelle ville haute[16]?

Au XVIIIe siècle on y embarquait du grain à destination de Mari, parfois en quantité importante. Un document mentionne l'envoi de 10 bateaux de 36 tonnes d'Emar vers Mari[17] : la location de chaque bateau coûte 250 gr d'argent, ce qui, au tarif du Code de Ḥammurabi, serait énorme pour la seule location d'un bateau «avalant»[18].

Nous savons par les textes que le royaume de Mari était en relations commerciales avec Canaan et la côte: Gubla/Byblos, Ugarit et le royaume de Ḥaṣura/Ḥaṣôr dont nous avons même le nom d'un souverain: Ibni-Addu[19]. Les échanges s'effectuaient totalement ou partiellement par caravanes. Palmyre/Tadmer servait de relais, avec d'autres oasis dont l'importance a été oblitérée dans la suite des temps par la fortune historique de la cité de Zénobie[20].

La voie du désert imposait de se munir de provisions importantes, ne fût-ce qu'en eau. De surcroît, les bédouins pillards la rendaient dangereuse. Même l'oasis de Palmyre n'était pas à l'abri de leurs coups de main[21]. Aussi, quitte à allonger le trajet, les caravanes gagnaient-elles volontiers Emar; le reste du voyage se faisait par terre le long du fleuve, qui assurait au moins le ravitaillement en eau, ou par bateau. Les deux solutions valaient également pour les voyages d'aval vers l'amont. Lorsqu'il est question d'acheminer de Mari vers l'«autre côté du fleuve», sans doute à destination d'Alep, un groupe de jeunes filles, on choisira

---

[16] Peut-être sous les niveaux romains ou byzantins selon M. HELTZER, *RLA* V, p. 65 *b*. Cette hypothèse serait confirmée par un sondage conduit par J. Margueron sous la cité médiévale de Balis; il a fallu creuser sur 8 mètres les niveaux successifs arabe, byzantin et romain pour trouver le sommet de la couche du bronze récent. Les recherches ont été interrompues, faute de temps (J. MARGUERON, *Archéologia* 176, p. 23 *a*; voir n. 14). Il est peu probable qu'elles puissent jamais être reprises.

[17] *ARMT* XIII, 35; voir note 12.

[18] Le Code fixe la location d'un bateau de 18 tonnes à moins de 3 grammes d'argent seulement par jour (§ 277). Si on inclut le coût de la main-d'œuvre dans les 250 grammes d'argent, le voyage d'Emar à Mari ne prendrait que deux jours, ce qui est impensable.

[19] *Ib-ni-*[d]*IM, A. 1270, 22 (= *RA* 64 [1970], p. 98-99). Pour Gubla, Ugarit, Ḥaṣurā, voir les références *s.v.* dans *ARMT* XVI/1.

[20] Comme Našalā/Nazalā/Qariyatein au Sud de Palmyre; voir aussi n. 8.

[21] *ARM* V, 23,14-18.

l'une ou l'autre voie suivant la décision de Zimri-Lim suite aux présages
défavorables[22].

Le gouverneur du district de Mari signale le passage d'un groupe de
voyageurs. Il écrit notamment au roi: «2 messagers babyloniens qui
résident depuis longtemps à Haṣôr, et un homme de Haṣôr, leur guide,
sont passés en direction de Babylone»[23]. D'aussi longs déplacements
n'étaient pas sans aléas. Il y avait bien les voleurs, mais il y avait aussi des
douaniers rapaces qui contrôlaient pour leurs souverains respectifs le
trafic des marchandises et prélevaient de substantielles taxes de passage.
Ces contributions alimentaient pour une bonne part le trésor de Mari.
Les missions royales officielles pouvaient en être dispensées à condition
d'être munies d'un laisser-passer[24]. La «valise diplomatique» n'est pas
seulement d'aujourd'hui.

Il y a tout lieu de supposer que les autres royaumes n'agissaient pas
autrement. La route du désert était plus périlleuse, mais moins coûteuse
à condition que les marchandises arrivent intactes à destination, puisque
les caravanes qui l'empruntaient n'empiétaient pas sur le puissant
royaune de Yamḥad, par ailleurs en mauvais termes avec Qatna au
temps de la domination assyrienne à Mari[25].

La situation politique jouait donc, par les fluctuations éventuelles des
zones d'influence, ou par le jeu des alliances, un rôle important dans les
transactions commerciales et la fixation de l'itinéraire. C'est à dessein
que j'emploie l'expression de «zones d'influence» et que je ne parle pas
de «frontières». En effet, les limites entre les royaumes sont généralement
floues et toujours instables, de même que les alliances sont souvent
sujettes à révision.

Pour l'époque qui nous intéresse, en gros de 1820 à 1760, les textes de
Mari ne nous apprennent rien sur le royaume de Haṣôr, sauf qu'il s'agit
d'une place importante et réputée puisqu'un texte traitant d'envoyés
du pays d'Amurru signale explicitement ceux de Haṣôr — et ceux-là

---

[22] *ARM* II, 134. Si la destination finale est bien Alep, comme semble l'indiquer le nom
du chef de mission Warad-ilišu, le voyage se fait par Emar qui appartient au royaume de
Yamḥad. Un autre itinéraire vers Alep faisait étape à Zalpah — dépendant de Mari — sur
le Baliḥ (voir P. VILLARD, *Un voyage de la Cour de Mari vers l'Ouest?*, dans *ARMT* XXIII,
p. 457-475). M. FALKNER avait proposé de retrouver Zalpah à Tell Hammām et Turkmān;
c'est aussi l'hypothèse de M. VAN LOON qui y fouille aujourd'hui (voir *Akkadica* 27 [1982],
p. 30-45).

[23] *ARM* VI, 78,13-17.

[24] Ainsi une mission du roi de Karkémiš envoyée dans le royaume de Mari au temps
de la domination assyrienne (*ARM* V, 11).

[25] Voir *Recueil Georges Dossin*, p. 326.

seulement — par leur «nationalité»[26]. Nous en savons davantage sur Qatna — près de la ville actuelle de Homs[27]. Au temps de la suprématie assyrienne à Mari, le roi d'Assyrie Šamši-Adad Iᵉʳ avait scellé son alliance avec le riche royaume de Qatna par une union matrimoniale : il avait choisi la fille du roi de Qatna pour son fils cadet, Yasmaḫ-Addu, le vice-roi de Mari, et des expéditions militaires communes étaient envisagées dans les régions occidentales. Ce même Yasmaḫ-Addu entretenait de bonnes relations avec le royaume de Karkémiš dont nous avons signalé l'importance comme centre commercial et port du Haut-Euphrate[28]. Lorsque Zimri-Lim aura reconquis le trône de son père, les rapports continueront d'être bons entre Mari et Karkémiš, au point que Zimri-Lim se propose d'envoyer au roi Aplaḫanda une jeune femme qui est précisément un «morceau de roi» et qu'il avait d'abord destinée à son beau-père[29].

Cependant la ville-clé des échanges entre le Nord et l'Ouest d'une part, le Sud-Est d'autre part, c'est bien l'emporium d'Emar et on s'explique les convoitises dont la ville était l'objet. Apparemment indépendante au temps des roi d'Ebla[30], elle a subi l'assaut des rois de Mari dans la seconde moitié du IIIᵉ millénaire et l'un d'eux l'aurait conquise[31]. Il est probable qu'elle est tombée aux mains de Narām-Sin, le petit-fils de Sargon, lorsqu'il a écrasé Ebla. Nous n'avons plus de mention d'Emar — redevenue indépendante ou tombée dans la mouvance de Ḫalab ou de Qatna — jusqu'au temps de Yaḫdun-Lim, roi de Mari, qui se glorifie d'y avoir remporté une victoire digne d'être commémorée dans les annales de son règne[32]. Ce puissant souverain avait mené ses troupes jusqu'à la

---

[26] C'est une lettre du roi d'Assyrie enjoignant à son fils Yasmaḫ-Addu de faire accompagner par un délégué de Qatna de retour chez lui des messagers de Ḫaṣôr et «des messagers de quatre rois amorrhéens» (lettre A. 2760, encore inédite; *Recueil Georges Dossin*, p. 87-88).

[27] Voir *Le royaume de Qatna au XVIIIᵉ siècle avant notre ère d'après les «archives royales de Mari»*, dans *Recueil Georges Dossin*, p. 320-328.

[28] Voir *Aplaḫanda, roi de Carkémiš*, dans *Recueil Georges Dossin*, p. 293-299; J.D. HAWKINS, *Karkamiš*, dans *RLA* V, p. 426-446, notamment p. 426b-428b.

[29] *ARM* X, p. 139.

[30] A. ARCHI, *Les 17.000 tablettes des Archives Royales*, dans *Histoire et Archéologie. Les dossiers: Ebla* (n° 83, mai 1984), p. 32.

[31] A. ARCHI, *Les tablettes d'Ebla et Mari*, dans *Histoire et Archéologie. Les dossiers: Mari* (N° 80, févier 1984), p. 33. Du même auteur: *I rapporti tra Ebla e Mari*, dans *Studi Eblaiti* 4 (1981), p. 129-166.

[32] MU *Ia-aḫ-du-Li-im da-*PI*-da-am ša I-ma-ar*ki *i-du-ku-ú* = n° 4 dans G. DOSSIN, *Studia Mariana*, Leiden 1950, p. 52.

Méditerranée[33]; c'est sans doute antérieurement qu'il avait remporté la victoire d'Emar puisque le récit de son expédition vers l'Ouest n'y fait pas allusion. Plusieurs noms d'années de son règne le montrent préoccupé d'assurer sa frontière occidentale[34], sans doute déjà contre le roi d'Alep qui avait mis à profit le raid de Yaḫdun-Lim vers la Méditerranée pour appuyer une coalition de ses adversaires[35]. Yaḫdun-Lim les balaie au retour, démantèle les places-fortes, annexe leurs territoires et y installe peut-être déjà des «résidents»[36]. Son royaume est suffisamment puissant pour qu'il mette un frein provisoire aux visées de Šamši-Adad et le contienne au Nord-Est[37].

Une fois son pouvoir solidement assis en Assyrie, Šamši-Adad aura sa revanche; il s'emparera du royaume de Mari[38] qu'il fera gouverner par son fils Yasmaḫ-Addu. Un document de cette époque fait mention d'un voyage du roi à Emar[39]. Sans doute ce port fluvial n'était-il pas encore tombé sous la mouvance d'Alep ou y avait-il provisoirement échappé, étant donné les rapports hostiles entre l'Assyrie et le royaume de Yamḫad. Les relations n'étaient pas meilleures entre Alep et Mari au temps de Yaḫdun-Lim. Cependant, lorsqu'un nouveau souverain montera sur le trône d'Alep, Zimri-Lim, le fils en exil de Yaḫdun-Lim,

---

[33] G. Dossin, L'inscription de fondation de Iaḫdun-Lim, roi de Mari, dans Recueil Georges Dossin, p. 263-292.

[34] Des raisons économiques et militaires l'ont amené à contrôler Emar. Ses noms d'années (voir G. Dossin, Studia Mariana, p. 52) signalent qu'il «a pris Paḫudar» (= n° 1; sans doute dans le secteur occidental de la Haute Mésopotamie, ARMT XVI/1, p. 26, d'après K. Veenhof, Aspects of Old Assyrian Trade, Leiden 1972, p. 241), qu'il «a détruit le rempart de Zalpaḫ» (= n° 3) et «brûlé sa récolte» (ARM VII, 1, 4'-8'; Zalpaḫ est située sur le Baliḫ en amont de Tuttul), peut-être qu'il a pris le pays de Zalmaqum, dans la région de Ḥarrân (cf. Paḫudar; selon une restitution de J.T. Luke, Pastoralism and Politics in the Mari Period, Ann Arbor 1965, p. 227, n. 22).

[35] Il s'agit du roi Sūmu-Epuḫ, prédécesseur de Yarīm-Lim.

[36] Inscr. de fondation de Yaḫdun-Lim, col. III, 3-27. Sur le ḫazannum, «résident» de Samānum et celui de Tuttul du Baliḫ, voir A. Finet, dans Les pouvoirs locaux en Mésopotamie et dans les régions adjacentes, Bruxelles 1982, p. 146-147.

[37] Voir Studia Mariana, p. 52, n° 7: «l'année où [Yaḫdun]-Lim a incendié la moisson du pays de Samsi-Addu», et G. Dossin dans RA 61 (1967), p. 20: MU Ia-aḫ-du-Li-im da-PI-da-PI ša Sa-am-si-ᵈIM i-na bâb Na-ga-ar i-tu-ku-ú (T 199, 8-12), «l'année où Yaḫdun-Lim a infligé une défaite à Samsi-Addu à la porte de Nagar».

[38] Sūmu-Yamam, le successeur de Yaḫdun-Lim, avait entrepris des travaux de défense en fondant ou fortifiant Ḥalabit (au Nord-Ouest de Terqa: Studia Mariana, p. 52, n° 8) et en construisant ou réparant le rempart de Sagarātum sur le cours inférieur du Ḫabur (ibid., p. 53, n° 9; cf. G. Dossin, RA 64 [1970], p. 19). Ces activités défensives visaient peut-être Šamši-Adad (G. Dossin, ibid., p. 19-20), mais elles protégeaient aussi contre une éventuelle incursion du royaume de Yamḫad.

[39] Il s'agit de réception d'huiles «le jour où le roi est parti pour Emar», i-nu-ma šarrum a-na I-ma-arᵏⁱ il-li-ku (ARM VII, 7,7-9).

y trouvera un refuge et une épouse. Lorsqu'il remporte la victoire sur
l'assyrien Yasmaḫ-Addu, vers 1775, et récupère le royaume de Mari, on
peut supposer que c'est avec l'aide de son beau-père[40]. Il ne semble pas
cependant que les relations entre le roi d'Alep et son gendre soient
toujours idylliques. Le royaume de Mari n'est plus ce qu'il était sous le
père de Zimri-Lim[41]. Le port d'Emar est à présent sous la dépendance
d'Alep. Le long de l'Euphrate il n'y a pas de frontière commune entre le
pays de Yamḫad et le royaume de Mari. Des états tampons les séparent,
telle la principauté d'Abattum[42] ou bien celle où règne un certain
Yarīm-Šakim, vassal de Zimri-Lim[43].

Tout ce qui transite par Emar est contrôlé par le roi d'Alep. Mari se
trouve vis-à-vis d'Alep dans la situation où se trouve Babylone à l'égard
de Mari. C'est une dépendance bien lourde pour un souverain ambitieux.
C'est une des raisons de la hargne de Ḫammurabi de Babylone contre
Zimri-Lim; celui-ci devait éprouver des sentiments du même genre envers
son beau-père. D'autant plus que le beau-père n'était pas commode.

Ainsi, en période de disette à Mari, le roi d'Alep s'oppose au départ
vers la capitale de son gendre de bateaux chargés d'orge achetée aux
marchands d'Emar. Zimri-Lim est bien conscient de tout ce qu'il doit à
son beau-père; il comprend d'autant moins que celui qui l'a aidé à
remonter sur le trône, se refuse à le faire quand son peuple souffre de la
disette. «Depuis, écrit-il, que je suis remonté sur mon trône, je ne livre
que combats et batailles, et jamais encore je n'ai pu faire rentrer à mon
pays une récolte dans la paix». En revanche, l'occasion a paru propice au
rusé roi de Babylone, Ḫammurabi, qui a proposé de faire amener à Mari
d'énormes quantités de blé. Zimri-Lim a hautement décliné cette
offre: il ne veut d'aide que de son beau-père[44].

Nous ne savons pas pour quelle raison le roi d'Alep avait retenu les
bateaux à Emar. Serait-ce par représailles? Les différends n'étaient pas

---

[40] Il l'écrit expressément dans A 1153, 8-11 (lettre publiée par G. DOSSIN dans *La
voix de l'opposition en Mésopotamie*, p. 180-183). Cette récupération est attribuée à
l'intervention du dieu Adad, la grande divinité d'Alep, dans A 1121 + A 2731, 49-51 (ces
deux documents ont été reconnus comme jointifs et l'ensemble a été republié par B.
LAFONT, *Le roi de Mari et les prophètes du dieu Adad*, dans *RA* 78 [1984], p. 7-18).

[41] Sur la cession de la localité d'Alaḫtum par Zimri-Lim au pays de Yamḫad, voir
B. LAFONT, *art. cit.*, notamment p. 16-17.

[42] Sur Abattum, voir *ARMT* XVI/1, p. 3, et M.C. ASTOUR, *The Rabbeans* (SMS 2/1),
Malibu 1978, p. 2.

[43] S 115,72-17; aperçu dans M. BIROT, *Syria* 50 (1973), p. 9-10.

[44] Il s'agit de la lettre A 1153 écrite à Yarīm-Lim par son gendre Zimri-Lim. Voir G.
DOSSIN, *Une opposition familiale*, dans *La voix de l'opposition en Mésopotamie*, Bruxelles
1973, p. 179-188.

exceptionnels, ni entre les états, ni entre les marchands. Dans de telles circonstances, le royaume dont les ressortissants sont brimés exerce des mesures de rétorsion contre les citoyens qui relèvent de l'état vexateur. Le cas s'est déjà produit, comme l'atteste une lettre du gouverneur de Sagarātum au roi Zimri-Lim. Les bateaux qui sont allés charger du grain à Emar y sont retenus. Il semble que les sévices qu'on exerce à Mari ou dans le royaume contre un habitant d'Emar ne soient pas étrangers à cette mesure[45]. S'agit-il ici d'une affaire semblable? De même, pour une raison qui n'est pas indiquée, 30 moutons, 50 jarres de vin et même l'épouse du batelier dont la cargaison venait de Karkémiš ont été arrêtés à Tuttul, ville située au confluent du Baliḫ et de l'Euphrate et dépendant de Mari. Aplaḫanda, roi de Karkémiš, signale à Yasmaḫ-Addu, vice-roi de Mari, que cette nouvelle a fait grand bruit à Karkémiš. On y a retenu «de très nombreux marchands» qui devaient descendre à Tuttul ou à Mari. Que Yasmaḫ-Addu intime donc à Tuttul l'ordre de relâcher les biens et la personne détenus pour que cessent les mesures de rétorsion[46]. Une autre lettre des Archives de Mari concerne un différend du même genre, cette fois encore entre Mari et Emar, c'est-à-dire qu'il met en scène le roi Zimri-Lim et son beau-père, le roi d'Alep, qui détient Emar. Il s'agit d'un document très vivant et piquant, dont une première analyse avait été publiée par M. Birot et dont l'étude a été faite par A. Malamat dans le volume d'hommage à Yigaël Yadin et ensuite reprise dans un numéro récent du *Biblical Archaeologist*, suivant une interprétation améliorée dont nous avions discuté de concert[47].

La missive que Zimri-Lim adresse à Alep relate les faits suivants. D'après un message du roi d'Alep à son gendre — message que nous n'avons pas conservé ou pas encore retrouvé — quelqu'un de Mari, sans doute un émissaire de Zimri-Lim, est allé à Ḥaṣôr pour s'approvisionner en or, en argent et en pierres précieuses. Une fois ces biens en sa possession, il se serait enfui auprès de Zimri-Lim. Telle est la version du roi d'Alep. Ce à quoi Zimri-Lim rétorque qu'il n'a jamais rien reçu. La version des faits qu'il présente et qu'il tient vraisemblablement de

---

[45] *ARM* XIV, 33,1′-11′. En tout cas l'irritation d'un ressortissant d'Emar ne se traite pas à la légère (*ARM* XIV, 91).

[46] *ARM* V, 9.

[47] Il s'agit du document 72-16 de la salle 115, présenté par M. BIROT, *Nouvelles découvertes épigraphiques au palais de Mari (salle 115)*, dans *Syria* 50 (1973), p. 10-11. Sa translitération a été publiée et commentée par A. MALAMAT, «*Silver, Gold and Precious Stones from Hazor*». *Trade and Trouble in a New Mari Document*, dans *Essays in honour of Yigael Yadin* = *JJS* 33 (1982), p. 71-79. Sous le même titre l'auteur en a présenté une interprétation revue dans *Biblical Archaeologist* 46 (1983), p. 169-174.

l'intéressé est fort différente. Celui-ci se serait rendu à Ḥaṣôr, il y aurait
acheté or, argent et pierres précieuses. Sur le chemin du retour, dans
la ville d'Emar, il aurait été malmené et dépouillé de tout ce qu'il
transportait, y compris le document scellé attestant qu'il avait bien payé
les marchandises achetées. Totalement démuni, il avait du moins réussi à
sauver sa vie et à gagner Mari, les mains vides.

Selon la version du roi d'Alep, lorsque l'homme de Mari avait quitté
Ḥaṣôr, les gens de Ḥaṣôr avaient saisi les ânes et quiconque venait au
marché de Ḥaṣôr pour y faire commerce. Ces représailles donnent à
penser que si l'homme de Mari avait quitté Ḥaṣôr, c'était subrepticement
et avec des biens précieux qu'il n'avait sans doute pas — ou pas
totalement — payés. Et s'il a bien été assailli à Emar, ce n'est probablement pas par des voleurs, mais par des gens de Ḥaṣôr lancés à sa
poursuite ou bien par des représentants de la ville cananéenne qui
tenaient comptoir à Emar et lui ont fait rendre gorge. J'ai bien
l'impression que ce reçu prétendument volé, et la seule preuve de son
payement, n'a jamais existé. Zimri-Lim, qui y croit, demande à son
beau-père de faire le nécessaire pour récupérer ce qui aurait été dérobé et
se le faire déposer chez lui, au palais d'Alep.

Soyons moins naïfs que le roi de Mari. Certes nous avons vu que le
commerce n'était pas sans aléas et que les caravanes et les simples
messagers voyageant en petits groupes se faisaient souvent agresser,
dépouiller, voire même réduire en esclavage ou assassiner. Les grands
marchés internationaux du XVIIIᵉ siècle avant notre ère devaient être —
comme ils le sont toujours et partout — repaire d'escrocs, de filous et de
margoulins de tout acabit. Il n'était pas difficile d'y perdre et d'y
dépenser de l'argent: prostitués et prostituées n'y étaient pas rares. La
version des faits présentée à son souverain par le citoyen de Mari n'était
pas invraisemblable. Autre chose est pourtant de lui accorder foi.

SUMMARY

The ancient harbour-city of Emar was situated on the great Euphrates bend,
where the river is at its closest to Ḥalab, the North-Syrian metropolis, nowadays
Aleppo, and to the Mediterranean coast. The city flourished from the mid-third
millennium B.C., the time of the Ebla archives, to the 18th century, period the
Mari documents date from, and it remained prosperous throughout the 13th-
12th centuries, when it became a Hittite provincial capital. Though no longer
known under the name of Emar, the city played an important role also during
the Greek, Roman, Byzantine, and Arab periods. Thanks to its geographical
situation, in fact, Emar was the gateway for trade between the West or the
North, on the one side, and the South-East, on the other, at the time when the

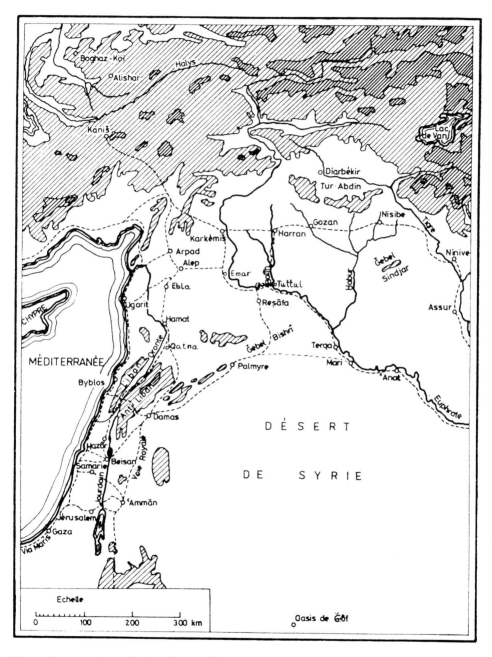

Réseau de routes internationales de Haute-Mésopotamie, de Syrie, de Palestine et de Transjordanie.

river was the main trade route. To be sure, there were caravan tracks leading from the Land of Canaan to the Middle Euphrates, but the presence of plundering beduins made them unsafe, and during the 18th century Emar was the main trans-shipment centre for river and land traffic. The river-harbour of Emar had been in the sphere of influence of Yaḥdun-Lim, king of Mari, but during the reign of his son Zimri-Lim the city belonged to the powerful lord of Ḥalab. In spite of the fact that the latter was Zimri-Lim's father-in-law, the two kings were not always on good terms and the control the king of Ḥalab had on Emar and on her merchants hampered the kingdom of Mari. The cosmopolitan harbour of Emar was not without risks — and also, perhaps, not without attractions — for the merchants from Mari, even when they were the king's envoys. This is proved by the misadventures which occurred to one of them on his way back from Ḥaṣôr, at least if we are to believe what he writes in his letter.

André Finet
Institut de Philologie et d'Histoire Orientales
Université Libre de Bruxelles
Av. Fr. Roosevelt, 50
B-1050 Bruxelles

LE DOSSIER ÉGYPTIEN DES PHILISTINS*

CLAUDE VANDERSLEYEN

Les Philistins sont un peuple auquel se heurtèrent les Israélites lors de leur installation en Canaan, choc illustré par des épisodes fameux de l'histoire biblique: Samson luttera vigoureusement contre eux avant de leur être traîtreusement livré par Dalila (*Juges* 13-16); David, jeune berger, abattra d'une balle de fronde le géant philistin Goliath (*I Sam.* 17). Par la suite, ils perdront leur importance politique, mais donneront leur nom à l'ensemble de la région, la Palestine, terme déjà utilisé par Hérodote.

Le nom des Philistins ne se lisait jadis que dans la Bible, mais l'éclosion de l'égyptologie est venue apporter de nouvelles informations à leur sujet. Ces informations datent exclusivement du règne de Ramsès III (1184-1153) sous lequel une guerre opposa l'armée égyptienne à un groupe de peuples dont faisaient partie les Philistins[1]: elles proviennent de textes accompagnés de figurations, gravés sur les murs du temple de Médinet Habou[2], d'une stèle de Deir el-Medina[3], ainsi que d'un résumé du règne qui, dans le Grand Papyrus Harris[4], fait suite à l'énumération des bienfaits accordés par le roi aux temples d'Égypte.

Quand Champollion visita Médinet Habou en juin 1829, il vit ces scènes, lut le nom des *Pourosato*, sans y reconnaître les Philistins[5]; plus

---

* Je tiens à remercier ici pour leur aide précieuse mon collègue Yves Duhoux, ainsi que mes anciens étudiants Jacques Vanschoonwinkel et Michel Defossez.

[1] Ces peuples sont — outre les Philistins — les *Tjekker*, les *Shekelesh*, les *Denyen* et les *Weshesh*; cf. K. KITCHEN, *Ramesside Inscriptions* (ci-après *KRI*) V, Oxford 1972, p. 40,3 = H.H. NELSON, dans *Medinet Habu* (ci-après *MH*) I, Chicago 1930, pl. 46,18.

[2] Les mentions des Philistins à Médinet Habou sont: *MH* I, pl. 28,51 = *KRI* V, p. 25,5; *MH* I, pl. 29 = *KRI*, p. 28,4; *MH* I, pl. 44 = *KRI*, p. 36,7 et 37,2-3; *MH* I, pl. 46,18 = *KRI*, p. 40,3; *MH* II, pl. 107 = *KRI*, p. 73,9; *MH* II, pl. 118c = *KRI* V, p. 102,8.

[3] Cf. B. PORTER-R. MOSS, *Topographical Bibliography* (ci-après *PM*) I, Oxford 1964, p. 707, stèle C; *KRI* V, p. 91 s.

[4] Pap. Harris I, 76,7. Cf. W. ERICHSEN, *Papyrus Harris I. Hieroglyphische Transkription* (Bibliotheca Aegyptiaca 5), Bruxelles 1933, p. 92,18.

[5] Cf. J.F. CHAMPOLLION, *Lettres et journaux écrits pendant le voyage d'Égypte*, Paris 1833, p. 339 = éd. H. HARTLEBEN, Paris 1909, p. 358-359; dans l'ensemble des peuples de ces scènes, «plusieurs voyageurs ..., ajoute Champollion, ont cru reconnaître des peuples hindous».

Philistins capturés par Ramsès III, d'après un bas-relief de Médinet Habou
(*Medinet Habu* I, pl. 44).

tard, dans son *Dictionnaire égyptien* et dans sa *Grammaire égyptienne*[6], il transcrivit le même nom *Polosté* ou *Pholosté*, mais contrairement à ce qu'affirmait Brugsch en 1858[7] et tous les auteurs postérieurs, Champollion n'a nulle part écrit que ces *Pholosté* étaient les Philistins de la Bible[8]. Quel que soit l'auteur véritable de cette identification[9], celle-ci

[6] Respectivement en 1841, p. 314, et 1836, p. 180; H.R. HALL (cf. ci-après, n. 12) donne respectivement comme références, p. 314,66 et 180,151; je n'ai pas pu deviner ce que signifiait le nombre suivant chaque fois la pagination.

[7] H. BRUGSCH, *Geographische Inschriften altägyptischer Denkmäler*, Leipzig 1857-60, vol. II, p. 86.

[8] Dans l'*Égypte ancienne*, publiée par son frère J.J. CHAMPOLLION-FIGEAC en 1839, p. 156, le terme *Pourosato* est repris tel quel aux *Lettres*, sans autre commentaire. Cf. aussi la note suivante.

[9] À ma connaissance, les plus anciens savants qui ont proposé explicitement l'identification des *Pourousta* avec les Philistins sont William OSBURN Jr., *Ancient Egypt, Her Testimony to the Truth of the Bible* ..., Londres 1846, p. 99, 107, 137, et Edward HINCKS, *An Attempt to ascertain the Number, Names, and Powers of the Letters of the Hieroglyphic or Ancient Egyptian Alphabet*, Dublin 1847, p. 47; ce dernier écrit à propos du nom *Pourousta* : «It is given by Champollion, p. 180, from Medinet Abu (aet. Rameses III), fig. 118, PuRusaTa ... I identify this with the פלשתי, *Plishti*, of 1 Sam. XVII. 4, *et al.*». Ces deux auteurs sont mentionnés par G. MASPERO, *Histoire ancienne des peuples de l'Orient classique* II, Paris 1897, p. 463, n. 1; il écrit : «Les Poulasati ont été rapprochés des Philistins par Champollion dans son dictionnaire hiéroglyphique, puis par les premiers égyptologues

est généralement admise[10]. Toutefois la documentation égyptienne sur les Philistins est réduite et peu explicite; en outre, ce peuple n'était pas seul quand il s'est heurté à Ramsès III: il était associé aux *Tjekker*, aux *Shekelesh*, aux *Denyen* et aux *Weshesh*. Or les *Shekelesh* et les *Denyen* figuraient déjà parmi les peuples que vainquit Merenptah, lors d'une guerre antérieure. Le cas des Philistins a donc été souvent traité globalement avec celui de tous ces peuples. Certains d'entre eux sont dits venir soit des «îles au milieu de *ouadj-our*» (*w'ḏ wr*), soit «de *pa ym*» (*p' ym*), deux termes couramment traduits par «la mer». Ainsi sont nés les «Peuples de la Mer», expression due à Emmanuel de Rougé[11] et aujourd'hui universellement employée[12]. Rougé donna, dès 1867, une orientation ethnique et géographique générale au problème des Philistins en proposant pour les divers peuples combattus par Merenptah et Ramsès III les identifications suivantes, souvent encore acceptées aujourd'hui (sauf les Osques): Sardes (*Sherden*), Sicules (*Shekelesh*), Étrusques (*Touresh*), Achéens (*Akawasha* ou *Ekouesh*), Lyciens (*Lukka*), puis[13] Danéens (*Denyen*), Osques (*Weshesh*), Teucriens (*Tjekker*). La documentation égyptienne promettait donc d'apporter des lumières

anglais Osburn ... Hincks ...» La référence à Champollion étant à écarter, Maspero ne semble connaître personne avant les deux Anglais.

[10] Dans son célèbre *Mémoire sur les attaques dirigées contre l'Égypte par les peuples de la Méditerranée vers le quatorzième siècle avant notre ère*, dont des «Extraits» ont paru dans la *Revue archéologique* de 1867, p. 38-81 (réimprimés dans E. DE ROUGÉ, *Œuvres diverses* IV [Bibliothèque égyptologique 24], Paris 1911, p. 417-458), Emmanuel DE ROUGÉ parle essentiellement des guerres menées par Ramsès II et Merenptah; le nom des Philistins n'y est donc pas mentionné. Une lettre manuscrite de la main de son fils Jacques, datée du 21 février 1884, est insérée dans le tiré-à-part de cet article que possède la Fondation Égyptologique Reine Élisabeth; cette lettre (dont le destinataire n'est pas nommé, mais ce pourrait être Félix Robion, qui s'est intéressé à la question dans le *Recueil de Travaux* 2 [1880], p. 56-59) répond à une demande de renseignements concernant les peuples agresseurs et spécialement les «Pelestas»; Jacques de Rougé écrit que son père était revenu sur ces problèmes dans ses cours au Collège de France, mais qu'il avait renoncé à identifier les «Pelestas». «Mon père énonça timidement à un cours comme simple hypothèse l'assimilation avec les Pélasges ...; mon père voyait de grandes difficultés philologiques à cette assimilation. Depuis cette époque, Mr Chabas a complètement adopté cette manière de voir ... Mr François Lenormant, je crois, avait proposé de reconnaître les Philistins dans ces *Pelesta*, mais personne ne l'a suivi dans cette voie». François Lenormant n'a pu faire une telle suggestion qu'après la publication de Brugsch, qu'il semble pourtant ne pas connaître. Tenait-il l'idée de Charles Lenormant, son père, compagnon de Champollion en Égypte?

[11] E. DE ROUGÉ, *op. cit.* (n. 10), p. 419 = p. 4-5 du tiré à part.

[12] Cf. H.R. HALL, *The Peoples of the Sea. A Chapter of the History of Egyptology*, dans *Recueil Champollion*, Paris 1922, p. 299-300: «There is now nobody to dispute the general probability of the French identifications of the 'Peoples of the Sea'».

[13] Cf. ci-dessus, n. 10.

nouvelles sur l'origine des Philistins. La Bible, elle, les faisait venir de
Kaphtor, nom qu'on rapprocha des *Keftiou* des sources égyptiennes et
de *Kaptara* des sources akkadiennes[14]. Les *Keftiou* sont figurés dans
des tombes égyptiennes, notamment celle de Rekhmiré, sous Touthmosis
III[15], et les découvertes de Cnossos au début du siècle révélèrent des
analogies frappantes entre les personnages figurés dans ces tombes et
ceux des peintures crétoises[16]. Donc le pays des *Keftiou* et Kaphtor
furent identifiés à la Crète et la présence de têtes «philistines» sur le
célèbre disque de Phaestos[17] vint corroborer l'opinion que la Crète avait
été une étape dans les migrations de ce peuple marin.

Cet exposé extrêmement schématique fait illusion; on pourrait croire
que les problèmes sont résolus. Mais depuis un siècle, des voix discordan-
tes ont critiqué les identifications, en ont proposé d'autres, tantôt simples
nuances par rapport aux précédentes, tantôt bouleversements complets.
En fait, la vue d'ensemble du problème des Philistins, telle qu'elle a été
brièvement rappelée, est bâtie sur des rapprochements souvent superfi-
ciels. L'opinion généralement adoptée aujourd'hui concernant l'origine
des Philistins, les Peuples de la Mer et la localisation des *Keftiou*, opinion
répétée malgré les incertitudes et les objections avec une sorte de
résignation au moindre mal, dépend d'une série d'idées préconçues.
L'idée préconçue principale, c'est le mirage égéen.

On aura noté que les premières identifications, celles de Rougé, nous
orientent vers la Grèce et la Méditerranée centrale. Un revirement
d'importance eut lieu quand on se rendit compte que même en acceptant
la plupart de ces identifications, il fallait situer ce moment de l'histoire
des Sardes, Sicules, Étrusques à une époque où ils n'étaient pas encore
installés dans leur territoire définitif; ils se seraient plutôt rendus en
Afrique à partir de leur terroir originel, du côté de l'Asie. Néanmoins,
des expressions comme «les îles», surtout «les îles qui sont au milieu de la
mer», faisaient irrésistiblement penser à la mer Égée d'où seraient venus
ces «Peuples de la Mer», et l'association de la Crète (les *Keftiou*) aux îles
semblait confirmer cette orientation. La plupart des raisonnements ont
été faussés par ce qu'on prenait pour le point de repère géographique le
plus inébranlable de toute la documentation. Or, il n'est pas du tout sûr
que les îles de la mer Égée ou la Crète doivent intervenir ici, et il n'est

[14] Cf. ci-après, p. 46-50.
[15] *PM* I, p. 207, tombe n° 100 (4).
[16] Sur ces questions, cf. les ouvrages de J. VERCOUTTER, cités ci-après, n. 42 et 46.
[17] Cf. ci-après, p. 50.

pas du tout sûr qu'il ait été question d'îles, ni qu'il y ait eu des «Peuples de la Mer».

La majorité des arguments nécessaires pour démontrer tout cela ont été formulés et publiés naguère par Alessandra Nibbi. Malheureusement, une certaine présentation des problémes et parfois trop d'imagination dans la recherche de solutions ont provoqué contre les écrits de Mme Nibbi une réaction totalement négative[18]. Si ses propositions sont souvent surprenantes, trop catégoriques ou même impossibles, la critique qu'elle fait des opinions traditionnelles est généralement pertinente et ses objections méritent d'être prises en considération. Bien des idées ici défendues ont leur point de départ dans ses écrits.

La documentation égyptienne sur les Philistins consiste donc en textes et en images. On peut reconnaître un Philistin à un certain uniforme : une coiffure peut-être faite de plumes, une tunique courte bordée de galons décoratifs et formant à son bord inférieur trois pointes auxquelles pendent des glands. L'identification est donnée par les légendes nommant Philistins les guerriers ainsi accoutrés. Toutefois, les noms des *Tjekker* et des *Denyen* peuvent apparaître aussi à côté de guerriers absolument identiques, et les *Shasou*, dont la coiffure est distincte, portent parfois la même tunique[19]. Il n'est donc pas possible de distinguer par l'image les Philistins, les *Denyen*, les *Tjekker* et peut-être aussi les *Weshesh*, le nom de ceux-ci ne se lisant jamais à côté d'une figuration. Le fait qu'un siècle plus tard, dans l'histoire d'Ounamon[20], les *Tjek(k)er* sont installés à Dor, ville contiguë au territoire philistin, indiquerait qu'il s'agit bien d'une population qui leur était associée. Quand le nom de Philistin n'accompagne pas la figuration de ces guerriers, c'est par convention que j'appellerai ceux-ci Philistins. En se fondant sur ces figurations, on constate que les Philistins ou les peuples apparentés que je viens de citer étaient connus des Égyptiens avant le choc de l'an 8 de Ramsès III. Dans les scènes qui concernent la campagne de ce roi contre les Libyens, en l'an 5, on trouve déjà des Philistins parmi

---

[18] La plupart des auteurs qui ont traité récemment des «Peuples de la Mer» passent complètement sous silence les articles et livres d'Alessandra Nibbi, sauf pour les rejeter en bloc, par exemple W. HELCK, *Die Beziehungen Ägyptens und Vorderasiens zur Ägäis bis ins 7. Jahrhundert v. Chr.*, Darmstadt 1979, p. 299, G. 2 (sans citer l'auteur); ou R. STADELMANN, *Seevölker*, dans *LÄ* V, col. 819, n. 1 *in fine*.

[19] Cf. R. GIVEON, *Les Bédouins Shosou des documents égyptiens*, Leyde 1971, pl. XI-XII et XVIa et b, et W. Max MÜLLER, *Asien und Europa nach altägyptischen Denkmälern*, Leipzig 1893, p. 376-377.

[20] Cf. G. LEFEBVRE, *Romans et contes égyptiens de l'époque pharaonique*, Paris 1949, p. 208.

les soldats égyptiens[21]. Plus étrange est le fait que dans l'inscription où Ramsès III raconte cette campagne de l'an 5 et où il cite les noms de deux chefs libyens qui ont combattu jadis contre Merenptah (à moins qu'ils ne portent seulement les mêmes noms que ceux-là), les hiéroglyphes qui représentent ces deux chefs ont exactement l'aspect de Philistins[22].

Avant d'aborder le problème crucial, c'est-à-dire les sens qu'on peut donner à l'expression *iouou heryou-ib ouadj-our* (*iww ḥryw-ib wȝd-wr*), traduite habituellement par «les îles qui sont au milieu de la mer», et aux termes qu'on traduit généralement par «mer», c'est-à-dire *ouadj-our* (*wȝd-wr*) et *pa ym* (*pȝ ym*), il faut souligner qu'il n'existe aucun texte qui lie les Philistins ou les *Tjekker* à ces deux derniers termes. Parmi les divers peuples groupés sous le nom de «Peuples de la Mer», les *Sherden* sont dits «de *ouadj-our*»[23]; ils sont également appelés «de *pa ym*»[24], comme le sont aussi les *Ekouesh* (*Akawasha*)[25], les *Touresh*[26] et les *Weshesh*[27]. Cette appellation «de *pa ym*» est très individuelle : au bas de la façade de la porte fortifiée précédant le temple de Médinet Habou, sur les six chefs asiatiques qui sont figurés et dont l'inscription est bien visible, seuls les *Sherden* et les *Touresh* sont ainsi qualifiés[28]. Donc sur les cinq peuples impliqués dans la campagne de Ramsès III, deux seulement sont «de *pa ym*»; si on y joint ceux que combattit Merenptah, cela en fait quatre[29]

---

[21] *MH* I, pl. 17. On trouve aussi des Philistins au combat avec les Égyptiens contre les Nubiens (pl. 9), et lors de la guerre contre Amor, il y a des Philistins parmi les prisonniers (*MH* II, pl. 98 et 125), mais la date de ces événements, dans le règne, n'est pas connue.

[22] *MH* I, pl. 28, 47; cf. *KRI* V, p. 24, 47.

[23] Pap. Anastasi II, v° de r° 7-8, cf. A.H. GARDINER, *Late-Egyptian Miscellanies* (Bibliotheca Aegyptiaca 7), Bruxelles 1937, p. 20.

[24] Médinet Habou, façade de la porte fortifiée; *PM* II, p. 483 (13) et Pap. Harris I, 76, 7.

[25] Cf. l'inscription de Merenptah à Karnak, ligne 52 = *KRI* IV, p. 8,9, et la stèle d'Athribis, v° ligne 13 = *KRI* IV, p. 22,8.

[26] Stèle de Deir el-Médina, ligne 8 = *KRI* V, p. 91,11-12; Médinet Habou, *PM* II, p. 483 (13).

[27] Pap. Harris I, 76,7.

[28] Cf. ci-dessus, n. 23, 24 et 26.

[29] Quand des noms de peuples se suivent, par exemple sur la stèle de Deir el-Médina, *KRI* V, p. 91,11-12, *Poursati* et *Toursha em hery-ib pa ym*, il n'y a aucune raison grammaticale de faire porter la dernière expression sur les deux peuples, comme le faisait W. Max MÜLLER, *op. cit.* (n. 19), p. 363. Dans l'inscription de Merenptah à Karnak (ligne 52 = *KRI* IV, p. 8, 9), l'énumération des *Sherden*, *Shekelesh* et *Ekouesh* est suivie de l'expression «les peuples étrangers de *pa ym*» (*nȝ ḫȝstyw n pȝ ym*); on pourrait penser que les *Shekelesh* sont englobés dans l'expression, mais J.H. BREASTED, *Ancient Records of Egypt* III, Chicago 1906, p. 249, n. *a*, s'y oppose à juste titre, soulignant que dans la stèle d'Athribis (ligne 13, *ibid.*, p. 255, § 601) l'expression ne se rapporte manifestement qu'aux *Ekouesh*.

sur neuf. C'est donc par une regrettable généralisation qu'on parle de
«sea-borne forces» ou qu'on écrit: «All these peoples are described as
'of the Sea'»[30]. Philistins et *Tjekker* ne sont donc jamais appelés «de la
mer (*ym*)»[31].

Il se pourrait d'ailleurs qu'*aucun* des peuples impliqués dans ces
guerres ne mérite le nom de «Peuple de la Mer», car le sens de *ouadj-our*
et de *pa ym* est moins sûr qu'on ne le pense. Fondamentalement, *ouadj*
(wȝḏ) est lié à la couleur verte non de la mer, mais de la végétation, et
les figurations d'un génie de fécondité nommé *ouadj-our* l'associent à la
production de nourriture végétale et donc à l'eau douce[32], alors que l'eau
de mer rend la terre stérile. Textes et figurations de *ouadj-our* ont été fort
bien réunis et assez sobrement commentés par A. Nibbi[33]; c'est vrai que
dans la grande majorité des contextes la traduction «mer» ne s'impose
pas, alors que souvent le Delta se présente comme une identification très
plausible. A. Nibbi va trop loin quand elle estime que *ouadj-our* ne
signifie jamais «la mer», mais toujours le Delta[34], mais à part cette
question de proportions, elle a raison. Le mot *ym* non plus ne doit pas se
traduire en toute circonstance par «mer»; il est lui-même emprunté aux
langues sémitiques; en hébreu, le mot peut désigner non seulement la
mer, mais aussi un lac, un étang, ou un fleuve, comme le Nil ou
l'Euphrate[35]; on se souviendra que *pa ym* est le nom du Fayoum, qui en
est directement dérivé[36]. En somme, les peuples dits «de *pa ym*»

[30] R.D. BARNETT, dans *CAH* II/2, Cambridge 1975, p. 366-367.

[31] Ce qui n'interdit évidemment pas la navigation; dans le *Récit d'Ounamon*, à peu
près un siècle plus tard, des navires *Tjekker*, dont le port d'attache était sans doute Dor,
sur la côte palestinienne, menacent le voyageur égyptien, mais il est abusif d'en faire
des pirates: ils ont «une affaire à régler avec lui». G. LEFEBVRE, *op. cit.* (n. 20), p. 219;
Guy BUNNENS, dans *Rivista di Studi Fenici* 6 (1978), p. 13.

[32] Il serait surprenant qu'une libation se fasse à l'eau de mer. Or l'eau de *ouadj-our* est
mentionnée dans une énumération de liquides dont il faut faire une libation, les cinq
premiers étant de l'eau (l'eau de *ouadj-our* est le cinquième) et les sept suivants, du vin; cf.
L. HABACHI, *Tavole d'offerta* ... (Catalogo del Museo Egizio di Torino II/2), Turin 1977,
inv. n° 22053, section E, p. 66 et 75 (E 72b).

[33] A. NIBBI, *The Sea Peoples: A Re-examination of the Egyptian Sources*, Oxford 1972,
p. 11-32, et *The Sea Peoples and Egypt*, Park Ridge (New Jersey) 1975, p. 35-48.

[34] A. NIBBI, *op. cit.* (n. 33), p. 45; il y a au moins — à une époque très tardive, il est vrai
— un passage du Décret de Canope (ligne 9) où l'île de Chypre est désignée en hiéroglyphes
par *iw ... nty m ḥr-ib wȝḏ wr.*

[35] W. GESENIUS-F. BUHL, *Hebräisches und aramäisches Handwörterbuch*, 17e éd.,
Leipzig 1915, p. 302. Un bon exemple de *yam* désignant des étendues d'eau douce se lit dans
Ézéchiel 32,2, où le pharaon est comparé à un crocodile, animal d'eau douce, dans les *lacs*
(*yammîm*, évidemment pas *mers*), se mouvant aussi dans les fleuves et les canaux.

[36] A.H. GARDINER, *Ancient Egyptian Onomastica* I, Oxford 1947, p. 163*, pense aussi
à «lac» pour traduire *ym*.

pouvaient être installés au bord d'un lac, au bord d'un canal ou d'un bras de rivière, pas nécessairement au bord de la mer.

Il est donc probable qu'il ne faille traduire ici ni *ouadj-our*, ni *pa ym* par «mer», ce qui pourrait exclure par le fait même les «îles de la mer Égée». Le mot égyptien *iou (ìw)*, traduit par «île», peut d'ailleurs avoir d'autres sens. Son correspondant hébreu *'î* (אֿ) désigne aussi bien la côte, le rivage, qu'une île et il en va de même en égyptien[37]. En outre, même quand il s'agit bien d'îles, ce n'est pas nécessairement dans la mer. *Iouou heryou-ib* se lit dans la stèle du conquérant koushite Piyé pour désigner expressément la région centrale du Delta, entre l'est et l'ouest. N. Grimal traduit l'expression par «territoires du centre (du Delta)»[38], se référant à un commentaire d'A. Gutbub qui avait rendu la même expression, dans un texte de Kom Ombo, par «régions centrales» ou «régions inter-médiaires»[39], sans même employer le mot «île». Dans un autre passage de la stèle de Piyé, le roi égyptien Tefnakht, qui s'est retiré vers le Nord devant le conquérant koushite, lui fait savoir qu'il fuira devant lui jusqu'à ce qu'il atteigne *iouou nou ouadj-our*, que Grimal traduit ici: «les îles de la mer»[40]. Pourquoi pas les îles du Delta? Tefnakht ne parle pas de fuir jusqu'aux îles de la mer Égée, comme on l'a parfois pensé; il est en fait acculé à la mer. Vandier, sans traduire littéralement le texte, l'interprète sainement en écrivant que Tefnakht «s'était réfugié dans les marais du Delta, près de la mer»[41].

On le voit, *iou* ne désigne pas nécessairement des îles, surtout pas celles de la mer Égée.

Il nous reste à traiter, à propos des Philistins, de la Crète et de son éventuelle identification au terme égyptien *Keftiou* et au terme biblique Kaphtor. Avant que les documents égyptiens et akkadiens ne viennent étoffer le dossier, on avait proposé pour Kaphtor diverses identifica-tions: Crète, Chypre, Cilicie, Syrie du Nord[42]. Brugsch, en 1858, citait

---

[37] Cf. W. SCHENKEL, *Die Bewasserungsrevolution im Alten Ägypten*, Mayence 1978, p. 62-64.

[38] Cf. N. GRIMAL, *La stèle triomphale de Pi('ankh)y au Musée du Caire* (MIFAO 105) Le Caire 1981, p. 36, ligne 19; p. 140, ligne 107; p. 172, ligne 146; cf. p. 38, n. 88; autres références à cette même signification dans D. MEEKS, *Année lexicographique*, s.v. ìw. Ce sens était déjà celui donné par *Wb* I, 47,10.

[39] A. GUTBUB, *Textes fondamentaux de la théologie de Kom Ombo* (Bibl. d'Étude 47), Le Caire 1973, p. 202 (p).

[40] Ligne 129; N. GRIMAL, *op. cit.* (n. 38), p. 160 et 166, n. 493.

[41] E. DRIOTON-J. VANDIER, *L'Égypte*, Paris 1938, p. 543.

[42] Cf. J. VERCOUTTER, *L'Égypte et le monde égéen préhellénique* (Bibl. d'étude 22), Le Caire 1956, p. 33-123, qui donne un état des recherches détaillé et tous les textes

aussi la Pamphylie, et même, d'après un certain Dr Stark, le Delta
égyptien; les Kaphtorîm, ou Philistins, étaient «tantôt considérés —
continue Brugsch — comme indo-germains (comme Pélasges), tantôt
comme sémites, tantôt comme les restes des Égyptiens qui auraient
émigré avec les Hyksos et donc d'origine égyptienne, cette dernière idée
s'accordant à l'information de l'Ancien Testament selon laquelle ils
seraient des descendants de Mizraim (*Gen.* 10,14)»[43]. La découverte
et la fouille des sites crétois au début de ce siècle ont mis en évidence
l'importance de la Crète, et l'analyse par J. Vercoutter des figurations
«crétoises» de certaines tombes égyptiennes a entraîné l'acceptation
quasi unanime de l'équivalence *Keftiou*-Kaphtor-Crète[44]. «La documentation épigraphique égyptienne ne permet pas, par l'étude des seuls
textes, d'arriver à une certitude», écrit Vercoutter[45], et ce sont les
figurations des tombes qui apportent le plus de poids à l'identification,
figurations dont il a donné une analyse approfondie[46]. Encore faut-il
que soit établi le lien entre les figures et les noms géographiques. Les
deux plus anciennes tombes, Senmout (tombe nᵒ 71) et Pouyemré
(nᵒ 39), n'ont pas conservé de noms; celles d'Amenemheb (nᵒ 85), de
Menkheperreseneb (nᵒ 86), d'Aanen (nᵒ 120) mentionnent les *Keftiou*;
celle d'Amenouser (ou Ouseramon) (nᵒ 131) mentionne les «îles» qui
sont au milieu de *ouadj-our*; celle de Rekhmiré (nᵒ 100) fait la jonction
entre ces divers éléments en accompagnant des figurations assez égéennes
(les tombes postérieures ne figurent pas toujours les *Keftiou* ainsi) de la
légende: «princes du pays *Keftiou* et des îles qui sont au milieu de la
mer (*ouadj-our*)»[47]. C'est donc sur la tombe de Rekhmiré que repose
l'identification des Égéens avec les *Keftiou* et l'apparentement de ceux-ci
avec les habitants des «îles». Que les Égyptiens aient eu connaissance de
la civilisation crétoise et de personnages de cette nation ne fait pas de
doute; mais ceux-ci ont pu venir en Égypte dans le cadre d'une visite de
tributaires venus d'ailleurs que de Crète; ces personnages d'allure

égyptiens concernant *Keftiou*; et J. STRANGE, *Caphtor/Keftiu. A New Investigation*, Leyde
1980, p. 11: celui-ci donne, en plus des textes égyptiens, toutes les mentions de Kaphtor,
Kaptara et mots apparentés dans toutes les langues. L'identification à la Crète a été
proposée dès 1722, cf. *ibid.*, p. 118.

[43] H. BRUGSCH, *op. cit.* (n. 7), p. 86.

[44] Cf. W. HELCK, *Ägäis und Ägypten*, dans *LÄ* I, Wiesbaden 1975; ID., *op. cit.* (n. 18),
p. 32-33.

[45] J. VERCOUTTER, *op. cit.* (n. 42), p. XV.

[46] *Ibid.*, p. 185-368; cf. aussi une première présentation de ses recherches dans son *Essai
sur les relations entre Égyptiens et Préhellènes*, Paris 1954, p. 93-140.

[47] J. VERCOUTTER, *op. cit.* (n. 42), p. 57.

égéenne pouvait être au service d'autres nations : qu'on pense aux Gardes suisses du Vatican ou aux troupes coloniales jadis au service de la France ou de l'Angleterre. On reconnaîtra le caractère exceptionnel des figurations, limitées pratiquement à l'époque de Touthmosis III ; l'usage du mot *Keftiou* est beaucoup plus large que cela[48] et il accompagne plus souvent des personnages de type syrien qu'égéen. L'identification des *Keftiou* n'est donc pas pleinement assurée par ces figurations exceptionnelles. On trouve chez Vercoutter lui-même la trace de grandes hésitations : «Seule l'expression composée 'îles qui sont au milieu de la mer' reste unanimement reconnue comme devant s'appliquer au monde égéen»[49], et c'était là, même dans ses recherches sur les figurations, le point d'appui qui lui semblait le plus sûr[50]. Or on a vu que les *iouou heryou-ib ouadj-our* n'étaient probablement pas des îles. Le point d'appui principal de l'identification des *Keftiou* et des Crétois se révèle donc d'une extrême faiblesse.

La découverte d'une liste de sites préhelléniques sur une base de statue d'Amenhotep III a pourtant semblé confirmer que les *Keftiou* étaient les Crétois[51]. Parmi les cinq bases retrouvées dans le temple funéraire du roi, toutes appartenant au côté nord du temple et conservant donc des noms de peuples nordiques, celle qui nous intéresse est seule à avoir conservé la ligne d'inscription qui surmonte l'énumération des noms géographiques. La décoration des faces de ces bases était toujours organisée en deux parties symétriques qui ont comme axe, au centre de la face antérieure, l'emblème de l'Union des deux Égyptes ; à cet emblème étaient liés ici deux prisonniers identiques, d'allure asiatique. Autre caractéristique de cette base : la partie droite est inachevée[52] ; tant la ligne supérieure que la liste de peuples s'arrêtent avant la fin de la face et tout le long côté est nu ; la partie gauche est au contraire complète. Sur la partie droite, on lit : «toutes les terres difficiles d'accès de l'extrême nord de l'Asie» et, en dessous, les deux noms : *Keftiou* et *Tinayou* ; à gauche on lit «toutes les terres des *Fenkhou*, (et) *Khenthennefer*, (sont) sous les pieds de ce dieu parfait, etc. ... ». Sous cette ligne-là, Kitchen, puis Edel ont lu

[48] Depuis la Ire Période Intermédiaire, si les «*Admonitions*» datent bien d'alors, sinon depuis Touthmosis III jusqu'à l'époque ptolémaïque, cf. J. STRANGE, *op. cit.* (n. 42), p. 108-109.

[49] J. VERCOUTTER, *op. cit.* (n. 46), p. 28.

[50] *Ibid.*, p. 109.

[51] E. EDEL, *Die Ortsnamenlisten aus dem Totentempel Amenophis' III.* (Bonner Biblische Beiträge 25), Bonn 1966, p. 33-60.

[52] Cf. la photo publiée par J. STRANGE, *op. cit.* (n. 42), p. 23, fig. 1.

des noms dont l'interprétation a donné Amnisos, Phaestos, Kydonia, Mycènes, Cnossos, etc. ...[53]. La situation réciproque des deux listes et leur contenu ont suggéré à Edel l'idée qu'elles étaient liées; Helck reprenait l'idée et l'exprimait ainsi: «La disposition des inscriptions sur la face antérieure de la base montre que les deux noms *Ka-f-tù* et *Ta-na-ju*, indiqués à droite pour l'observateur, comme désignation de pays, devraient constituer en quelque sorte le titre général pour les noms indiqués à gauche»[54]. Comme ces noms nous orientent vers la Crète et que ni Edel ni Helck ne doutaient que *Keftiou* ne désigne la Crète, il était logique qu'ils cherchent à situer *Tinayou* aussi du côté de la mer Égée. Edel suggérait Rhodes et Helck, rapprochant *Ta-na-ju* des Danaoi, y voyait le Péloponnèse. En fait, la partie droite de l'inscription est assurément inachevée et c'est par hasard qu'elle ne comporte que deux noms; en outre, ce serait un cas unique parmi les nombreuses listes de peuples conservées sur des bases de statue si la partie droite servait en quelque sorte à synthétiser la partie gauche. Il y a en outre cercle vicieux à voir en *Keftiou* une justification des identifications de sites égéens, tout en considérant ensuite que l'identification de ces sites confirme que *Keftiou*, c'est la Crète. Quand à *Tinayou*, sa situation est moins incertaine qu'on ne le dit, à condition d'accepter les documents tels quels. En dehors de la présente liste, le nom est cité deux fois. D'abord dans les Annales de Touthmosis III, en l'an 42[55], quand ce roi a fait une ultime expédition en Asie; parmi les noms conservés, on trouve Tounip et Qadesh que le roi a prises, les princes du Naharina dont elles dépendaient, puis le butin pris au Retenou, la moisson du Djahi, toutes régions bien connues de Syrie, puis après la description d'autres peuples asiatiques dont le nom a disparu (Sethe propose les Hittites [* Htš*] ou *Isy*) vient le tribut de *Tinayou* comportant des vases d'argent en travail *Keftiou*, suivi des tributs africains (*Koush* et *Ouaouat*). L'autre mention se lit dans une liste de peuples sur la base d'une statue, au nord du 10e pylône de Karnak, statue d'Horemheb usurpée par Ramsès II[56]. D'un côté il s'agit de peuples du nord, de l'autre, du sud. La liste des peuples du nord commence par *(San)gar*, la Babylonie; quatre emplacements n'ont pas été gravés; puis viennent les *Meshouesh* et les *Timehy*, probablement

---

[53] E. EDEL, *op. cit.* (n. 51), p. 54.

[54] W. HELCK, *op. cit.* (n. 18), p. 30.

[55] K. SETHE, *Urkunden der 18. Dynastie* (*Urk*. IV 3), Leipzig 1927, p. 733,4-7.

[56] *PM* II, p. 187 (582); J. SIMONS, *Handbook for the Study of Egyptian Topographical Lists relating to Western Asia*, Leyde 1937, liste XII; relevé complet par G. LEGRAIN, dans *ASAE* 14 (1914), p. 40-43.

deux peuples Libyens, donc d'Afrique du nord, *Tekhti* (pour *Tekhsi?*), *Tounip, Qadesh, Qatna, Ougarit, Paher, Tinayou* et *I(r?)sa*. Même si des obscurités subsistent dans cette liste, les noms précédant *Tinayou* sont ici aussi des sites assurés de la Syrie; rien n'autorise à penser à Rhodes ou au Péloponnèse. En conclusion, la base de statue d'Amenhotep III n'apporte absolument pas la preuve que *Keftiou*/Kaphtor est la Crète.

Reste, comme dernier lien éventuel entre les Philistins et la Crète, le fameux disque de Phaestos, cet objet daté archéologiquement entre 1850 et 1600 et où se voit, parmi les 45 signes hiéroglyphiques, une tête dont la coiffure rappelle fort celle des Philistins[57]. L'écart d'un demi-millénaire entre ce document et l'apparition des Philistins en Égypte n'enlève rien à l'intérêt de ce témoignage. Il faut remarquer que cette coiffure n'est pas propre aux Philistins, que le disque est un monument assez isolé, même si certains de ses signes ont été trouvés sur d'autres objets crétois également très anciens; cela ne prouve pas nécessairement que les Philistins ont séjourné en Crète et cela pose surtout le problème de l'origine des Crétois.

Kaphtor, d'où la Bible fait sortir les Philistins, est probablement la patrie des *Keftiou*, mais il n'y a aucune raison d'y voir la Crète. John Strange, dans une étude approfondie sur Kaphtor et *Keftiou*[58], démontre fort bien que la documentation n'oriente nullement vers la Crète, mais vers l'Asie, et plus précisément vers la Syrie. Malheureusement, il mène son étude avec l'idée préconçue — due encore une fois au mirage des «îles de la mer» — que c'était Chypre, et pour arriver à cette conclusion, il doit forcer la documentation[59].

Je pense donc qu'il faut cesser désormais de parler des «Peuples de la Mer». D'ailleurs, les Philistins sont probablement venus en Égypte non comme une première version des Vikings, mais principalement par voie de terre. «Aucun pays ne pouvait tenir devant leurs bras: depuis le Haïti, Kode, Karkemish, Yereth et Yeres»[60], c'est-à-dire les Hittites, la

[57] Sur ce disque, cf. Y. DUHOUX, *Le disque de Phaestos*, Louvain 1977; le signe: p. 57. Sur le rapprochement du signe avec les Philistins, cf. E. MEYER, *Der Diskus von Phaestos und die Philister auf Kreta*, dans *Sitzungsberichte der K. Preuss. Ak. d. Wiss.* 41 (1909), p. 1022-1029.

[58] J. STRANGE, *op. cit.* (n. 42).

[59] *Ibid.*, p. 40-41, de pures spéculations pour faire de Kamaturi Caphtor et Chypre; p. 111, où il évoque judicieusement l'obstacle que constitue le fait que le mot *Keftiou* en hiéroglyphes n'est jamais déterminé par le signe de l'île, mais bien par celui de la triple montagne désignant les pays étrangers, en concluant néanmoins: «This difficulty need not, however, prove Keftiu not to be an island».

[60] *MH* I, pl. 46 = *KRI* V, p. 39,15 - 40,1.

Cilicie Trachée ou bien la région voisine, à l'est du golfe d'Issus ou d'Alexandrette[61], Karkemish sur l'Euphrate, à la même latitude, puis Arzawa sur la côte sud de la Turquie, peut-être la Pamphylie[62], et Alasiya, souvent identifiée à Chypre, sans certitude[63]. Ceci n'est peut-être pas un itinéraire, mais Hatti et Karkemish sont des lieux logés trop loin à l'intérieur des terres pour avoir été détruits par de simples actes de piraterie. En outre, nous ignorons la durée de ces événements dramatiques et s'ils ont précédé immédiatement les guerres de Ramsès III. Après cette énumération de lieux, le texte mentionne l'installation (?) des troupes menaçantes à l'intérieur d'Amor, région côtière au nord du Liban[64]. Quant à la bataille de l'an 8, s'il est certain que l'épisode naval eut lieu dans les bouches du Nil, donc dans le Delta, on a tendance à penser que le combat terrestre eut lieu beaucoup plus loin, en Syrie[65]. Pourtant, le Djahi vers lequel marche le roi pour rencontrer les ennemis commence de l'autre côté du bras oriental du Nil, la branche Pélusiaque[66], et il est fort possible que les deux batailles aient eu lieu à peu près au même endroit et en même temps. Ici se repose la question des «îles» (iouou). Les peuples ennemis étaient-ils déjà dans les «îles» du Delta quand ils «conspiraient»[67]? Ramsès III dit qu'il a «écrasé les Denyen dans leurs îles»[68]; il n'est toutefois jamais allé en mer Égée, ni même à Adana où l'on place parfois aujourd'hui l'habitat des Denyen[69]. Le seul endroit où il ait pu les écraser est aux abords du Delta. Il est bon de se remémorer dans quelles circonstances Merenptah a rencontré, un peu auparavant, la «première vague» de ces envahisseurs; les Libyens avaient reçu l'aide de «peuples du nord venant de tous les pays»: Ekouesh, Teresh, Lukka, Sherden, Shekelesh[70], et l'opinion première est que ces troupes ont dû aborder la côte africaine bien à l'ouest du Delta égyptien[71]. Ce n'est pas sûr. Par les inscriptions mêmes de Merenptah,

[61] Cf. respectivement H. GAUTHIER, Dictionnaire des noms géographiques, Le Caire 1925-31, vol. V, p. 180, et A.H. GARDINER, op. cit. (n. 36) I, p. 134*-136*; cf. la carte, p. 133*.

[62] A.H. GARDINER, op. cit. (n. 36) I, p. 129*-132*.

[63] Cf. J. LECLANT, Le nom de Chypre dans les textes hiéroglyphiques, dans Salamine de Chypre. Histoire et archéologie (CNRS, Colloque n° 578), Paris 1980, p. 131-135.

[64] Cf. A.H. GARDINER, op. cit. (n. 36) I, p. 133* et 136*.

[65] Cf. R. STADELMANN, Die Abwehr der Seevölker unter Ramses III., dans Saeculum 19 (1968), p. 164-166.

[66] Ibid., p. 165.

[67] MH I, pl. 46 = KRI V, p. 39,14.

[68] Pap. Harris I, 76,7, cf. ci-dessus, n. 4.

[69] Cf. E. EDEL, dans Studien zur altägyptischen Kultur 3 (1975), p. 63 s.

[70] Cf. Inscription de Karnak, ligne 1 = KRI IV, p. 2,13-14.

[71] Cf. O. BATES, The Eastern Libyans. An Essay, Londres 1914, p. 19, n. 1.

on apprend que le Delta avait été laissé longuement à l'abandon «à cause des Neuf Arcs», c'est-à-dire, d'une manière générale, les ennemis traditionnels de l'Égypte, et il semble que le roi ne s'est décidé à agir que parce que les Libyens et leurs alliés menaçaient déjà Héliopolis[72]. Il devait leur être loisible de passer à travers le Delta, d'ouest en est ou dans l'autre sens, et les peuples alliés, s'ils venaient de l'est, ont pu faire leur jonction avec les Libyens quelque part dans ce Delta. La victoire de Merenptah sur les Libyens est encore célébrée dans une stèle appelée «stèle d'Israël», parce qu'elle contient la seule mention de ce nom dans toute la documentation égyptienne[73]. La stèle n'ajoute rien à ce qu'on savait déjà sur la guerre contre les Libyens, lit-on chez les historiens[74]. Spiegelberg, premier éditeur et traducteur du document, avait noté qu'il ne contenait pas la moindre mention des alliés nordiques des Libyens[75]. Pourtant, le texte s'achève par une énumération lyrique de tous les vaincus, parmi lesquels les Libyens tiennent peu de place; ce sont: les Neuf Arcs, les Libyens, les Hittites, Gaza (*Pakanan*), Askalon, Gézer, Yénoam, Israël et la Syrie (*Kharou*). Selon Breasted[76], cette finale révèle que Merenptah a fait aussi une campagne, distincte, en Palestine. Pourquoi ne pas voir dans cette énumération les lieux d'où seraient venus les alliés des Libyens?

Une fois oublié le mirage égéen et maritime, des indications éparses, écartées naguère parce qu'elles ne cadraient pas avec les théories généralement acceptées, reprennent un sens. Gardiner[77], étudiant le nom *Tjekker*, n'acceptait pas d'en voir une première mention sous Touthmosis III dans une liste de Karnak[78]; «c'est — écrit-il — sans aucun doute un simple homonyme, car les quelques noms identifiables dans la liste appartiennent tous à la Syrie du nord». C'est en fait un bon argument en faveur de l'identification! Dans le Décret de Canope, le mot *Keftiou* est rendu par «Phénicie»[79]. Je ne suis pas si sûr que la principale raison — selon Maspero — de ne pas accepter cette identification, «c'est que les scribes égyptiens de l'âge ptolémaïque l'ont faite et que ces

---

[72] Karnak, lignes 8, 9 et 6 = *KRI* IV, p. 3, 6-10 et 4-5.
[73] Stèle Caire CG 34025, v°; cf. *KRI* IV, p. 12 ss.
[74] Cf. J.H. BREASTED, *Ancient Records* III, Chicago 1906, § 602; R.O. FAULKNER, dans *CAH* II/2, Cambridge 1975, p. 233.
[75] J.H. BREASTED, *op. cit.*, § 602.
[76] *Ibid.*, § 606.
[77] A.H. GARDINER, *op. cit.* (n. 36) I, p. 200*.
[78] K. SETHE, *Urk.* IV/3 (n. 55), p. 788, 136.
[79] Lignes 9-10; K. SETHE, *Hieroglyphische Urkunden der griechisch-römischen Zeit* (*Urk.* II), Leipzig 1904-16, p. 131; cf. J. VERCOUTTER, *op. cit.* (n. 42), p. 100.

Égyptiens ne savaient ce qu'ils faisaient»[80]. Il faut se souvenir que pour l'époque classique, la Phénicie commençait à l'extrême nord de la côte syrienne, au golfe d'Alexandrette[81].

En conclusion, le dossier égyptien des Philistins n'est pas aussi clair qu'on le voudrait. Certaines certitudes se dégagent pourtant. Les Philistins et leurs associés dans les guerres contre l'Égypte ne sont originaires ni de la Crète, ni des îles de la mer Égée, ni même des côtes égéennes de l'Asie Mineure, mais plutôt de la région sud de cette partie de l'Asie, aux alentours du golfe d'Alexandrette, peut-être même à l'intérieur des terres[82]. C'est de ce côté, je pense, qu'il faut chercher les *Keftiou* et Kaphtor, et donc l'origine des Philistins.

Dans un si vaste sujet, il aurait été démesuré et en partie inutile de reprendre point par point tout ce qui a été dit, de peser toutes les hypothèses et de réfuter toutes les objections. Mais on peut espérer qu'après lecture de ces lignes, ce qui a été écrit ailleurs sur ce sujet sera apprécié autrement.

SUMMARY

The Egyptian documents supplying us with information concerning the Philistines date from the reign of Ramses III (1184-1153). Besides the Philistines, other populations, some of them related to them and others not, assailed Egypt in the time of this monarch or at a slightly earlier period, during Merenptah's reign (1224-1204). Some of these peoples, though not the Philistines, are said to be «from *wꜣḏ-wr*» or «from *pꜣ ym*», expressions usually translated by «from the sea». Thus, the problem as a whole has become that of the «Sea Peoples». However, of the nine peoples concerned by these wars, only four were actually defined as coming «from *wꜣḏ-wr*» or «from *pꜣ ym*». Furthermore, these

---

[80] Cité par J. VERCOUTTER, *op. cit.* (n. 46), p. 37.

[81] HÉRODOTE IV, 38. Le fait que dans *Amos* 9,7, les Septante traduisent Kaphtor par Cappadoce est peut-être plus significatif qu'on ne le pense, car cette région est contiguë aux territoires que les peuples combattus par Ramsès III ont dévastés (cf. sur ce texte, J. STRANGE, *op. cit.* [n. 42], p. 75-76).

[82] En somme, c'est presque la solution proposée par W. Max MÜLLER, *Asien und Europa*, en 1893; cf. la carte à la fin de son ouvrage. On verra aussi à quel point tout ceci correspond à ce qu'on sait de Mopsos (cf. R.D. BARNETT, dans *CAH* II/2, Cambridge 1975, p. 363-366).

Outre les ouvrages cités dans les notes, ont été aussi consultés :

P. MERTENS, *Les Peuples de la Mer*, dans *CdÉ* 35 (1960), p. 65-88.

K. A. KITCHEN, *The Philistines*, dans *Peoples of Old Testament Times* (éd. D. J. WISEMAN), Oxford 1973, p. 53-78.

M. GÖRG, *Philister*, dans *LÄ* IV, Wiesbaden 1982, col. 1029-1030.

T. DOTHAN, *The Philistines and their Material Culture*, Jérusalem 1982.

expressions seem to be linked more often to vegetation and sweet water than to sea water, and it seems clear that the term «Sea Peoples» has to be abandoned. Some will object to this, basing themselves on the expression *iww ḥryw-ib wꜣḏ-wr*, usually translated by «islands situated in the middle of the sea», where some of the Sea Peoples are said to have come from. Indeed, it is this expression which supported the persistent idea that the «Sea Peoples» came from the Aegean islands or at least from an East-Mediterranean island. Now, these terms are misleading, not only because *wꜣḏ-wr* and *pꜣ ym*, quite likely, do not designate «the sea» here, but also because the term *iw* itself does not always mean «island»; it can also be used to indicate other kinds of territories, not necessarily maritime ones. The argument based on these alleged «sea islands» is thus groundless. The Bible, for its part, says that the Philistines come from Kaphtor, a term the Egyptian word *Keftiu* was compared to, already long ago. In their turn, Kaphtor and *Keftiu* were identified with Crete, mainly because of the representations found in Egyptian tombs and depicting Cretan looking persons, some of which were called *Keftiu*. This identification seemed to be confirmed by the word *Keftiu* and by a list of pre-Hellenic place names, both of them inscribed on the very same base of a statue of king Amenhotep III. Whatever the explanation for the representations found in the tombs, nothing actually proves that *Keftiu* is to be identified with Crete. Likewise, the «Philistine heads» represented on the Phaestus disk do not prove that the Philistines went through Crete.

To conclude, the Philistines came neither from Crete nor from the Aegean islands or coasts, but probably from the southern coast of Asia Minor or from Syria.

Claude VANDERSLEYEN
Rue Baron Dhanis 31
B — 1040 Bruxelles.

ASPECTS OF EGYPTIAN AND PHILISTINE PRESENCE IN CANAAN DURING THE LATE BRONZE — EARLY IRON AGES

TRUDE DOTHAN

INTRODUCTION

This speech will focus on the excavations at Deir el-Balaḥ and Tel Miqne-Ekron, two sites which have been excavated under the auspices of the Institute of Archaeology of the Hebrew University of Jerusalem. Of particular interest is the nature of occupation at each site during the Late Bronze and early Iron Ages (14th-12th centuries B.C.E.), a time period which witnessed widespread international trade, the collapse of empires, and the migration of large population groups. Deir el-Balaḥ, located in an area that was under close Egyptian domination, is a type-site for the Egyptian presence in Canaan during the Amarna Age and Ramesside period (14th-12th centuries). Miqne also serves as a type-site, but for a different aspect of the history of Canaan. It offers evidence that enhances our understanding of the coming of the Philistines to Canaan and the initial phase of their settlement there at the close of the 12th century.

DEIR EL-BALAḤ

Deir el-Balaḥ is located about ten miles southwest of Gaza amid the massive sand dunes on the coast of Israel. The site was excavated between 1972 and 1982 by a team from the Institute of Archaeology under the direction of the author. The excavators uncovered both the Late Bronze Age settlement and the cemetery associated with it. The finds from the excavation, together with those that surfaced through illicit digging, form one of the most varied collections in Israel.

Deir el-Balaḥ's ancient identification remains unknown. The excavation of the site was extremely difficult due to the surrounding, towering dunes — a fraction of which was removed. Since only two dunams (0,2 ha) of the settlement itself were excavated, the resulting picture forms but a window on the history of the site and not a complete picture (figs. 1-2).

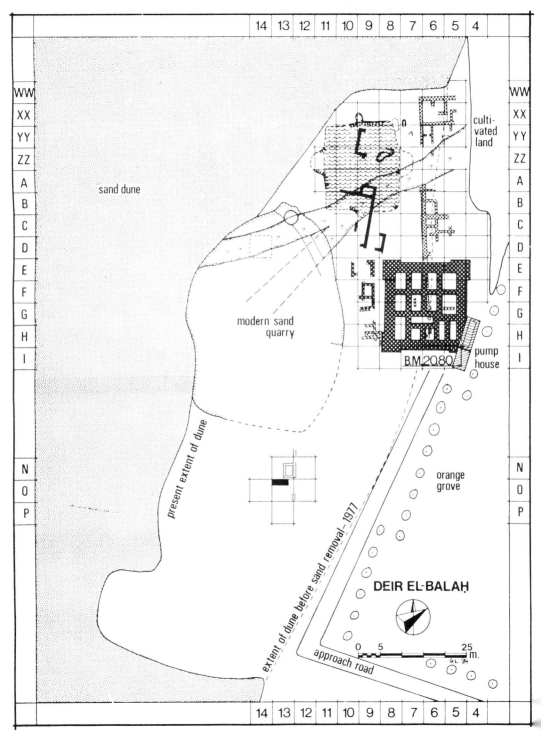

Fig. 1. — Site map of the excavated settlement of Deir el- Balaḥ.

The site was strategically located on the major route leading from the Egyptian Delta to Canaan. This highway, which was established during the 18th dynasty, was systematically settled and fortified by the Egyptians to provide safe passage for the trade caravans and companies of soldiers who frequented it. During various phases of its existence, Deir el-Balaḥ functioned both as an economic and administrative centre and as a military outpost. The site lay just south of Gaza, the Egyptian capital of Canaan during the New Kingdom, and was considered to be just within the borders of Egypt. Hence, it was an Egyptian border outpost manned by Egyptians who came into contact with the surrounding Canaanite population. Philistines settled at the site as the Egyptian presence declined. The incorporation of Philistines into Egyptian out-

Fig. 2. — Aerial view of the site of Deir el-Balah, looking to the north-west. On the upper left, the area of the cemetery, now covered by guava plantations. In the centre, the settlement at the time of excavation surrounded by the sand dunes which had accumulated after the Byzantine period. Below, orange groves (Z. Radovan).

posts is a pattern well known from other sites in Canaan dating to the same period (*e.g.*, Beth Shean).

The excavators uncovered nine major settlement phases with subdivisions at Deir el-Balaḥ. We shall review Strata IX-III with an eye to the site's function as a model of the settlement of Egyptians in Canaan during the Late Bronze Age and the incoming and settlement of the Philistines at the close of the era.

Stratum IX

The earliest phase at the site, Stratum IX, is contemporary with the late 18th dynasty/the Amarna Age in Egypt. During this phase, the site functioned as an administrative centre (fig. 3).

The Amarna Age in Egypt was a troubled time marked by far-reaching religious, political, and social changes. While researchers have generally felt that Egypt under Akhenaten withdrew from a strong foreign policy, recent investigations are showing otherwise. The systematic re-evaluation of the literary and archaeological data underway since the mid-60's has shown that preparations for military campaigns and building activity took place on the eastern and southern borders of Egypt during Akhenaten's reign[1]. This building and preparation for military activity provides a vivid backdrop against which to view the settlement founded at Deir el-Balaḥ.

The major architectural feature from Stratum IX was a large residence built next to a manmade pond, similar in design to building complexes of the Amarna period in Egypt. This residence was composed of three mudbrick buildings set at a right angle whose rooms together total more than twenty. The buildings border the pond on its eastern and southern perimeters. It is probable that they are part of a larger settlement, although the westernmost and northernmost boundaries of the complex are as yet undetermined since they continue under the sand dunes.

The large crater-pond is approximately 400 m². The boundaries of the crater were traced and partially defined on all four sides. The quarried sides slope steeply into the virgin marl to a depth of 5 m. Both archaeological observation and geological investigation confirm that the

---

[1] See, *e.g.*, the recent studies by H. REVIV, *The Planning of an Egyptian Campaign in Canaan during the Days of Amenhotep IV*, in *Yediot* 30 (1965-66), p. 45-51 (Hebrew); J.M. WEINSTEIN, *The Egyptian Empire in Palestine: A Reassessment*, in *BASOR* 241 (1982), p. 1-28, esp. p. 17; A. R. SCHULMAN, *'Ankhesenamūn, Nofretity, and the Amka Affair*, in *JARCE* 15 (1978), p. 43-48; M. SEVERAL, *Reconsidering the Egyptian Empire in Palestine during the Amarna Period*, in *PEQ* 104 (1972), p. 123-133.

Fig. 3. — Excavated settlement of Deir el-Balaḥ, looking to the south (Z. Radovan).

crater is manmade. Since many of the mudbricks from the buildings had been formed from the same marl as the crater, it seems that the crater served as a quarry, at least in its initial phase. After the marl had been quarried, the crater served as a water reservoir (so, too, in Strata VIII-VII). The use of the crater as a pond or reservoir is confirmed on the one hand by the hydrological investigation and on the other by the known building pattern of Amarna Age Egypt, evident in the residences excavated at Tell el-Amarna, in which building complexes were designed adjacent to a pond or lake.

A number of special finds from in and around the residence have close links to Tell el-Amarna proper and reveal the highly Egyptian character of the inhabitants of this phase. Four worked stone *kurkar* bases were found on the beaten earth floor of one room of the residence. They measured 13 × 13 cm and had sloping sides and a slightly depressed top. It is likely that they served as the supports for the four legs of a bedstead. Although many well-known and well-preserved beds have been found in Egypt, the only other stone bases known are from Tell el-Amarna, where an identical set was found in a bedroom niche.

A clay bulla (seal) was found just west of the residence in a *favissa* (pit) in the open area alongside the building. It bore four hieroglyphs, two *udjats* and two *nefers*. The closest parallel to this seal comes from Amarna and provides a good chronological indication of the date of the pit and of the buildings of Stratum IX. This seal also significantly indicates possible correspondence between Amarna proper and Deir el-Balah, since bullae were used to seal papyrus letters.

Ten cylindrical pieces of jasper (carnelian?) and blue frit were found scattered on the floor in another room of the residence. Traces of gold dotted the blue frit and all the pieces were pierced through by a square aperture. The size of the pieces and the nature of the aperture indicated that they were not beads for a necklace but rather should be reconstructed as a staff or flail, similar to the ones found in the tomb of Tutankhamun. The frit and carnelian would be mounted on a wooden rod in an alternating sequence. The size and beauty of the objects give additional evidence of the specifically Egyptian character and high culture linking this stratum with the Amarna Age.

The pottery from the residence found on a number of well-preserved beaten-earth floors was of both Egyptian and Canaanite types (fig. 4). Among the Egyptian vessels were those painted with the so-called «Amarna blue». Some of the vessels, such as a chalice and a small drop-shaped painted vessel, have exact parallels at Amarna proper.

In addition, a razor-knife was recovered from the floor of the Amarna residence, again with an exact parallel from Tell el-Amarna.

Although the cemetery associated with this phase of the settlement's existence was not located by our team, material relevant to Stratum IX has surfaced in private collections including coffins, a number of scarabs, alabaster vessels strongly reminiscent of those crafted during the Amarna era, and Aegean pottery types.

The strategic location of Deir el-Balah on the furthest border of Egypt, just before the entry to Canaan at Gaza, coupled with its unique architectural and special finds, indicate that during the 14th century Deir el-Balah was an Egyptian administrative centre, perhaps with links to the very capital itself at Tell el-Amarna.

Fig. 4. — Egyptian and Canaanite vessels associated with Stratum IX (Z. Radovan).

Stratum VII

Egypt experienced a renewed interest and involvement in her Asian holdings with the beginning of the 19th dynasty. The strategic military and trade route along the northern Sinai coast was refurbished during Seti I's reign; a series of fortresses and way stations were established with accompanying wells or reservoirs. Against this background of strategic renewal and construction, the remains of Stratum VII at Deir el-Balaḥ stand out in clear relief.

The character of the site in the excavated area changed clearly and dramatically from that of Stratum IX. Where once an elaborate residence had stood, an isolated, fortified structure had later been built, again purposely adjacent to the water reservoir.

The structure itself was monumental in size and shape. It measured 20 × 20 m, with fourteen rooms and a tower at each of its four corners.

Clearly, it was a fort or tower complex. The massive mudbrick walls were preserved to a height of 1 m and served as the foundations of a structure which stood at least two stories high, while the main outer walls of the complex were 2.4 m wide. The highly indicative construction technique of placing a layer of sand along the base of the foundation trench, a well-known feature of Egyptian building methods, pointed to the Egyptian construction of this fortress.

The function and nature of this isolated structure became evident in the light of the Egyptian activity along the coastal route during the early 19th dynasty. The northern Sinai route, called by the Egyptians «the Ways of Horus», was vividly depicted by Seti I on a wall relief in the Amun Temple at Karnak. Here, on the northern wall of the Great Hypostyle Hall, one of the earliest «maps» depicts a series of fortresses and their accompanying wells or reservoirs running from the Egyptian frontier town of Sile (Qantara) to the Canaanite border town of Gaza. Though scholars had long been aware of this «map» and had attempted to identify the modern site or location of these ancient fortresses, little progress was made until the last decade, when our fortress and water complex at Deir el-Balaḥ was systematically excavated. It proved to be the veritable picture-image of the depictions at Karnak and provided stark evidence for the resurgence of Egyptian military activity in Sinai and Canaan in the 13th century. The plan of the building, the «Egyptianizing» feature of the layer of sand along the base of the foundation trench, and the correlation with the Sinai relief indicate that the fortress was built by the 13th century.

Strata VI-IV

Seti I was succeeded by his son Ramesses II, whose lengthy reign of sixty-six years witnessed a vast array of empire building and consolidation. These activities, in conjunction with his lengthy and costly wars against the Hittites, neccessitated the upkeep and constant use of the fortresses and way stations along the northern Sinai coast.

Strata VI-IV of the settlement were basically contemporary with the primary use of the cemetery. The two dunams (0,2 ha) section excavated exhibited a marked shift in character in this period. The water reservoir was filled in and subsidiary structures were built on top. Private buildings, as well as a water-installation, heavy ash layers, and kilns were excavated and indicated the transformation of the area into an industrial quarter. Coffin fragments found in and around the three excavated kilns indicate that they were not used for ordinary pottery vessels but rather to fire coffin lids. Neutron activation analysis of the coffins and the fragments from the settlement indicate that all were locally made. The evidence for coffin construction at the site, therefore, is clear-cut.

Specific finds from the settlement provided concrete evidence that many of the burial gifts were locally made as well and that the industrial quarter served as an artisan's quarter, housing a thriving and varied crafts industry. Evidence for nearly every type of burial gift was recovered including figurines, molds, modelling clay, coloring pigments, and bronze scrap. Fragments of spinning bowls, used to weave the linen which wrapped the bronze items and a stamp carved with the image of the god Ptaḥ, the patron of artisans (figs. 5-6), were also found.

The Ramesside era at Deir el-Balaḥ first came to light in the cemetery excavations. Four anthropoid pottery coffins with their accompanying burial gifts were recovered by the excavation team (fig. 7). These four coffins were of distinctly Egyptian style and form a small fraction of the more than forty that surfaced through illicit diggings together with their rich burial gifts. Of particular interest are four locally made burial stelae, one found *in situ*, made of *kurkar* with hieroglyphic inscriptions and depictions of Mut and Osiris, strikingly similar to 19th dynasty stelae from Deir el-Medina in Egypt.

A wide variety of exquisite burial gifts was recovered from the cemetery by the excavation team. Wrought in primarily Egyptian style, they included bronzes and alabasters, and jewelry and amulets in gold, carnelian and faience. All the gifts have close analogies in New Kingdom Egypt. While the cemetery likely reflects burials from various eras grouped together, the period of Ramesses II was especially well represented and was confirmed by a seal of this pharaoh found *in situ*. Though distinct Canaanite traits were manifest in the workmanship of some of the jewelry and in some of the common pottery vessels, the predominant culture of the people buried in the cemetery was clearly Egyptian. The combined evidence of the coffins and the burial gifts points to an affluent population steeped in Egyptian religion and culture.

Stratum III

Following the flourishing Egyptian settlement of Strata VI-IV during the Ramesside era, Philistine presence at the site is indicated by a number of pits containing large quantities of typical Philistine pottery dating to

Fig. 5. — Stamp seal with the image of the god Ptaḥ from Strata V-IV pit.

Fig. 6. — Carved image of the god Ptaḥ on the stamp seal from Strata V-IV pit.

Fig. 7. — Closed anthropoid coffin (tomb 301) from the cemetery of Deir
el-Balaḥ (Z. Radovan).

the 12th-11th centuries B.C.E. The pits also contained a quantity of
Egyptian pottery types, the sole indicators of the sounding of the final
chord of Egyptian presence at the site during the early Iron Age and
silent witnesses to the oft-observed pattern of the incorporation of
Philistines into contemporary and former Egyptian settlements. Such
an incorporation of Philistines in an Egyptian settlement is also seen
at Beth Shean where the Philistines served as mercenaries during the
12th century. Anthropoid pottery coffins associated with Philistine
burials were found in the northern cemetery there. The facial depictions
on the lids of these coffins is strongly reminiscent of the depictions of
Philistines in the reliefs at Medinet Habu of Ramesses III's great battle
against the Sea Peoples.

   While the ceramic evidence from the pits clearly indicates Philistine
presence at Deir el-Balaḥ, the Philistine settlement and cemetery remains

buried under the massive dunes adjacent to the excavated area. Pits containing Israelite pottery dating to the 11th-10th centuries were also excavated, indicating their subsequent arrival at the site.

MIQNE

New evidence clarifying the arrival and settlement of the Philistines in the land of Canaan during the 12th century B.C.E. has been produced by the recent excavations at Tel Miqne.

The site is located about 3 km east of Kibbutz Revadim on the southern bank of the Nahal Timna. Its strategic location on the border of the Shephelah, separating the coastal plain from the inner coastal plain, overlooks the ancient network of highways leading northeast from Ashdod to Gezer and inland to Beth Shemesh.

In 1924, W.F. Albright surveyed this low-lying tell and, on the basis of ceramic finds, identified it with biblical Eltekeh. However, following the survey conducted in 1957 for the Department of Antiquities, J. Naveh suggested an identification with Ekron, one of the five capital cities of the Philistines. The well-stratified finds from the recent excavations conducted jointly by the Institute of Archaeology of the Hebrew University and the W.F. Albright Institute of Archaeological Research in Jerusalem have further strengthened this identification. Two pilot seasons (1981 and 1982) and the first of ten major seasons (1984) have been conducted by this joint American/Israeli project, directed by T. Dothan of the Institute of Archaeology and S. Gitin of the Albright Institute.

In Field I NE, the occupational profile of this tell, which at 50 acres (20 ha) is one of the largest in Israel, was clarified in a probe carried out on its north-eastern slope (fig. 8). Thirteen phases of occupation have been discerned ranging from the Chalcolithic period up to the Iron Age. The earliest phases (13-12; Chalcolithic-Early Bronze I and II) have been attested by ceramic and lithic finds only. A geologic probe 30 meters east of Field I NE uncovered for the first time monumental fortifications which have been tentatively dated to the MB II periods. Further excavation will clarify whether this wall formed part of the fortifications of a MB II city. This probe, together with two additional probes, confirmed that the tell was at least 4 meters higher in antiquity than is presently visible. Its «low profile» is merely the tip of the iceberg of a much larger tell buried beneath the alluvial buildup which was completed in the Byzantine period.

Fig. 8. — Tel Miqne-Ekron. Field I NE : probe carried out on the north-eastern
slope of the acropolis, looking westwards.

The 1984 season also brought a fresh understanding of the nature of the settlement of the tell during the Late Bronze I and II periods (Phase 10). The previously held view of the site as having been first settled by the Philistines (like Tell Qasile, for example) has been changed on the evidence of the excavation. Occupation spanning LB I to the end of LB II was recorded, indicating the presence of Canaanite settlers at Miqne during these periods. The last Canaanite city met a violent end as the heavy destruction layer found in Area 5 attests. It covered a floor with an assemblage of diagnostic vessels of the period including local Canaanite painted vessels and Cypriote and Mycenaean imports. A new, fortified city was immediately built on the destruction of the last Canaanite city, with a new town plan and a distinctly different material culture. The Phase 9 (Iron I) mudbrick city wall, 3.25 m wide, was associated with this new city and was also traced in Field I SE and Field III SE, suggesting that the city wall encompassed the entire 50 acre tell during this phase. The change in material culture was seen in the cessation of imported vessels and in the appearance of a distinctive, new type of pottery — Mycenaean III C: 1b. These modifications in fortifications, planning and material culture signify a change in the identity of the inhabitants of Miqne and may possibly be related to the coming of the Philistines. The pattern and phases of settlement seen at Miqne parallel closely that of Ashdod, another of the Philistine pentapolis cities.

Large amounts of Mycenaean III C: 1b pottery together with Iron Age I plain wares were found in Area 5 associated with the earliest surface from this phase. Small bell-shaped bowls with horizontal handles are predominant in the Miqne Mycenaean III C: 1b assemblage, which also includes large kraters with horizontal handles and a small number of stirrup jars and strainer spouted jugs. The pottery is well levigated and thoroughly fired. The decoration is monochrome, ranging in shade from black to brick-red. The decorative repertoire includes geometric spirals and loops as well as fish and bird motifs. Without the results of the neutron activation analysis of this pottery which indicate that it was all locally made, it would be very hard to distinguish it from similar ware found in an ever-growing number of sites outside Palestine such as Maa, Enkomi and Kouklia on Cyprus, and Ras Ibn Hani in Syria[2].

---

[2] For a discussion of the sequence of Philistine migration into Philistia and comments on absolute chronology, see my article, *The Philistines Reconsidered*, in *Biblical Archaeology Today*, Jerusalem 1985, p. 165-176.

Mycenaean III C: 1b is an important indicator of the appearance of new ethnic elements — likely Philistines — at sites such as Ashdod and Miqne and precedes the appearance of the distinctive Philistine bichrome ware. Mycenaean III C: 1b preserves Mycenaean traditions in forms, motifs and colors. The initial appearance of the monochrome Mycenaean III C: 1b pottery at Miqne and Ashdod and throughout the eastern Mediterranean points to the immigration of peoples who had a common cultural background manifested primarily in their pottery. The unity of technique, style, and decoration in the many sites at which this pottery has been found indicates the short chronological period in which the dispersion of these elements took place. But, while one might assume that this pottery was brought to the many diverse areas in which it was found, testing by neutron activation analysis of the abundant materials from Miqne, Ashdod, and Cyprus has confirmed that in each place it was locally made, reaffirming that the potters who made the ware shared a common background and ceramic tradition which they brought with them and utilized in their new homes in a relatively short period of time.

One of most remarkable features of the appearance of Philistine material culture — as seen in its most distinctive form, the pottery — is its sudden popularity; it appears fully-developed and with elaborate decoration in phases containing diminishing quantities of the monochrome Mycenaean III C: 1b, characteristic of the initial phase of settlement. The dominant traits in shape and decoration of Philistine bichrome ware were derived from the Mycenaean repertoire and point to the Aegean background of this pottery type. The ware of Philistine pottery, however, is much coarser and cruder, perhaps indicating the production of the pottery on a large-scale. Philistine pottery exhibits much more elaborate decoration than Mycenaean III C: 1b and a larger number of closed vessels were produced (fig. 9).

Phase 8 at Miqne, which dates to the 12th-11th centuries B.C.E., was observed in Area 4. Though it was architecturally poor, a well-stratified sequence of surfaces and stone walls and a clear ceramic sequence were recorded. While Iron Age I plain wares were found throughout the phase, the earliest surface in this sequence produced no Philistine bichrome ware but did produce a rich assemblage of Mycenaean III C: 1b pottery. The second sub-phase contained both Mycenaean III C: 1b and Philistine bichrome ware. This evidence is extremely important for it clearly confirms the typological and stylistic development from Mycenaean III C: 1b to Philistine bichrome pottery. Selected fragments from Miqne exhibit for the first time transitional features between the

Fig. 9. — Fragment of an early Philistine krater with the bird motif, from Tel Miqne-Ekron.

two pottery types and serve as a «missing link» in reconstructing the ceramic evolution from Mycenaean III C : 1b to Philistine bichrome ware. While this typological sequence parallels that at the Philistine coastal city of Ashdod, the evidence from Miqne enables a much more refined reconstruction of the sequence.

Two phases at Miqne (7 and 6) are dated to the 11th century. While only traces of architectural features dating to Phase 7 were found, enormous amounts of pottery were recovered. The bulk was Philistine bichrome ware indicating the substantial presence of the Philistines at the site during the Iron Age I. A significant architectural feature was discovered in Area 3 — a rectangular-shaped room with a plastered floor running up to two oblong sockets (which may indicate the presence in antiquity of standing architectural features which did not survive), and two plastered drainage channels. Two large adjacent stones, one of which had a hemispherical depression, had been set in the west section of the floor. The function of these stones is under investigation. Six vessels, some of which have parallels from the Stratum X sanctuary at Qasile, were found lying on the plaster floor — one a small votive juglet. Nearby were two incised bovine scapulae; a third was later reconstructed. These scapulae closely parallel those from the 12th century temple at Enkomi where they were found in large quantities on and around the sanctuary benches. The cultic character of the Enkomi finds is clear. This plastered room at Miqne, with its special architectural features (the plastered floor, the drainage channels, and the fixed stones), its small finds, and the scapulae may indicate that a small shrine existed here which shows links with features from contemporary Cypriote sanctuaries.

The Iron Age I period was represented in Field III SE by the 3.25 m wide mudbrick wall, whose extension had been traced in Field I NE. The wall had an off-set and lower platform, all of mudbrick, and a massive stone tower. A thick, sharply angled, plastered revetment of compacted fill was laid up against the outer face of the wall and tower and covered the platform. It may have served as a water run-off device. The entire unit may have been part of a fortification system with a monumental entrance.

The evidence for dating this fortification system to the 12th-11th centuries was based on the large homogeneous assemblage of Iron I plain and Philistine bichrome wares contained within the revetment (the latest structural element), which were similar to those of Phases 7 and 6 in Field I NE. While the construction and first use of the city wall may be linked to Phases 9 and 8 in Field I NE, dated to the 12th century B.C.E., these

Fig. 10. — Tel Miqne - Ekron. Assemblage of wares from the final phase of the Philistine city, destroyed in the 7th century B. C. E.

levels have not yet been reached in Field III SE. It seems, however, that the city was fortified on a large scale during the earliest phase of Philistine habitation at Miqne. Further excavation will reveal more fully the plan of the mudbrick city wall and confirm the probable location of the gate. From the evidence at hand, it appears that the fortification system spans the 12th-11th centuries, the *floruit* of the Philistine city of Ekron, which remained a predominantly Philistine city until its destruction in the 7th century (fig. 10).

CONCLUSION

The combined histories of Deir el-Balaḥ and Miqne span many centuries. Yet each in its own way especially functions as a type-site for a particular aspect of the Bronze - early Iron Ages — a critical time of political, ethnic, and economic transition in Canaan. Deir el-Balaḥ served as an Egyptian outpost on the border of Canaan and subsequently experienced Philistine and Israelite occupation. It contributes significantly to our understanding of the meeting of the Egyptian and Canaanite cultures and their impact on each other. Miqne illustrates clearly the transition from a Canaanite to a Philistine city in the heart of Philistia at the junction of these two periods — a pattern seen at other significant Canaanite sites.

Moreover, these sites serve to remind us of the diversity of cultural traits and settlement patterns within Late Bronze - early Iron Age Canaan. They caution us against building too homogeneous a picture of the peoples and the period and encourage us, instead, to search for regional patterns of settlement which will serve to clarify political and ethnic transitions as well.

BIBLIOGRAPHY

DOTHAN, T., *Anthropoid Clay Coffins from a Late Bronze Age Cemetery near Deir el-Balaḥ (Preliminary Report)*, in *IEJ* 22 (1972), p. 65-72.
—, *Anthropoid Clay Coffins from a Late Bronze Age Cemetery near Deir el-Balaḥ (Preliminary Report II)*, in *IEJ* 23 (1973), p. 129-146.
—, *Excavations at the Cemetery of Deir el-Balaḥ* (Qedem 10), Jerusalem 1979.
—, *The Philistines and their Material Culture*, New Haven 1982.
—, *Deir el-Balaḥ, Preliminary Report of the 1979 and 1980 Campaigns*, in *IEJ* 31 (1981), p. 126-131.
—, *Lost Outpost of Ancient Egypt*, in *National Geographic Magazine* 162 (1982), p. 739-769.

—, *Some Aspects of the Appearance of the Sea Peoples and Philistines in Canaan*, in S. DEGER-JALKOTZY, ed., *Griechenland, die Ägais und die Levante während der « Dark Ages » vom 12. bis zum 9. Jh. v. Chr.*, Wien 1983, p. 99-120.

—, *Digging in the Land of Canaan*, in *The Illustrated London News* 272 (1984), p. 80-81.

—, *The Philistines Reconsidered*, in *Biblical Archaeology Today*, Jerusalem 1985, p. 165-176.

—, *Aspects of Relations between Egypt and Canaan during the Late Bronze Age in Light of the Excavations at Deir el-Balaḥ*, in *Proceedings of the Israel Academy of Sciences and Humanities*, forthcoming.

—, with I. PERLMAN and F. ASARO, *Provenance of the Deir el-Balaḥ Coffins*, in *IEJ* 23 (1973), p. 147-451.

—, with S. GITIN, *Tel Miqne (Ekron), 1981*, in *IEJ* 32 (1982), p. 150-153.

—, with S. GITIN, *Tel Miqne (Ekron), 1982*, in *IEJ* 33 (1983), p. 127-129.

—, with S. GITIN, *Tel Miqne, 1984*, in *IEJ* 35 (1985), p. 67-71.

—, with I. GUNNEWEG, I. PERLMAN, and S. GITIN, *On the Origins of Pottery from Tel Miqne-Ekron*, in *BASOR*, in press.

—, with B. BRANDL, B. GOULD, G. LIPTON, and A. KILLEBREW, *Excavations of Cemetery and Settlement of Deir el-Balaḥ* (Qedem), forthcoming.

Trude DOTHAN
Institute of Archaeology
The Hebrew University
Jerusalem, Israel.

THE ISRAELITE CONQUEST:
TEXTUAL EVIDENCE
IN THE ARCHAEOLOGICAL ARGUMENT

ANTOON SCHOORS

The topic of this paper was first suggested to me, when, preparing a course of lectures, I looked into the late Prof. Yadin's *Hazor. The Rediscovery of a Great Citadel of the Bible*. As everyone knows, he dates stratum XIII of the tell at Hazor (stratum IA of the lower city) in the 13th century B.C. More in particular, he presents the following arguments, as to the historical interpretation of this archaeological stratigraphy and date:

> «The discovery of the Mycenaean IIIB fragments in the topmost stratum shows that the city existed while such pottery was still extant, namely until 1230 B.C. Most probably the city was destroyed sometime in the second third of the thirteenth century ... The striking similarity between the size of Hazor as revealed by the excavation and its description in the Bible as 'the head of all those kingdoms', plus the insistence of the biblical narrator that Hazor — and only Hazor — had been destroyed by Joshua and burned, leave little doubt, it seems, that we actually found the Canaanite city of Jabin that was destroyed by Joshua. In that case, the excavations of Hazor provided, for the first time, decisive archaeological data for fixing both Joshua's dates and, indirectly, the date of the Exodus from Egypt[1]».

The reading of this text left me with a certain feeling of dissatisfaction. First of all, the quoted passage contains a clear case of circular reasoning. On archaeological grounds the destruction of Hazor XIII is fixed about the middle of the 13th century. Then this destruction is ascribed to Joshua on the unexpressed assumption that the Israelite conquest of Canaan is to be dated at the end of the Late Bronze Age. And hence it is concluded that the excavations of Hazor provided — for the first time! — decisive data for fixing the date of Joshua's campaign and of the Exodus. But, how does Yadin know that Hazor XIII was destroyed by Joshua? Here the main argument is the Bible, in casu *Jos.*

---

[1] Y. YADIN, *Hazor. The Rediscovery of a Great Citadel of the Bible*, New York 1975, p. 145. Cf. *Hazor* II, Jerusalem 1960, p. 160.

11,10-13. But is such an argument conclusive, especially if, according to Yadin himself, there are as yet no decisive archaeological data for fixing Joshua's dates? The question has two sides: What exact historical information do we obtain from the biblical account? And which archaeological data do match these historical facts?

The statement in *Jos.* 11 that Hazor was destroyed and burned by Joshua has met and is still meeting with considerable doubt. J.M. Miller sums up the situation as follows:

> «The account of the battle by the waters of Merom in Joshua 11 may recall an incident which occurred in connection with the settlement of Naphtali. But verses 10-15 of the account are to be seen as primarily, if not entirely, secondary redactional expansion. Certainly it is gratuitous to attribute the destruction of Hazor XIII to Israel on the basis of verses 10f.[2]».

Also Yadin is aware of some literary problems in this respect. He notes that a compiler or editor added a gloss to emphasize that of all the cities of northern Canaan, Hazor alone was burned, for Hazor 'formerly was the head of all those kingdoms'[3]. It is not quite clear how far, in his opinion, the gloss extends and he certainly does not draw any historical conclusions from this literary fact. As do many Bible critics, Yadin also notices the problem created by some striking parallels in *Jud.* 4, where verse 2 mentions «Jabin king of Canaan, who reigned in Hazor» and verse 24 states: «And the hand of the people of Israel bore harder on Jabin the king of Canaan, until they destroyed Jabin king of Canaan». But he offers no literary analysis of the two texts in order to clarify their mutual relationship. On the contrary, he restates that the excavation of Hazor proves *Jos.* 11 to be correct and hence he concludes:

> «The narrative in the Book of Joshua is therefore the true historical nucleus, while the mention of Jabin in Judges 4 must have been a later editorial interpolation».

Yet the literary-critical picture relating to *Jos.* 11 and *Jud.* 4 is much more complicated, as V. Fritz has shown in a thorough and balanced analysis[5]. In *Jud.* 4, Jabin is mentioned in verses 2.7.17 and 23-24. Verses 2 and 23-24 belong to the redactional frame, which is character-ized by fixed formulas that occur several times in the Book of Judges.

---

[2] J.M. MILLER, *The Israelite Occupation of Canaan*, in J.H. HAYES-J.M. MILLER (ed.), *Israelite and Judaean History*, Philadelphia 1977, p. 282.

[3] Y. YADIN, *op. cit.*, p. 12 and 249.

[4] Y. YADIN, *op. cit.*, p. 255.

[5] V. FRITZ, *Das Ende der spätbronzezeitlichen Stadt Hazor Stratum XIII und die biblische Überlieferung in Josua 11 und Richter 4*, in *UF* 5 (1973), p. 123-139.

Irrespective of the exact date of that redactional frame (deuteronomistic, pre-deuteronomistic, Jahwistic)[6], it is definitely younger than the account itself. The mention of Jabin in the corpus of the chapter (vss. 7 and 17) is due to a later redaction which depends on the frame : this is particularly clear in vs. 7, where the formulation repeats that of vs. 2, whereas vs. 17b is an addition that points out the *šālôm* between Jabin and Bêt Heber, in order to explain why Sisera flees to Heber. All this matches the fact that Jabin is not mentioned in the poetical account of the battle in *Jud.* 5, the Song of Deborah. So far, Fritz follows the same line as Yadin. Thus the information on Jabin in *Jud.* 4 is eliminated as historically unreliable. If it is borrowed from a written source, *Jos.* 11,1-15 does hardly qualify for that function, for it positively states that Hazor is completely destroyed and that its king is dead. Thus the interpolated notes on Jabin in *Jud.* 4 are older than *Jos.* 11,1-15 in its present form. In other words, the account of *Jos.* 11,1-15 is relatively late and the additions on Jabin in *Jud.* 4 are probably taken from an oral tradition in which the importance of king Jabin was extolled. But it remains to be investigated whether *Jos.* 11,1-15 does not contain an ancient tradition on the capture of Hazor by the tribes of Israel.

Jos. 11,12b: «except Hazor only, that Joshua burned», qualifies 11,13a: «But none of the cities that stood on mounds did Israel burn». Verse 13a in its turn is a qualification of vs. 12: «And all the cities of those kings, and all their kings, Joshua took, and smote them with the edge of the sword, utterly destroying them». Thus vs. 13 betrays the intention to adapt the text to historical reality, viz. the co-existence of Israelite settlements and Canaanite cities. In 11,10-11, the mention of the king of Hazor is in contradiction with the account of 11,1-9, according to which the king has already been killed. Also the mention of the destruction of the city is out of place since the capture of the cities of the coalition is told only in vs. 12. Therefore, verses 10-11 are clearly interpolated in the account of the battle by the waters of Merom. But also this account, *Jos.* 11,1-9.12a.14, is hardly reliable from a historical point of view: its language and contents point to a relatively late construction, and some traditio-historical features betray a dependency on literary strands which excludes the origin of the tradition in or shortly

---

[6] Deuteronomistic according to M. NOTH, *Überlieferungsgeschichtliche Studien*, Tübingen 1957, p. 49-54; pre-deuteronomistic according to W. BEYERLIN, *Gattung und Herkunft des Rahmens im Richterbuch*, in *Tradition und Situation*, Göttingen 1963, p. 22-23; W. RICHTER, *Die Bearbeitung des «Retterbuches» in der deuteronomistischen Epoche*, Bonn 1964, p. 114; related to J according to V. FRITZ himself, *art. cit.*, p. 127.

after the period of the Israelite conquest. The mention of Jabin of Hazor can very well have been taken from *Jud.* 4. Fritz concludes his literary analysis as follows:

«Die Erzählung von der Schlacht an den Wassern von Merom enthält somit keine zuverlässigen Nachrichten, sondern ist wahrscheinlich eine Bildung in Analogie zu Jos 10,1-15 unter Übernahme des in Ri 4 genannten Jabin von Hazor und einiger Ortsnamen aus der Jos 12 verarbeiteten Liste unter Verwendung des allgemeinen Sprachgebrauchs im Zusammenhang mit dem Jahwekrieg. Die Erzählung wurde geschaffen, um die Landnahmeerzählung mit einem siegreichen Unternehmen Josuas im Norden des Landes abzuschliessen[7]».

The image of a mighty king Jabin probably originated in oral tradition because of the impressive ruins of the Late Bronze city. The Israelite historiography has in the account of *Jos.* 11,1-15 ascribed the ruins of the city to its capture by Joshua, which matches the general picture of the conquest, created by the Jahwist and strongly promoted by David's military successes. Even if this picture is only one of the possible explanations of the origin of the account in *Jos.* 11,1-15, it is definitely clear that this account did not originate as an immediate report of the facts and that its historical information should not be taken at face value.

Thus, at the utmost, the destruction of Hazor XIII by Joshua is a mere possiblity, and not even a strong one, since the historical fact of such a destruction is, to say the least, open to doubt. And there are alternative possibilities. V. Fritz *e.g.* makes a good case for ascribing the destruction of Hazor XIII to the Sea Peoples, who destroyed also Carchemish, Ugarit, Alalakh, Tunip and Kadesh on the Orontes.

This problem can be broadened to the more general question of how the biblical story of the exodus and the conquest can be used in interpreting archaeological data. Archaeologists sometimes tend to forget that certain historical theses concerning these important biblical episodes have not been proven and thus remain only working hypotheses. To begin with, the date of the exodus itself is not beyond doubt. The present consensus to date it in the second half of the 13th century is based on the mention of Pithom and Ramses in *Ex.* 1,11. «The implication that there was some specially energetic activity in building leads to the assumption that the pharaoh who displayed it was Ramesses II (1304-1237 B.C.)», thus W.F. Albright, summing up the *sensus communis*, and he continues: «The mention of the cities Pithom and

---

[7] V. FRITZ, *art. cit.*, p. 133.

Ramses makes the conclusion a practical certainty». Then he argues as follows: «If the inclusion of the Israelites among those compelled to do forced labour is to be assigned to the decade 1300-1290 B.C., or thereabouts, then their entry into Egypt must be dated to about the end of the fourteenth century. The exodus will then fall in the second half of the thirteenth century»[8]. Another argument in favour of this dating is the stele of Merneptah, the so-called Israel stele, found at Thebes. In this poetic eulogy we read that «Israel is laid waste, his seed is not»[9]. This proves that about 1230 Israel was present in Canaan, since it is mentioned together with Canaan, Ashkelon, Gezer and Yano'am. Since the word Israel is written with the determinative of people rather than land, we may accept that Israel was not yet settled in the days of Merneptah. This would mean that at that time the conquest of Canaan was under way but not yet completed. Both arguments are valuable but not conclusive. The Israel stela gives no direct information concerning a conquest but only concerning the presence in Canaan of a people called Israel. The determinative «people» can be due to the carelessness of the engraver of the stela, who is notorious for his blunders of writing. There is also the question what the name «Israel» could stand for in Merneptah's time. It is certainly not the whole community of the twelve tribes, which did not yet exist. Placed between the southern cities of Ashkelon and Gezer and the northern one of Yano'am, it must be in the North or in the centre. It thus seems to refer to the Israel-Rachel group, centred around Shechem and Bethel, which was perhaps not yet fully settled in the days of Merneptah[10]. As to the exodus, the biblical account is beset with problems. Some scholars have concluded from the analyses of the exodus traditions that there were at least two different exoduses[11] and there is a widely accepted opinion that only a portion of the later Israel actually participated in the Egyptian experience. Also the concept of an initial conquest of the whole land of Canaan is a systematization confined to the later strata of Joshua. The materials underlying the final redaction of Numbers, Joshua and Judges 1 reflect individual tribal movements primarily in the central hill country. Some of them are aetiological sagas which are told in order to explain a still existing

[8] W.F. ALBRIGHT, *Palestine in the Time of the Nineteenth Dynasty*, in *CAH* II/2, Cambridge 1975, p. 321-322.

[9] Cf. *ANET*, p. 378.

[10] R. DE VAUX, *Histoire ancienne d'Israël. Des origines à l'installation en Canaan*, Paris 1971, p. 366-367.

[11] Cf. R. DE VAUX, *op. cit.*, p. 352-353.

custom, or landmarks, such as heaps of stones or impressive ruins. From all this J.M. Miller rightly concludes:

«On the one hand, it follows that any attempt to date the conquest which assumes that it occurred in direct sequence with the exodus is methodologically problematic. In fact the character of the Israelite occupation of Canaan may have been such as to preclude the assignment of an absolute date. On the other hand, some of the materials in the books of Genesis and Judges may have more direct relevance for the study of the conquest than their present literary contexts imply[12]».

All in all, if there has been a conquest of a certain importance, following an exodus out of Egypt, the best date we can obtain for it from the Bible and Egyptian material is the second half of the 13th century B.C. Let us now see which use has been made of this date in archaeology. The Israelite conquest of Canaan is now generally connected with the end of LB and the transition to Iron I. In archaeology, this transition has been dated about 1200 B.C. No wonder that the conquest, which is dated at the end of the 13th century, has been connected with the transition from LB to Iron Age. Especially W.F. Albright has vigorously enunciated this opinion. In Bethel he found that somewhere in the 13th century the second phase of LB was destroyed by a tremendous conflagration. He also considered the break between this and the following stratum to be more complete than in any other case except between Iron II and Hellenistic. On these facts he based his conclusion:

«When we consider the masonry, building-plans, pottery, and culture of the following three phases, which are in these respects homogeneous, the break becomes so much greater that no bridge can be thrown across it, and we are compelled to identify it with the Israelite conquest. In reaching this obvious and inescapable conclusion, the writer abandons a position which he has held for eleven years, and adopts the low date of the Israelite conquest of central Palestine[13]».

There is no single argument which shows that the destruction of Bethel at the end of the 13th century must be ascribed to acts of war, and still less that it should be ascribed to the Israelites. The masonry of the early Iron Age phases is described as very rude in comparison with that of the preceding Canaanite city and the pottery as monotonous, with the conspicuous exception of the store-jars with collared rim, characteristic of the 12th century B.C. This is of great help for an exact dating of the

---

[12] J.M. MILLER, op. cit., p. 242.
[13] W.F. ALBRIGHT, The Kyle Memorial Excavation at Bethel, in BASOR 56 (1934), p. 2-15, esp. p. 9-10; cf. BASOR 58 (1935), p. 13.

first IA-phases at Bethel, but rude masonry and collared rims are not a clear testimony of Israelite occupation. Albright is convinced that his «inescapable conclusion» extends to Jericho also, and that his findings at Bethel increase the probability that the destruction of stratum C at Tell Beit Mirsim by fire was also due to the Israelite conquest. And that notwithstanding the fact that, in his opinion, the fall of Canaanite Jericho took place somewhere between 1375 and 1300 B.C., which is at least half a century before the destruction of LB Bethel. From a later article on archaeology and the date of the Israelite conquest it appears that the argument is based on an uncritical acceptance of the biblical story[14]. At the time this lack of a critical approach to the biblical account was already criticized by M. Noth, but W.F. Albright replied by simply repeating his archaeological evidence[15]. He has, of course, a problem with Ai, the destruction of which is related immediately after that of Jericho (*Jos.* 8), contradicting the archaeological evidence of et-Tell[16]. But, as is well known, he supposes that, originally, the story told the capture of Bethel and was later on shifted to Ai, in order to explain the important ruins of Ai, which in fact date from the 22nd century B.C. So he is forced to abandon at least the absolute historical reliability of *Jos.* 8, and the suggestion that it originally told the capture of Bethel is purely conjectural. Hence we have no reliable information as to the historical and chronological background of this clearly aetiological story. The same of course applies to the account of the capture of Jericho.

The idea that the destruction of LB Bethel, Jericho, Beit Mirsim and Lachish should be identified with the Israelite conquest has been dissiminated into secondary literature through Albright's *The Archaeology of Palestine* and similar works. But the *caveat* formulated by others has not always received due attention. K.M. Kenyon, for one, is much more circumspect in her approach of the conquest. She emphatically states that archaeology provides surprisingly little evidence of the Israelite entry into Palestine[17]. Albright should have been aware of a problem, *e.g.* at Tell Beit Mirsim. He states himself that there is no

---

[14] W.F. ALBRIGHT, *Archaeology and the Date of the Hebrew Conquest of Palestine*, in *BASOR* 58 (1935), p. 10-18.

[15] M. NOTH, *Grundsätzliches zur geschichtlichen Deutung archäologischer Befunde auf dem Boden Palästinas*, in *PJ* 34 (1938), p. 7-22; W.F. ALBRIGHT, *The Israelite Conquest of Canaan in the Light of Archaeology*, in *BASOR* 74 (1939), p. 11-23.

[16] J. MARQUET-KRAUSE, *Les fouilles de ʿAy (et-Tell)*, Paris 1949, p. 23-24; cf. J.A. CALLAWAY, *BASOR* 178 (1965), p. 27-28.

[17] K.M. KENYON, *Archaeology in the Holy Land*, London 1979, p. 204.

evidence for a drastic change in the fortunes of the town until late in B_2, when Philistine pottery appears on the site[18]. In plain language this means that there is no archaeological evidence for a new population having settled on the site at the beginning of Iron I, after the destruction of stratum C (LB II). And this remark has a broader application than to Beit Mirsim only:

> «It is not possible to deduce on the existing evidence any spread of conquest or, on grounds of material remains, to say that at any time a certain district fell under the control of invaders[19]».

The problem is a methodological one. The recognition of archaeological evidence for the conquest, and especially of material remains pointing to the presence of a new population, viz. Israel, is of course based on the excavation of individual sites. So, when the evidence in the individual excavation is shaky, the general picture of the conquest is even more impressionistic and open to doubt. It is more the result of the archaeologist's vision than of a set of ascertained material data explained according to strictly scientific, i.e. verifiable, rules and standards. Of course, archaeology and history have close connections: we can say that archaeology belongs to the family of the historical sciences. But for the sake of sound method, the two sciences should not be mixed, only confronted. For the historian ascertained archaeological facts are part of his historical information, they are a historical source next to written documents, and he can occasionally be forced to adapt his interpretation of the textual evidence because of well established archaeological finds. But the archaeologist must have examined his material according to strictly archaeological standards before confronting his results with the historical evidence drawn from written sources. Therefore, a carefully established stratification should first be fitted into a chronology by comparing this particular archaeological sequence with other sites which have already been classified. These are universally known basic rules of archaeological methodology. But if the result is not from the start to be prejudiced by non-archaeological factors, the archaeologist must avoid projecting the history of a biblical site, which is supposed to be identical with the archaeological site, onto the archaeological finds. The identification of the site and confrontation with history should always be a *second* step. As M. Weippert has formulated it tersely: «The first step

---

[18] W.F. ALBRIGHT, *The Excavations of Tell Beit Mirsim* III (AASOR 21-22), New Haven 1943, p. 36.

[19] K.M. KENYON, *op. cit.*, p. 206.

can only be the interpretation of the archaeological findings on the basis of internal criteria and by analogy with other findings»[20].

When we apply these standards in the critical assessment of Albright's work, we must admit that he made his first step very carefully. When judged according to the standards of that time, his stratigraphical and chronological approach is excellent, and, on the whole, his results are still standing. But his second step is not above all suspicion. The conflagration levels he found only prove that the LB city of Bethel was destroyed by fire. Such fires can have many causes. The closely packed houses, built of clay mixed with straw, with roofs supported by wooden beams, can catch fire by sparks from any kitchen or industrial oven, and what starts as a relatively small fire can reduce a whole city to ashes. A general conflagration can also be caused by an earthquake. Thus the destruction of the LB sanctuary at Tell Deir 'Allā in the 12th century, which *prima facie* could be connected with events of the Israelite occupation or even with the activity of the Philistines, has been ascribed with some probability to an earthquake by the excavator[21]. Therefore, when we ascribe a burnt layer to acts of war, we should prove it with evidence other than fire, such as concentrations of arrowheads or destructions which show to be caused by siege engins. But even supposing that the LB cities have been destroyed by war, it is too superficial a procedure to establish the identity of the enemy without further specific evidence. Here, it seems, Albright made a methodological mistake. He ascribed the destruction under discussion to the invading Israelites, simply because of the biblical account of the conquest. As we have seen, in his days, the date of the exodus and the conquest was still under discussion, so that even the congruency of archaeological and historical dates was not an argument. On the contrary, his identification of the destruction of cities, dated at the end of the 13th century on archaeological grounds, with the activity of the Israelite invaders, brings him to abandon his former position concerning the date of the exodus and the conquest and to adopt the low date. However, with no other archaeological information on the actual destroyers, there are other historical events which could account for the destructions. They might have taken place in connection with Merneptah's raid or with the

---

[20] M. WEIPPERT, *The Settlement of the Israelite Tribes in Palestine*, London 1971, p. 129.

[21] Cf. H.J. FRANKEN, *The Excavations at Deir 'Allā*, in *VT* 11 (1961) p. 363-367; 14 (1964), p. 418.

incursion of the Sea Peoples or with Egyptian expeditions under Ramesses III aimed at chasing them out[22]. Owing to the weakness of Egyptian rule in Palestine of that time, the destructions could also be due to internal troubles. M. Weippert has summed up this point quite well:

«Since the rule of the Pharaohs in most parts of Palestine in the thirteenth to twelfth century was scarcely even nominal, we must in any case reckon with the fact that the general state of war between the city-states and territorial states could have continued even without organized attacks from without. Wright himself[23] admits this with regard to the twelfth century and would like to think what must not be excluded as a possibility, namely that the 'Israelites' participated in the wars; nor is there any reason for not admitting a similar situation with regard to the thirteenth century. The conflagration levels, therefore, could have been caused by very different people who cannot be immediately identified from the written sources and among whom, of course, there may well have been 'Israelites'[24]».

A different but related problem is that of the identification of the new settlers after the destruction of the LB cities. Albright stressed the difference in masonry, building-plans and pottery in order to conclude that they are the Israelites. We have seen that he himself qualified the importance of the break as far as Beit Mirsim is concerned. But granted that the difference between the last LB cities and the new settlements is considerable, there remains the same methodological problem: from a comparison of the archaeological material one cannot conclude to the identity of the new settlers. It is thought that the primitive wall and pottery techniques of Iron I reflect the nomadic background of the Israelites. This is one possible explanation but the archaeological material and the historical conditions in the area, as we know them, allow of a different one. The deterioration in the material culture of Palestine had already begun some centuries before and the break between LB I and LB II seems to be more important than between LB and Iron I. This deterioration is probably connected with the decline in political and economic stability, specifically the internal wars between city-states which undermined the political stability of the country. Such a state of affairs was favourable for the infiltration of nomadic tribes and the settlement of the Israelites *could* be understood in this context[25].

[22] Cf. *ANET*, p. 262-263; K.M. KENYON, *op. cit.*, p. 207.

[23] G.E. WRIGHT accepted Albright's conclusions; cf. his *Biblical Archaeology*, Philadelphia 1962, p. 69-84.

[24] M. WEIPPERT, *op. cit.*, p. 130-131; cf. R. DE VAUX, *op. cit.*, p. 450-452; H.J. FRANKEN, *Van Aartsvaders tot Profeten*, Amsterdam 1962, p. 95-96.

[25] M. WEIPPERT, *op. cit.*, p. 132-133; K.M. KENYON, *op. cit.*, p. 204; H.J. FRANKEN, *op. cit.*, p. 99.

The question is totally different with respect to the Philistine occupation. There is archaeological material which is to be associated with the Philistines, viz. a type of pottery with characteristic decoration. K.M. Kenyon clearly summarizes the evidence:

«It cannot be accepted without question that this pottery is necessarily associated with the Philistines, but the evidence does seem to be strongly in favour of this ascription. It has just been shown that it must be dated about 1200 B.C., while the historical date given for the repulse of the invaders by Rameses III is c. 1191 B.C. Secondly, the distribution of the pottery corresponds well with the area occupied by the Philistines. It is concentrated in the coastal plain and the borders of the hill country, which was the area of the primary Philistine conquests, while in the hill country proper it occurs only sporadically. Finally, archaeological evidence shows that it appears suddenly at the end of the Late Bonze Age on the coast, but rather later farther inland[26]».

M. Weippert has thrown some doubts on this approach of the Philistine pottery. In his opinion, it is not obvious that it was introduced into the country as the result of mass immigration. One should rather think of the migration of individual families of potters or of imports or of local imitations of imported articles[27]. It seems that this judgment is too sceptical in the case of the Philistines, since the date and distribution of that pottery exactly fits the biblical and extrabiblical historical evidence[28].

Do we have anything similar in connection with the Israelites? We have seen that Albright mentioned the store-jars with collared rim among the characteristics of the new Israelite occupants. Since, the collared rim has become a major criterion in establishing the presence of the new Israelite tribes in Canaan. In his *Archaeology of Palestine*, Albright mentions the presence of this pottery in Iron I sites of central Palestine in connection with the pre-monarchic period in Israel : Bethel, Tell el-Fûl, Tell en-Nasbeh, Ai, Shilo, Beth Shemesh, Beth Zur, Tell Beit Mirsim, Shechem and Megiddo (sparsely in stratum VII, abundantly in stratum VI)[29]. He clearly expressed his opinion on the subject in 1940:

«As it happens, this collared store-jar is a «type-fossil» of great importance for Israelite chronology in the time of the Judges and the United Monarchy,

---

[26] K.M. KENYON, *op. cit.*, p. 215.

[27] M. WEIPPERT, *op. cit.*, p. 134.

[28] Cf. T. DOTHAN, *The Philistines and their Material Culture*, New Haven 1982, p. 94-217.

[29] W.F. ALBRIGHT, *The Archaeology of Palestine*, Harmondsworth 1949, p. 118.

since it is found all over the hill-country proper in the twelfth and early eleventh century, but went out of fashion between ca. 1050 and ca. 1020 B.C.[30]».

Also Y. Aharoni, in his studies of the Israelite settlement in Galilee, considered it as a type of genuine Israelite pottery, because of its high frequency in new settlements of Iron Age Age I[31]. In his last work on the archaeology of Israel, he stresses again the importance of this pottery type. He states that it is still quite difficult to fix the date for the founding of the various conquest settlements. The widely accepted date, the beginning of the twelfth century, he says, is influenced by the identification of the Israelite period with the Iron Age and has no archaeological basis. (Why then does he call Iron Age I Israelite I?). This strikingly critical view on the identification of the historical Israelite conquest with the archaeological period called Iron Age I is in accordance with what we have been exposing all along in this paper. Therefore it is the more amazing to read on the same page: «In the conquest settlements there is a special type of ware worthy of the designation 'conquest ware'». Aharoni then specifically mentions a cooking pot with an elongated and triangular rim and the «collared rim jar»[32]. But we may ask whether the collared-rim jar has not been identified too rashly as typically Israelite. Again, this identification suffers from an unwarranted connecting of textual and archaeological evidence. As a matter of fact, the role of the collared-rim jar as a witness to Israelite occupation of a site harks back to the fact that it was found in levels which Albright has identified as Israelite. But, as we have seen before, this was without satisfactory archaeological proof. Even if this pottery form appears for the first time in the oldest Iron Age levels, there is no conclusive proof that it must be associated with the Israelites with the exclusion of other groups[33]. In this case there is even archaeological counter-evidence. This type, as Aharoni himself admits, seems to represent a continuous development from LB forms, so that it would be unwarranted to assign it to newcomers at the end of LB. The more so, since it has been found in Canaanite contexts, *e.g.* in Aphek or in Megiddo, which remained Canaanite in stratum VII and, according to

---

[30] W.F. ALBRIGHT, Review of *Megiddo I* and G.M. SHIPTON, *Notes on the Megiddo Pottery*, in *AJA* 44 (1940), p. 548.

[31] Y. AHARONI, in *Eretz Israel* 4 (1956), p. 63-64; ID., *The Settlement of Israelite Tribes in Upper Galilee* (in Hebrew), Jerusalem 1957, p. 21-23.

[32] Y. AHARONI, *The Archaeology of the Land of Israel*, London 1982, p. 174.

[33] Cf. J.M. MILLER, *op. cit.*, p. 274; M. WEIPPERT, *op. cit.*, p. 134.

Albright himself and others, even in stratum VI[34]. The cooking pot to which Aharoni refers also seems to be a development of earlier Canaanite forms, from which it differs only by its longer rim. So it is a clear mark for stratigraphic and chronological analysis, but as far as I see, not yet for identifying new occupants of a site. For that matter, Aharoni weakens his own position when he states that «Archaeological research has proved that the Israelites did not bring a consolidated tradition of material culture with them. Instead, they borrowed everything from the previous inhabitants. The Israelite craftsman imitates the Canaanite product, and in the beginning creates more primitive vessels but in the same style»[35].

In more recent research, attention has been drawn to the Israelite occupation of the Negeb. It seems that the biblical Negeb was not occupied in the Late Bronze period. But the Iron Age levels at Beer-Sheba, Arad, Tel Malhata and Tel Masos play a considerable part in the latest theories about the Israelite settlement in that region. «The clearest information about one of the conquest settlements, thus Aharoni, is derived from the excavation at Tel Masos»[36]. Here a phase of semi-nomadic settlement, from which only cisterns and granaries have been preserved, was followed by pillared houses having pillars made of flat stones and showing the typical plan of the «four-room» house. Recently, this type of house has received some special attention, due in particular to the studies of Y. Shiloh[37]. His conclusion is that the four-room house must be considered an indigenous creation of early Israel. The excavators of Tel Masos, A. Kempinski and V. Fritz, adopt this view, and its large dissemination will be re-inforced through Aharoni's *Archaeology of the Land of Israel*, where he states:

> «It is still not known how this type developed or from whence it was brought. However, this is clearly a well-defined architectural feature which may be considered a characteristic Israelite house, a real trademark of Israelite occupation[38]».

[34] Cf. R. AMIRAN, *Ancient Pottery in the Holy Land*, Jerusalem 1969, p. 232; L.A. SINCLAIR, *An Archaeological Study of Gibea, Tell el-Fûl*, in *AASOR* 34 (1960), p. 16; G. LOUD, *Megiddo II*, Chicago 1948, pl. 83, H.J. FRANKEN, in *CAH* II/2, p. 332-333.

[35] Y. AHARONI, *The Land of the Bible*, London 1967, p. 219-220.

[36] Y. AHARONI, *The Archaeology of the Land of Israel*, p. 163.

[37] Cf. Y. SHILOH, *The Four-Room House. Its Situation and Function in the Israelite City*, in *IEJ* 20 (1970), p. 180-190; *The Four-Room House — The Israelite Type House?*, in *Eretz Israel* 11 (1973), p. 277-285; G.E. WRIGHT, *A Characteristic North Israelite House*, in *Archaeology in the Levant. Essays for K. Kenyon*, Warminster 1978, p. 149-154. The latter would limit the use of this type of house to the north. But Tel Masos clearly contradicts this; cf. V. FRITZ, *BASOR* 241 (1981), p. 61-73.

[38] Y. AHARONI, *loc. cit.*

Thus the four-room house became a new witness to Israelite occupation, which *e.g.* A. Kempinski mentions together with the collared-rim
jar[39]. But Aharoni's statement is not fully consistent. If it is not known
how this type developed nor from whence it was brought, how can we be
sure that it is a real trademark of Israelite occupation? No doubt, the
four-room house is a striking architectural feature on Israelite sites from
the early Iron Age throughout the period of the monarchy. But the
question is where it originated and how the Israelites came to use it.
Again I have the impression that the Iron Age I levels of the important
Negeb sites are assigned to the Israelites because of the general theory
that the Israelite conquest coincides with the beginning of the Iron Age.

V. Fritz is of the opinion that the four-room house represents the
culmination of a steady architectural development that may be reconstructed on the basis of houses that depart from this type. On Tel
Masos he found a number of interim stages in this development: 1. a
simple broad-room house with a row of pillars, sometimes extended by
adding rooms on the long side; 2. the relocation of the entrance on the
narrow side of the house and its orientation lengthwise; 3. the extension
of this type to the three-room and four-room house by the addition of
another room on the narrow side. Fritz surmises that the origin of this
house type was the broad-room tent. Thus one gets the impression that
the four-room house developed on the spot. But Fritz sees a similar
development at Ai and Khirbet Raddana[40]. This would mean that the
Israelite settlers did not bring with them the four-room house but that
it developed in different settlements of the early Iron Age. In order to
know whether it was developed by Israelites only, we need other evidence
that allows us to identify the settlers of that period.

In any case the architecture at Tel Masos displays a very complex
picture: it shows both the development of the «Israelite private house»
(understand: the four-room house), as well as a diversity of influences
from outside the Israelite architectural tradition[41]. And strikingly
enough, the pottery and metal-working show the continuation of LB
culture as it is found *e.g.* at Lachish and Tell Beit Mirsim[42]. This means
that, although Late Bronze settlement is lacking at the Negeb sites, the
Iron Age occupants of Tel Masos were in some way related to the pre-
Israelite population of Judah.

[39] A. KEMPINSKI, *Syrien-Palästina* (Archaeologia Mundi), München 1978, p. 76.
[40] Cf. V. FRITZ, *The Israelite «Conquest» in the Light of Recent Excavations at Khirbet
el-Meshâsh*, in *BASOR* 241 (1981), p. 61-65.
[41] V. FRITZ, *BASOR* 241 (1981), p. 68.
[42] Cf. A. KEMPINSKI-V. FRITZ, *Excavations at Tel Masos (Khirbet el-Meshâsh).
Preliminary Report on the Third Season, 1975*, in *Tel Aviv* 4 (1977), p. 142-143.

From the findings at Tel Masos, V. Fritz and Y. Aharoni conclude that the «conquest» of the Negeb proceeded in a peaceful manner. It is worthwhile to quote the first conclusion relating to the Negeb, formulated by Fritz:

> «The founders (of Tel Masos) brought with them their own style of architecture and continued to develop it. They created the «three-room» and «four-room house» design, a characteristic pillar-style building type that became typical for the entire Iron Age. One might conclude from this that the inhabitants were an ethnic group that was not part of the Canaanite population, but may have been related to it. However, the construction of the houses does not reveal their identity[43]».

This is a prudent conclusion. The most striking element of it is the last statement that the construction of the houses does not reveal the identity of the inhabitants. After all, Fritz draws a picture of the Israelite occupation of the Negeb which is different from previous theories, be it that of a conquest, a social revolution (G.E. Mendenhall and N.K. Gottwald) or a peaceful migration into the land. He supposes that the settlers of the Iron Age I sites were semi-nomads who, for a long time, had been living in symbiosis with the Canaanites, and who had migrated into the land in the 14th or 15th century. This is an interesting theory, which fits a number of historical data that have been drawn from the Bible and extra-biblical sources. But it means that the identification of the Israelites on the field is not so simple as it is suggested by some theories. Even if the new settlers in central Palestine were Israelites, that does not necessarily mean that also those in the Negeb were. We do not know when Israel as the whole community of the twelve tribes came into being. If the name Israel was originally limited to the central tribes, from what time on can we call the inhabitants of Tel Masos and, for that matter, of the Negeb Israelites? We should not exclude off-hand the possibility that Tel Masos was an Amalekite settlement, more in particular Ir-Amalek (*I Sam.* 15,5)[44].

Conclusion

In this paper, it was not my intention to contest the paramount importance of archaeology for the study of the historical problems connected with the conquest. On the contrary, a lot of work has been done during the last fifty years, following the excavations conducted by Albright. Especially the effort of Israeli scholars both in the archaeo-

---

[43] V. FRITZ, *BASOR* 241 (1981), p. 70.
[44] Oral suggestion of M. Kochavi.

logical field and in historical research about the conquest has been
massive and fruitful. We now know much more than when Albright
started his work and individual findings come together more and more
in a general picture, which is at the same time clearer and more
complicated. My intention was to warn against drawing too rash
historical conclusions from archaeological finds and against using those
conclusions in their turn as an argument when explaining other archaeological data. Such conclusions are often purely hypothetical, and in that
quality they cannot function as valid arguments in an archaeological
reasoning. Thus the conclusion that the destruction of practically all
LB cities was caused by the Israelite conquest is archaeologically
unwarranted, and therefore the ascription of the destruction of *e.g.*
Hazor XIII to Joshua, which is based on this conclusion, is also
unwarranted. But there is of course the testimony of *Jos.* 11. However,
I could also clarify my intention as a warning against the uncritical use
of the biblical text in archaeology. From the literary and historical
analysis of the Bible texts, including the Pentateuch, we get a rather
complicated picture of several migrations and conquests, and we have
to distinguish carefully the Israelite occupation of Galilee, Gilead, the
Central Mountains, Judah and the Negeb. And archaeological research
tends to confirm that picture. This means that it is an over-simplification
to assign every destruction of LB sites and every Iron I level to the
Israelites because of the unified picture of the conquest in the book of
Joshua. And the widespread presence of collared-rim jars or four-room
houses is a very important archaeological datum, but its historical
assessment supposes a careful confrontation with textual historical
evidence. But in order to obtain from the texts their historical evidence,
they must be critically analyzed on their own merits. So it is an uncritical
procedure to confront archaeological data with the biblical account in
its present form as well as with details of that account, that are not yet
settled in a consistent picture of the beginnings of Israelite history. As
I said, the problem is a methodological one, and therefore my remarks
apply to all periods. As one example belonging to another era, I simply
mention the rather general tendency to ascribe all destructions of cities
about the end of the 8th century to Sennacherib (701 B.C.), which is
totally unwarranted. In the confrontation of the two approaches, sound
methodology is for the benefit of both history and archaeology.

Antoon SCHOORS
Dunberg 50
B-3212 Lubbeek.

JUDA ET 'TOUT ISRAËL':
ANALOGIES ET CONTRASTES

E. LIPIŃSKI

Lors du Congrès international d'archéologie biblique, qui s'est tenu à Jérusalem du 1er au 10 avril 1984 à l'occasion du 75e anniversaire de l'*Israel Exploration Society*, le professeur Moshe Dothan a prononcé un plaidoyer en faveur d'une nouvelle nomenclature dans le domaine de l'archéologie palestinienne [1]. Il a proposé de remplacer l'appellation courante d'«âge du Fer» par celle d'«époque israélite». Cette terminologie, utilisée déjà dans l'*Encyclopedia of Archaeological Excavations in the Holy Land* [2], tient compte du fait que la présence discernable de clans israélites en Canaan coïncide avec l'âge du Fer et le caractérise d'une manière suffisamment claire et distincte sur les sites proprement israélites.

Il est cependant tout aussi évident que les plaines côtières d'Israël, du Torrent d'Égypte à Rosh-ha-Niqra', nous révèlent à la même époque des civilisations bien diverses de celles de l'intérieur du pays, où les tribus d'Israël s'étaient installées. Ces civilisations, en particulier celle des Philistins au sud et celle des Phéniciens au nord, ne peuvent être qualifiées d'«israélites», si l'on veut éviter des confusions regrettables et garder aux mots leur sens historique propre. On conçoit difficilement, par exemple, que l'on qualifie d'«Israélite II» l'ensemble des vestiges du Fer II relevés à Ḥorvat Rosh Zayit (Khirbet Ras ez-Zaitun) [3], dont la forteresse du Xe-IXe siècle est caractérisée par de la céramique chypro-phénicienne et correspond peut-être à la Kabul biblique (*I Rois* 9,13), que Salomon avait donnée au roi de Tyr. La conflagration, qui détruisit cette localité vers le milieu du IXe siècle av.n.è., pourrait être mise en relation avec le passage des armées assyriennes de Salmanasar III, en

---

[1] M. DOTHAN, *Terminology for the Archaeology of the Biblical Periods*, dans *Biblical Archaeology Today*, Jerusalem 1985, p. 136-141. — Je tiens à remercier le Dr Jacqueline Balensi, chargé de recherche au C.N.R.S., Centre de Recherche Français de Jérusalem, qui eut la gentillesse de me faire part de diverses suggestions précieuses.

[2] M. AVI-YONAH-E. STERN (éd.), *Encyclopedia of Archaeological Excavations in the Holy Land* I-IV, Oxford 1975-78.

[3] Z. GAL, *Ḥurvat Rosh Zayit, 1983*, dans *IEJ* 33 (1983), p. 257.

841 av.n.è.[4], mais cette destruction n'aurait pas plus de rapports avec le Royaume d'Israël que la poterie chypro-phénicienne trouvée sur le site.

Aux inconvénients qu'une telle terminologie présente pour les sites des plaines côtières et des collines avoisinantes, s'ajoutent deux autres difficultés. La première tient au fait que les vestiges israélites du Fer I sont relativement rares et d'un relief archéologique peu prononcé. Nous ne nous y attarderons pas, car ce fait nous paraît d'importance secondaire pour notre propos.

La seconde difficulté est peut-être plus subtile, mais historiquement très importante et aussi bien fondée que la première. Nombre d'archéologues, d'historiens et d'exégètes ont tendance à qualifier d'«israélites» tous les vestiges et toutes les manifestations de la civilisation du «Peuple de la Bible», comme si ce peuple avait constitué, aux temps bibliques, une unité culturelle et politique compacte, à peine différenciée par la division en douze tribus. Cette tendance, j'ai pu la relever dans mes propres publications, même très récentes[5].

Les auteurs n'hésitent donc pas à parler de la «Jérusalem israélite», d'«établissements israélites du Négev septentrional», du «centre de l'administration provinciale israélite à Béershéva», de la «citadelle israélite de Ḥorvat 'Uzza», dans le nord du Négev, ou de la «forteresse israélite de Qadesh Barnéa». Or, cette terminologie prête à confusion et contredit les témoignages historiques des *sources* de la Bible, dans lesquelles s'exprime la conscience d'une nette distinction entre le peuple d'Israël, établi dans les collines de la Cisjordanie centrale, et le peuple de Juda, habitant la Judée et le nord du Négev. Cette distinction, il faut le souligner, est antérieure à la scission du royaume de David et de Salomon, et l'histoire même de ces deux grands rois ne se comprend que dans la perspective d'une opposition entre Israël, au nord de Jérusalem, et Juda, au sud de la capitale davidique.

Il s'agit, en l'occurrence, d'une opposition, non pas entre deux races ou deux religions, mais entre deux peuples, le peuple étant défini comme une communauté liée par une tradition, des coutumes, une civilisation, un idiome et une certaine situation géographique. Considérée sous ces différents angles, la différence entre Israélites et Judéens est indéniable,

[4] Voir, à ce sujet, la reconstitution historique proposée par E. LIPIŃSKI, *An Assyro-Israelite Alliance in 842/841 B.C.E.?*, dans *Proceedings of the Sixth World Congress of Jewish Studies* I, Jerusalem 1977, p. 273-278; ID., *Aram et Israël du Xᵉ au VIIIᵉ siècle av.n.è.*, dans *Acta Antiqua Acad. Scient. Hung.* 27 (1979 [1981]), p. 50-102, voir p. 77-78.

[5] Relevons, p. ex., les «maisons israélites» de la Cité de David: E. LIPIŃSKI, *Vingt-cinq ans de recherches archéologiques en Israël*, dans *Recherches archéologiques en Israël — Archeologisch onderzoek in Israël*, Leuven 1984, p. 23-97 (voir p. 53).

et les données littéraires de la Bible, aussi bien que l'épigraphie,
permettent d'illustrer ce fait d'une manière, à notre sens, convaincante.

Le Cantique de Déborah (*Jug.* 5), dont on s'accorde à reconnaître
l'antiquité[6], énumère les six tribus qui ont pris part à la lutte contre
Sisera, à savoir Éphraïm, Benjamin, Makir, Zabulon, Issachar et
Nephtali, ainsi que les tribus qui se sont dérobées à la guerre sainte, à
savoir Ruben, Galaad, Dan, Asher et Méroz. Juda, Siméon et Lévi ne
sont point mentionnés et ne faisaient donc pas partie de la confédération
des tribus israélites[7]. En revanche, le cantique semble considérer Makir
(*Jug.* 5,14), Galaad (*Jug.* 5,17) et Méroz (*Jug.* 5,23) comme des entités
tribales au même titre que les tribus de la liste traditionnelle. La tribu la
plus méridionale du groupe était celle des Benjaminites, comme l'indique
leur nom de «fils de la droite», $b^e n\hat{e}$ $y\bar{a}m\hat{i}n$, c'est-à-dire «méridionaux»,
puisqu'on s'orientait en se tournant vers l'orient, et non vers le nord,
comme nous le faisons aujourd'hui tout en persistant à utiliser le verbe
«s'orienter». Il est donc normal qu'il n'y ait pas de tribus israélites vivant
au sud des Benjaminites.

Les étapes de l'accession de David à la royauté livrent une autre preuve
de la distinction entre Juda et Israël. Dans des circonstances qui nous
échappent, David s'était rendu maître d'Hébron (*II Sam.* 2, 1-3), «la ville
des quatre» quartiers calébites[8], et «les hommes de Juda vinrent et là ils
oignirent David comme roi de la maison de Juda» (*II Sam.* 2,4). Cet acte
n'a rien de surprenant si l'on songe que David était déjà un homme de
guerre renommé, qui avait fait ses preuves au service des Philistins, et il
venait de s'emparer d'Hébron, la principale ville de la montagne de Juda.
Lui-même provenait de Bethléem, le chef-lieu du territoire d'Éphrata,
dans le nord de Juda. Sa première femme, Ahinoam, appartenait au clan

---

[6] La datation la plus basse qui ait été proposée, au Xe ou IXe siècle av.n.è., a été
défendue récemment par G. GARBINI, *Il cantico di Debora*, dans *La Parola del Passato* 178
(1978), p. 5-31. Mais on admet communément que le poème remonte au XIIe siècle ou, à
tout le moins, à la fin du IIe millénaire av.n.è. Cf., entre autres, A. GLOBE, *The Literary
Structure and Unity of the Song of Deborah*, dans *JBL* 93 (1974), p. 493-512; J.A. SOGGIN,
Il canto di Debora, dans *Rendiconti dell'Accademia nazionale dei Lincei. Classe di scienze
morali, storiche e filologiche*, sér. VIII, 32 (1977), p. 97-112.

[7] D'après G.W. AHLSTRÖM, *Judges 5,20f. and History*, dans *JNES* 36 (1977), p. 287-
288, «one may conclude that the so-called Song of Deborah (Judges 5) was composed at a
time when Judah was not a part of Israel or had not yet come into closer contacts with the
peoples of central and northern Canaan».

[8] Sur cette notion de «ville des quatre», voir S. MOWINCKEL, *Die Gründung von Hebron*,
dans *Donum natalicium H.S. Nyberg oblatum*, Uppsala 1954, p. 185-194, et, dans un sens
très différent, E. LIPIŃSKI, *'Anaq - Kiryat 'Arba' - Hébron et ses sanctuaires tribaux*, dans
VT 24 (1974), p. 41-55, en particulier p. 48-55.

de Yizréël (*I Sam.* 25,43), vivant dans le Négev, en bordure des collines de Juda (*Jos.* 15,55-56; *I Sam.* 25,3), et sa seconde femme, Abigayil, provenait de Karmel (*I Sam.* 25,39-42), une ville située à 11 km au sud d'Hébron. L'origine de David, ses liens matrimoniaux et ses exploits en faisaient l'homme tout indiqué pour assumer le pouvoir au pays de Juda, qui prit corps et entra dans l'histoire avec David.

C'est seulement après plusieurs années de règne à Hébron que «toutes les tribus d'Israël» ou «tous les anciens d'Israël» vinrent auprès de David pour conclure un pacte avec lui et l'élever à la royauté sur Israël, en lieu et place d'Ishbaal, fils de Saül (*II Sam.* 5,1-3). Juda et Israël apparaissent ainsi comme deux entités géopolitiques distinctes et les deux groupes resteront distincts tout au long des règnes de David et de Salomon, malgré la conquête de Jérusalem, qui devait faire office de charnière entre Israël et Juda. Selon *II Sam.* 5,5, David «régna à Jérusalem trente-trois ans sur tout Israël et sur Juda», qui ne faisait manifestement pas partie de «tout Israël». Le royaume de David était donc un «Royaume-Uni», issu d'une union personnelle, cas dont on connaît d'autres exemples dans l'histoire du Proche-Orient ancien[9].

Bien que les rédacteurs bibliques se servent souvent du nom d'Israël pour désigner tout le royaume de David et de Salomon, plusieurs textes font voir qu'une distinction réelle subsista entre Israël et Juda tout au long de cette époque.

Le rédacteur de *II Sam.* 24 commence le récit du dénombrement du peuple en signalant que «la colère de Yahvé s'était enflammée contre Israël», mais dès qu'il cite sa source, il distingue Israël et Juda. Il rapporte les paroles divines de la manière suivante: «Va, fais le dénombrement d'Israël et de Juda». Quand le dénombrement était fait, «Joab donna au roi le chiffre obtenu pour le recensement du peuple: Israël comptait huit cent mille hommes tirant l'épée, et Juda cinq cent mille hommes». Quelle que soit la valeur des chiffres rapportés, il est évident qu'Israël et Juda forment deux entités distinctes et séparées. Quand David désigne Salomon pour lui succéder, il précise: «c'est lui que j'ai institué *nāgîd* sur Israël et sur Juda» (*I Rois* 1, 35).

Cette distinction subsista au temps de Salomon. Ceci résulte notamment d'un document d'archives repris en *I Rois* 4,7ss. Salomon avait établi «douze préfets sur tout Israël». Leurs noms et leurs préfectures sont énumérées, ce qui permet de constater que Juda n'est pas englobé

---

[9] G. BUCCELLATI, *Cities and Nations of Ancient Syria* (Studi semitici 26), Roma 1967, p. 137-193.

dans la liste. En effet, un treizième gouverneur était chargé du pays de Juda (*I Rois* 4,19b).

On aura remarqué que l'ordre habituel adopté par les auteurs bibliques est Israël, puis Juda. La raison ultime de cet ordre ne nous est pas connue, mais une anecdote reprise dans *II Sam.* 19,44 révèle l'idée que l'on se faisait des relations entre Israël et Juda. Le passage reflète les rivalités qui opposent les deux parties du Royaume-Uni au temps de David : «Les hommes d'Israël répliquèrent aux hommes de Juda et dirent : 'J'ai dix fois plus de droits sur le roi que toi! En effet, je suis ton aîné[10]! Pourquoi m'as-tu méprisé?'» Cette réplique indique que les rapports entre Israël et Juda pouvaient se concevoir comme celles de deux frères, dont Israël prétendait être l'aîné, sans doute en raison de son importance numérique. Cette conception réapparaît beaucoup plus tard en *Éz.* 23, où les capitales d'Israël et de Juda sont comparées à deux sœurs, l'aînée étant Samarie, la capitale d'Israël. Le prophète devait substituer ici l'image de deux sœurs à celle de deux frères, car les noms de villes sont en hébreu du genre féminin.

Si l'on accepte cette distinction radicale entre Israël et Juda[11], distinction bien antérieure à la scission du Royaume-Uni après la mort de Salomon, on comprend mieux les événements qui eurent lieu au temps de David.

Bien que David eût été élevé à la royauté sur Israël par les anciens d'Israël venus à Hébron, sa politique intérieure heurtait les traditions et les coutumes des tribus du Nord. Il avait basé son pouvoir sur des troupes mercenaires, composées surtout de Kérétiens et Pelétiens, apparentés aux Philistins dont Israël n'avait pas gardé le meilleur des souvenirs. S'étant emparé, à ce qu'il semble, des villes cananéennes de la plaine, qui avaient subsisté jusques alors au milieu des tribus israélites, il n'en avait pas massacré la population, mais l'avait intégrée aux sujets de

---

[10] La Septante et des manuscrits de la *Vetus Latina* ont préservé la leçon *bkwr* au lieu de *bdwd* du texte massorétique, leçon facilitante mais peu intelligible dans le contexte. La leçon *bdwd* s'explique aisément par une méprise du copiste, induit en erreur par le caractère insolite de la notice et la similitude des lettres *d*, *k* et *r* dans l'écriture araméenne du IVᵉ siècle av.n.è.; cf. F.M. CROSS, *The Development of the Jewish Scripts*, dans *The Bible and the Ancient Near East. Essays in Honor of W.F. Albright*, éd. G.E. WRIGHT, New York 1961, p. 133-202 (voir p. 137, ligne 1, cf. p. 142 et 143). Une confusion semblable explique, dans *Job* 41,12, la leçon massorétique *kdwd* (*kᵉdûd*), «comme un chaudron», au lieu de *kkwr* (*kᵉkûr*), «comme un fourneau», *Vorlage* de la Septante.

[11] Z. KALLAI, *Judah and Israel — A Study in Israelite Historiography*, dans *IEJ* 28 (1978), p. 251-261, s'efforce d'atténuer cette distinction : «It will be shown that the split between Judah and Israel is more abrupt, without a profound pre-history» (p. 253-254).

ses états, introduisant ainsi en Israël un élément étranger qui allait jouer
un rôle important dans l'évolution religieuse du Royaume du Nord aux
siècles suivants. Enfin, David s'était établi à Jérusalem, ville qui ne
relevait d'aucun territoire tribal, et il y avait même transféré le centre du
culte yahviste.

Ces mesures, auxquelles s'ajoutaient sans doute d'autres raisons,
créèrent en Israël un état de crise qui se manifesta au moins par deux
révoltes, celles d'Absalom et de Shéba, favorisées ou suscitées toutes
deux par les gens du Nord.

Absalom reçut l'onction royale des mains des anciens d'Israël (*II Sam.*
15 ss; cf. 19,11) et il fut soutenu par les Israélites. L'armée d'Israël fut
cependant battue par les mercenaires à la solde de David et Absalom fut
tué dans la région forestière d'Éphraïm (*II Sam.* 18,6ss). Juda ne semble
avoir joué aucun rôle actif dans cette lutte[12], qui ne présuppose donc
pas un conflit entre les deux peuples, mais une opposition d'Israël à
la politique de David. La seconde révolte fut dirigée par Shéba, un
Benjaminite (*II Sam.* 20,1-22). En cette occasion, David a cherché à
obtenir un appui effectif des Judéens, mais il semble avoir échoué (*II
Sam.* 20,4-5). Les mercenaires de David n'en eurent pas moins raison des
révoltés. L'intronisation même de Salomon eut lieu sous la protection des
Kerétiens et Pelétiens (*I Rois* 1,32-40), alors que les Judéens soutenaient
Adonias (*I Rois* 1,9) et que les Israélites paraissent totalement étrangers
à l'événement. Une monarchie héréditaire du type davidique ne devait
guère correspondre à l'idée que les anciens d'Israël se faisaient de la
royauté.

Salomon se rendait certainement compte du danger que les Israélites
pouvaient constituer pour son pouvoir. La fortification de Jérusalem, de
Hazor, de Megiddo et de Gézèr, toutes places fortes qui n'étaient pas
peuplées d'Israélites de vieille souche, renforçait encore son indépen-
dance vis-à-vis des institutions tribales d'Israël. Bien plus, au lieu
d'enrôler des Israélites dans l'armée, il préférait lever trente mille
hommes de corvée en Israël (*I Rois* 5,27; 11,26ss; 12,11ss). Ceci eut pour
résultat un rebondissement de la crise latente, dont Jéroboam sut tirer
parti (*I Rois* 11,26ss). Pour échapper à la mort, il se réfugia en Égypte,
auprès du pharaon Shéshonq Ier (945-924 av. n.è.) (*I Rois* 11,40), qui

---

[12] Les textes ne se prêtent pas à l'interprétation différente proposée par H. BARDTKE,
Erwägungen zur Rolle Judas im Aufstand des Absalom, dans *Wort und Geschichte.
Festschrift für Karl Elliger* (AOAT 18), Kevelaer-Neukirchen-Vluyn 1973, p. 1-8;
F. CRÜSEMANN, *Der Widerstand gegen das Königtum*, Neukirchen-Vluyn 1978, p. 94-104;
cf. F. LANGLAMET, dans *RB* 87 (1980), p. 419-423.

avait accordé aussi l'asile à Hadad l'Édomite (*I Rois* 11,18-22). Jéroboam demeura en Égypte jusqu'à la mort de Salomon (*I Rois* 11,40) et, le moment venu, c'est lui que l'assemblée d'Israël éleva à la royauté (*I Rois* 12). Roboam, le petit-fils de David, resta maître de Jérusalem et fut roi de Juda. La division était consommée, a-t-on coutume de dire, mais l'unité a-t-elle jamais existé, si l'on fait abstraction de l'union personnelle maintenue de force par le pouvoir central?

Une minutieuse analyse critique des chapitres pertinents de la Bible nous mènerait trop loin et, du reste, elle ne nous paraît pas requise en cette circonstance. Il est évident, en effet, que la dualité foncière d'Israël et de Juda est inscrite dans les sources anciennes et que les rédacteurs postérieurs l'ont oblitérée en employant souvent le nom d'Israël pour Israël et Juda.

S'il est relativement facile de se faire une idée générale de ce que fut Israël à l'époque du Fer I, — fédération plus ou moins lâche de tribus vivant dans les collines de la Cisjordanie centrale, — il est plus difficile de dire quelle est l'origine de la tribu de Juda qui n'entra dans l'histoire qu'avec David.

Juda, forme abrégée de *'ereṣ yᵉhūdā*, probablement «terre ravinée», est un nom géographique qui désignait à l'origine la région montagneuse, coupée de ravins, dont on peut fixer les limites au nord de Bethléem et au sud d'Hébron. Le nom ne semble être ni cananéen ni hébreu, mais il pourrait être nord-arabique, puisqu'il est apparenté, à première vue, à l'arabe *wahda*, «gorge, ravin»[13]. On le mettra donc en rapport avec les clans qenizzites et qénites qui avaient habité la région. De toute manière, ce n'est pas un nom de famille ou de clan. Ce n'est donc pas une tribu qui a donné son nom à la région; c'est la région qui a donné son nom à l'ensemble des clans qui y étaient installés et qui se sont constitués en tribu vers l'an 1000 av.n.è. La tribu s'est alors donné un ancêtre éponyme, Juda, qui est devenu fils de Jacob dans la synthèse panisraélite de la geste patriarcale[14].

---

[13] C'est l'explication que nous avons proposée naguère et que nous croyons pouvoir maintenir: E. LIPIŃSKI, *L'étymologie de «Juda»*, dans *VT* 23 (1973), p. 380-381. H.-J. ZOBEL, *jᵉhūḏāh*, dans *ThWAT* III, Stuttgart 1982, col. 512-533 (voir col. 515-516), lui objecte que le mot *wahda* ne se rencontre pas dans l'Ancien Testament, mais c'est précisément un terme qui n'est pas hébreu.

[14] Voir aussi R. DE VAUX, *L'installation des Israélites dans le Sud palestinien et les origines de la tribu de Juda*, dans *Proceedings of the Fifth World Congress of Jewish Studies* I, Jerusalem 1972, p. 150-156.

Les clans qui constituèrent la tribu de Juda étaient en réalité d'origine disparate. Rappelons qu'au moins deux clans rubénites, celui de Zarmi et celui d'Hèçrôn (*Gen.* 46,9; *Nomb.* 26,6; *I Chron.* 5,3), ont été agrégés à la tribu de Juda[15]. Ceci valut à Ruben d'être compté avec Juda, Siméon et Lévi parmi les enfants de Léa (*Gen.* 29,32-35). Par ailleurs, les Siméonites ont été intégrés à la tribu de Juda, comme *Jos.* 19,1-9 le laisse entendre[16]; ils se seraient établis dans la région de Béershéva. Parmi les autres clans, il faut mentionner en premier lieu les Calébites, qui ont occupé la région s'étendant d'un point situé un peu au nord d'Hébron jusqu'à la limite de la montagne judéenne, au nord de Béershéva[17]. Ils appartenaient à la tribu des Qenizzites[18], qui est attestée en Palestine méridionale[19] et était apparentée aux tribus d'Édom[20]. C'est sans doute dans le cadre de ces relations inter-tribales du pays de Juda qu'il faut chercher l'origine de l'insertion d'Ésaü-Édom dans la trame des récits patriarcaux de la Bible. Un autre clan qenizzite, celui d'Othniël, a occupé Debir[21], que l'on doit désormais localiser à Khirbet Rabūd[22], 15 km au sud-ouest d'Hébron.

D'autres clans qenizzites, notamment ceux de Yérahméel (*I Chron.* 2,9.42), paraissent avoir conservé plus longtemps une vie semi-nomade dans le Négev (*I Sam.* 27,10). Les «villes» des Yérahméelites, que mentionne *I Sam.* 30,29, devaient être de simples campements, à moins qu'elles ne correspondassent aux «agglomérations closes» mises au jour dans le Négev et datant du XIe siècle av.n.è. Ces agglomérations représentent, semble-t-il, un type d'installations sédentaires qui précédèrent l'aménagement administratif et militaire du Négev au temps de David et de Salomon[23].

Les Qenizzites voisinaient dans le Négev avec les Qénites[24], dont quelques clans s'étaient installés au sud-est d'Hébron, notamment en contre-bas d'Arad (*Jug.* 1,16; cf. *I Sam.* 30,28) et à Zanuah haq-Qayin (*Jos.* 15,56-57), c'est-à-dire Zanuah de Caïn, l'éponyme des Qénites (*Gen.* 4).

---

[15] Zarmi: *Jos.* 7,1.18; *I Chron.* 4,1. Hèçrôn: *Nomb.* 26,21; *I Chron.* 4,1.

[16] Cf. *I Chron.* 4,28-32; *Jug.* 1,4.17.

[17] *Jos.* 15,13-19; *Jug.* 1,20; *I Chron.* 2,42-50.

[18] *Nomb.* 32,12; *Jos.* 14,6.14; 15,17; *Jug.* 1,13; 3,9.11; *I Chron.* 4,13.

[19] *Gen.* 15,20; 36,11.15.42.

[20] *Gen.* 36,11.15; *I Chron.* 1,36.

[21] *Jos.* 15,16-19; *Jug.* 1,12-15.

[22] K. GALLING, *Zur Lokalisierung von Debir*, dans *ZDPV* 70 (1954), p. 135-141; M. KOCHAVI, *Khirbet Rabûd = Debir*, dans *Tel Aviv* 1 (1974), p. 2-33; cf. A. KUSCHKE, *Debir*, dans *Biblisches Reallexikon*, éd. K. GALLING, 2e éd., Tübingen 1977, p. 56-57.

[23] Z. HERZOG, *Enclosed Settlements in the Negeb and the Wilderness of Beer-Sheba*, dans *BASOR* 250 (1983), p. 41-49.

[24] *Gen.* 15,20; *Nomb.* 24,21; *I Sam.* 15,6.

Au nord du pays de Juda, Bethléem constituait le centre du territoire d'Éphrata, un nom géographique tout comme Éphraïm. Rien ne permet de croire, jusqu'ici, que la population de cette région n'était pas autochtone, vu qu'il n'est jamais question d'une conquête de Bethléem. Le clan le plus important devait y être celui de Pérèç[25], auquel la généalogie de *Ruth* 4,18-22 rattache le roi David[26], et dont le nom se retrouve dans celui du Baal des Peraçim qui permit à David de remporter une victoire décisive sur les Philistins[27].

Si^{uru}*Bêt-*^{d}NIN.URTA est bien Bethléem, **Bêt-Lāḥim*, «(lieu du) Temple du Guerroyeur»[28], la ville avait été une dépendance de Jérusalem à l'époque d'Amarna, mais elle s'était rendue indépendante au milieu du XIVe siècle[29]. Le «mariage» d'Éphrata avec Caleb (*I Chron.* 2,24), dont est issue la localité de Téqoa, sise 8 km au sud de Bethléem, atteste, en un second temps, un mélange d'éléments éphratéens et calébites dans la région située entre Bethléem et Hébron.

Le cas personnel de David, originaire de Bethléem et allié aux Calébites par ses femmes Abigayil de Karmel[30] et Ahinoam de Yizréel[31], explique qu'il ait pu réunir ces clans disparates, donner forme à une tribu de Juda et se faire reconnaître comme roi sur la

---

[25] *Gen.* 38,29; 46,12; *Nomb.* 26,20-21; *Ruth* 4,12.18; *Neh.* 11,4-6; *I Chron.* 2,4-5; 4,1; 9,4; 27,3.

[26] Cf. *I Chron.* 2,5-15; *Matthieu* 1,3-6; *Luc* 3,31-33. Dans la Bible grecque, tant dans la Septante que dans le Nouveau Testament, Pérèç porte le nom de Pharès.

[27] *II Sam.* 5,20; *I Chron.* 14,11; cf. *Is.* 28,21. Le Baal des Peraçim devait être le Baal du clan judéen de Pérèç, ce qui expliquerait que David ait vaincu les Philistins précisément aux abords de son sanctuaire. Amihai Mazar a récemment proposé de localiser ce dernier à Giloh, à 835 m d'altitude, site où les fouilles de sauvetage ont mis au jour des constructions du XIIe siècle av.n.è. Cf. A. MAZAR, *Giloh: An Early Israelite Settlement Site near Jerusalem*, dans *IEJ* 31 (1981), p. 1-36 et pl. 1-6 (voir p. 31-32).

[28] J.A. KNUDTZON, *Die El-Amarna-Tafeln*, Leipzig 1915, n° 290,16. Cette identification nous paraît actuellement préférable à celle que nous avons défendue naguère: E. LIPIŃSKI, *Beth-Schemesch und der Tempel der Herrin der Grabkamer in den Amarna-Briefen*, dans *VT* 23 (1973), p. 443-445. Ninurta étant un dieu de la guerre, son nom peut avoir servi de logogramme pour désigner une divinité guerrière locale. Le terme *lḥm* du toponyme Bethléem ne se rattacherait évidemment pas à *lḥm*, «pain», «viande» ou «poisson», suivant les langues, mais à *lḥm*, «combat» en sud-arabique; cf. A.F.L. BEESTON-M.A. GHUL-W.W. MÜLLER-J. RYCKMANS, *Dictionnaire sabéen*, Louvain-la-Neuve — Beyrouth 1982, p. 82. Le verbe moabitique *hlthm*, «faire la guerre» (*Mésha* 11.15.19.32), et le substantif hébraïque *milḥāmā*, «guerre», se rattachent à la même racine. En outre, l'épithète archaïque *Lāḥim*, «guerroyeur», se retrouve dans le chant de Déborah, en *Jug.* 5,8, où elle est employée en parallélisme avec *^{e}lōhīm*: «Que Dieu choisisse des armuriers (lire *ḥršym* au lieu de *ḥdšym*), puis, le Guerroyeur, des gardes portiers».

[29] C'est ce qui résulterait de la lettre du roi de Jérusalem: J.A. KNUDTZON, *op. cit.*, n° 290; cf. *ANET*, 3e éd., p. 489b.

[30] *I Sam.* 25,39-42.

[31] *I Sam.* 25,43; cf. *Jos.* 15,56; *I Sam.* 25,3.

«maison de Juda» (*II Sam.* 2,2-4). C'est la première fois que cette expression apparaît alors dans la Bible, car c'est par David que la tribu de Juda s'est constituée, s'identifiant avec le premier royaume de David à Hébron. Il va donc de soi que Juda n'a jamais fait partie de la fédération des douze tribus d'Israël et que le cantique de Déborah (*Jug.* 5) n'en fait aucune mention.

Si l'on définit un peuple comme une communauté liée par des traditions, des coutumes, une civilisation, un idiome et une certaine situation géographique, les origines diverses de Juda et de «tout Israël» devraient se refléter dans ces différents domaines socio-culturels, étant bien évident qu'il existait une nette démarcation géographique entre Juda et Israël.

Pour ce qui regarde les traditions, je me bornerai à évoquer les récits bibliques relatifs aux patriarches. De l'avis concordant des historiens critiques, les traditions sur Abraham et Isaac se réfèrent au sud palestinien, à la région de Gérar et de Béershéva, tandis que celles de Jacob sont localisées sur le Yabboq, à Sichem et à Béthel, c'est-à-dire dans les territoires habités par les tribus du Nord. L'association des trois patriarches Abraham, Isaac et Jacob-Israël dans l'histoire patriarcale panisraélite de *Gen.* 12-50 n'est que le résultat d'un agencement voulu et systématique de traditions d'origines et de dates diverses. Comme Abraham et Isaac sont des figures du terroir judéen, tandis que Jacob-Israël se rattache aux tribus du Nord, la systématisation actuelle ne peut dater que du temps de David et de Salomon. Elle avait vraisemblablement un but politique et visait à cimenter ces traditions d'origines diverses. Si cette opération, menée sans doute par des scribes royaux, avait réussi au plan littéraire, l'histoire d'Israël et de Juda montre qu'elle n'a guère eu d'influence sur le comportement des entités géopolitiques concernées.

Les sources dont nous disposons à l'heure présente ne nous permettent guère de différencier les coutumes et les institutions des Israélites du Nord de celles des Judéens du Sud, et il est probable qu'aucune découverte de documents écrits ne paillera d'une manière suffisante à ce manque actuel de données plus précises. Il y a pourtant une pratique coutumière d'Israël que les faits rapportés dans la Bible mettent suffisamment en relief pour qu'on puisse la comparer à la situation au pays de Juda. C'est l'institution monarchque que les anciens d'Israël ne rattachaient manifestement pas à un principe dynastique, alors que le «peuple du pays» de Juda l'avait en revanche accepté et défendu, quand le besoin s'en faisait sentir.

C'est l'assemblée d'Israël, représentée par ses anciens, qui avait élu Saül, puis David, à la royauté sur Israël. Salomon lui fut manifestement imposé et, à sa mort, l'élection de Jéroboam Ier, évinçant Roboam, le petit-fils de David, confirmait d'une manière éclatante l'autorité suprême que l'assemblée d'Israël s'attribuait en ce domaine.

Cette monarchie élective d'Israël était née de la nécessité de parer au danger philistin après le désastre d'Ében-ha-Ézer (*I Sam.* 4). Aux yeux des anciens d'Israël, le pays avait besoin d'un chef de guerre revêtu d'une autorité permanente, qui assumerait à la fois les fonctions de «suffète» et d'ataman, et porterait le titre de roi: «Notre roi nous 'jugera', il sortira à notre tête et combattra nos combats» (*I Sam.* 8,20). Les Livres de Samuel ont conservé deux récits de l'institution de la monarchie, l'un favorable à cette forme de l'État israélite, l'autre contraire à cette innovation dont les effets ne furent pas toujours perçus comme bénéfiques (cf. *I Sam.* 8,11-18). Les deux récits s'accordent cependant à reconnaître que Saül a été élu par l'assemblée du peuple, soit à cause de sa stature exceptionnelle, qui passait pour l'expression visible d'un charisme guerrier (*I Sam.* 10,23-25), soit à cause de la victoire remportée sur les Ammonites, succès qui avait fourni la preuve de ses qualités militaires (*I Sam.* 11,11.15).

Saül fut donc le premier roi électif d'Israël qui tirait son pouvoir de l'assemblée du peuple et des anciennes institutions prémonarchiques. En créant une armée de mercenaires (*I Sam.* 14,52; 22,7), qui lui restera fidèle même après sa mort (*II Sam.* 2,12ss), Saül tâcha cependant de jeter les fondements d'une monarchie héréditaire du type cananéen. Cet essai échoua: les anciens d'Israël élirent David comme roi (*II Sam.* 5,3), après que les hommes de Juda l'eussent d'abord élevé à la même dignité (*II Sam.* 2,1-4a). Une double monarchie élective était née de la sorte et, grâce à l'armée de mercenaires, notamment des Kerétiens et Pelétiens, elle survécut aux révoltes et passa par dévolution successorale à Salomon (*I Rois* 1,32-40). L'idéologie davidique[32] n'eut cependant pas raison des anciennes traditions du Nord, renforcées encore par l'opposition que suscita la politique de Salomon (*I Rois* 5,27ss; 11,26ss). À sa mort, l'assemblée du peuple réunie à Sichem réaffirma son droit d'élire le roi et désigna Jéroboam Ier comme successeur de Salomon, évinçant Roboam, le petit-fils de David (*I Rois* 12)[33]. L'histoire ultérieure d'Israël confirme

---

[32] *II Sam.* 7,12-16; 23,5; *Ps.* 89; 132. Cf. T.N.D. METTINGER, *King and Messiah*, Lund 1976, avec la bibliographie p. 312-332.

[33] Pour une interprétation de ce récit, interprétation que nous croyons pouvoir maintenir, on peut voir E. LIPIŃSKI, *Le récit de 1 Rois XII 1-19 à la lumière de l'ancien usage de l'hébreu et de nouveaux textes de Mari*, dans *VT* 24 (1974), p. 430-437.

l'autorité suprême que l'assemblée du peuple s'attribuait en ce domaine institutionnel.

Si Basha fit périr Nadab au milieu de «tout Israël» (*I Rois* 15,27) et si Omri fut proclamé roi par «tout Israël» (*I Rois* 16,16), c'est que l'assemblée du peuple ne reconnaissait pas le principe d'une monarchie héréditaire. Omri qui se construisit la ville royale de Samarie, soustraite à l'influence des anciennes institutions (*I Rois* 16,24), réussit pourtant à jeter les bases d'une monarchie héréditaire qui vécut plus de quarante ans. La réaction du yahvisme militant, dont Élie et Élisée furent les prophètes, y mit cependant fin d'une manière sanglante (*II Rois* 9-10), mais Jéhu parvint à son tour à établir une dynastie qui se maintint au pouvoir pendant près d'un siècle, malgré l'opposition du yahvisme traditionnel qui ne désarmait pas. Cette forme d'État monarchque lui paraissait manifestement inconciliable avec le principe de *vox populi, vox Dei*, défendu encore par *Osée* 8,4: «Ils ont fait un roi, mais sans mon accord; ils ont fait un prince, mais je ne l'ai pas reconnu».

La monarchie héréditaire instaurée par David reçut en revanche un accueil favorable au pays de Juda, demeuré étranger aux traditions prémonarchiques d'Israël et lié à la lignée du fils de Jessé provenant de la région même. L'assemblée générale des citoyens de Juda, distincte à l'époque monarchique de la population de Jérusalem, s'appelait *'am hā'āreṣ*, «le peuple du pays»[34]. C'est cette assemblée du «peuple du pays» qui proclama roi Joas (*II Rois* 11,14.18; *II Chron.* 23,13) et, plus tard, Josias (*II Rois* 21,24; *II Chron.* 33, 25), maintenant la lignée davidique sur le trône de Jérusalem en dépit de révolutions de palais. C'est elle aussi qui décida la démolition du temple de Baal à Jérusalem ou dans son voisinage immédiat, de même que l'exécution du prêtre de Baal et de la reine Athalie (*II Rois* 11,18.20; *II Chron.* 23,17.21). Le «peuple du pays» de Juda apparaît ainsi comme le gardien des traditions autochtones qu'il défend contre l'influence étrangère de l'entourage d'Athalie. Si l'on songe qu'Athalie était la fille et la sœur de rois d'Israël,

---

[34] Comparer *II Rois* 14,21 avec *II Rois* 23,30. Sur le *'am hā'āreṣ* on verra notamment les études de E. WÜRTHWEIN, *Der 'amm ha'arez im Alten Testament*, Stuttgart 1936; L.A. SNIJDERS, *Het «volk des lands» in Juda*, dans *Gereformeerd Theologisch Tijdschrift* 58 (1958), p. 241-256; J.A. SOGGIN, *Der judäische 'am-ha'areṣ und das Königtum in Juda*, dans *VT* 13 (1963), p. 187-195; ID., *Das Königtum in Israel* (BZAW 104), Berlin 1967, p. 106-111; R. DE VAUX, *Le sens de l'expression «peuple du pays» dans l'Ancien Testament et le rôle politique du peuple en Israël*, dans *RA* 58 (1964), p. 167-172; S. TALMON, *The Judaean 'am ha'areṣ in Historical Perspective*, dans *Proceedings of the Fourth World Congress of Jewish Studies* I, Jerusalem 1967, p. 71-76; T.N.D. METTINGER, *op. cit.* (n. 32), p. 124-129; A.H.J. GUNNEWEG, *'m h'rṣ — A Semantic Revolution*, dans *ZAW* 95 (1983), p. 437-440.

et que son nom même exprimait l'attachement au Dieu d'Israël, «Yahvé est seigneur»[35], on ne mesure que mieux le fossé qui séparait Israël et Juda. Le contraste portait même, semble-t-il, sur les coutumes religieuses et impliquait une certaine distinction entre le Dieu de Jérusalem, *'lhy yršlm*, comme l'appelle l'inscription de Khirbet Beit Lei[36], et le Dieu de Samarie, *yhwh šmrn*, dont le nom complet apparaît dans une inscription de Kuntillet 'Ajrūd qui pourrait remonter à l'époque d'Athalie[37]. On peut rappeler aussi que plusieurs textes d'Isaïe présentent Israël dans le rôle d'ennemi de Juda[38].

Les origines diverses de Juda et d'Israël doivent avoir laissé aussi des traces dans les vestiges de la civilisation matérielle, traces distinctes et susceptibles d'être discernées par des méthodes archéologiques. Bien que la céramique seule ne permette pas d'identifier un peuple, son homogénéité peut conduire à localiser une ethnie connue par l'épigraphie ou par des sources contemporaines reprises par les historiographes. Par exemple, la céramique grossière du Négev, modelée à la main sur des paillasses et cuite dans des fours provisoires creusés dans

---

[35] Le premier élément du nom d'Athalie, *'tl*, doit être rapproché de l'akkadien *etellu* ou *etallu*, «seigneur, prince», où le *e* initial révèle la présence d'une racine *'tl*. C'était déjà l'interprétation de FRIEDR. DELITZSCH, *Prolegomena eines neuen hebräisch-aramäischen Wörterbuchs zum Alten Testament*, Leipzig 1886, p. 212.

[36] J. NAVEH, *Old Hebrew Inscriptions in a Burial Cave*, dans *IEJ* 13 (1963), p. 74-92 et pl. 9-13 (voir p. 84-85 et 90-91). Cf. J.C.L. GIBSON, *Textbook of Syrian Semitic Inscriptions* I, 2ᵉ éd., Oxford 1973, p. 57-58; E. LIPIŃSKI, dans *Religionsgeschichtliches Textbuch zum Alten Testament*, éd. W. BEYERLIN, 2ᵉ éd., Göttingen 1985, p. 267-268. La même expression apparaît aussi dans *II Chron.* 32,19.

[37] Z. MESHEL, *Kuntillet 'Ajrud. A Religious Centre from the Time of the Judaean Monarchy on the Border of Sinai*, Jerusalem 1978, fig. 12. Cf. P. BECK, *The Drawings from Horvat Teiman (Kuntillet 'Ajrûd)*, dans *Tel Aviv* 9 (1982), p. 3-68 et pl. 1-16 (voir p. 45-47). Une datation plus tardive, entre *c.* 776 et 750 av.n.è., a été proposée par A. LEMAIRE, *Date et origine des inscriptions hébraïques et phéniciennes de Kuntillet 'Ajrud*, dans *SEL* 1 (1984), p. 131-143. — Il convient d'ajouter ici le *yhwh tmn*, «Yahvé de Témân» (cf. *Hab.* 3,3), mentionné aussi dans les inscriptions de Kuntillet 'Ajrūd d'après Z. Meshel; cf. M. WEINFELD, *Kuntillet 'Ajrud Inscriptions and Their Significance*, dans *SEL* 1 (1984), p. 121-130 (voir p. 125-126). Témân, qui pourrait être l'ancien nom de Kuntillet 'Ajrūd, est à tout le moins une spécification qui peut servir d'appoint à l'ancienne hypothèse de l'origine qénite ou madianite du Yahvisme. Voir à ce sujet H.H. ROWLEY, *From Joseph to Joshua*, London 1950, p. 149-163; ID., *Mose und der Monotheismus*, dans *ZAW* 69 (1957), p. 1-21 (voir p. 10-17); A.H.J. GUNNEWEG, *Mose in Midian*, dans *Zeitschrift für Theologie und Kirche* 61 (1964), p. 1-9; R. DE VAUX, *Sur l'origine kénite au madianite du Yahwisme*, dans *W.F. Albright Jubilee Volume* (Eretz-Israel IX), Jerusalem 1968, p. 28*-32*; J. KINYONGO, *Origine et signification du nom divin Yahvé*, Bonn 1970, p. 7-19, 39-41; cf. R. DE VAUX, *Histoire ancienne d'Israël* I, Paris 1971, p. 313-321.

[38] *Is.* 7,1-9; 8,1-4; 17,3; cf. aussi 10,27b-34; 17,4-6; 28,1-4. Voir Fr. HUBER, *Jahwe, Juda und die anderen Völker beim Propheten Jesaja* (BZAW 137), Berlin 1976, p. 10-31, cf. p. 32-34.

le sol, est attestée du XIIIe au VIe siècle av.n.è.[39] et pourrait être
attribuée aux Qenizzites[40], puisqu'on la rencontre sur le site édomite
de Tell el-Kheleifeh[41], près d'Aqaba. On la trouve au Négev, aux
XIe-Xe siècles, avec de la poterie réalisée à la tournette et attestée
communément au pays de Juda. Plutôt que de rapporter cette dernière
à David ou à Salomon[42], il faut peut-être la considérer simplement
comme qenizzite ou qénite, c'est-à-dire, en fin de compte, comme
judéenne. Nous préférons laisser la solution de ce problème aux
spécialistes de la céramique.

Selon Amihai Mazar, qui en est un, il n'est point difficile de discerner
un dépôt de poterie judéenne d'un dépôt contemporain israélite à
l'époque des deux royaumes séparés[43]. Il faudrait pousser les recherches
plus avant, afin de voir si des différences analogues n'existaient pas déjà
dans la poterie privée du temps de David et de Salomon, et même avant
cette date, à l'âge du Fer I[44]. Il serait logique de tirer ensuite les
conséquences pratiques de ces distinctions régionales et d'arriver à
qualifier, respectivement, d'israélites et de judéens les vestiges mis au jour
et dûment classifiés. Cela ne signifie point, bien sûr, que de nombreux
éléments de la culture matérielle ne sont pas communs à Israël et à Juda.
On a cependant tout avantage, pensons-nous, à pousser la distinction

---

[39] B. ROTHENBERG, *Timna*, London 1972, p. 180-182 (XIIIe siècle); R. COHEN, *The Iron Age Fortresses in the Central Negev*, dans *BASOR* 236 (1980), p. 61-78 (voir p. 75-77: VIIIe-VIIe siècles).

[40] R. COHEN, *art. cit.*, p. 77, l'a attribuée aux Qénites. Comme ceux-ci paraissent s'être établis dans la région d'Arad (*Jug.* 1,16; cf. *I Sam.* 30,29), à une époque qui pourrait correspondre au niveau XII d'Arad (cf. B. MAZAR, *The Sanctuary of Arad and the Family of Hobab the Kenite*, dans *JNES* 24 [1965], p. 297-303), où la céramique grossière du Négev n'est point attestée (M. AHARONI, *The Pottery of Strata 12-11 of the Iron Age Citadel at Arad*, dans *Y. Aharoni Memorial Volume* [Eretz-Israel XV], Jerusalem 1981, p. 181-204 [en hébreu] et 82*), nous préférons parler de Qenizzites. Les deux groupes étaient de toute manière apparentés.

[41] N. GLUECK, *The First Season of Excavations at Tell el-Kheleifeh*, dans *BASOR* 71 (1938), p. 3-17 (voir p. 14); ID., *The Third Season of Excavations at Tell el-Kheleifeh*, dans *BASOR* 79 (1940), p. 2-18 (voir p. 17-18).

[42] R. COHEN, *art. cit.*, p. 77-78; ID.-Z. MESHEL, *Two Iron Age Fortresses in the Northern Negev*, dans *Tel Aviv* 7 (1980), p. 70-81 (voir p. 80).

[43] A. MAZAR, *Archaeological Research on the Period of the Monarchy (Iron Age II)*, dans *Recent Archaeology in the Land of Israel*, éd. H. SHANKS-B. MAZAR, Washington-Jerusalem 1984, p. 43-57, voir p. 55: «It is a simple task, however, to differentiate between a cache of pottery originating in Judah and a contemporaneous one from the northern kingdom of Israel. We should persevere, however, in our attempts to investigate the slow but definite changes that occur in the pottery of each geopolitical entity, by constructing a series of exact typologies and by using quantitative analysis».

[44] C'est au fond le but des recherches archéologiques régionales, dont le nombre se multiplie actuellement en Israël.

aussi loin que possible, d'une manière systématique. Ceci permettrait de voir certains problèmes sous un jour nouveau.

Quelques exemples suffiront, je pense, à expliciter ma pensée.

On a fait remarquer à juste titre, semble-t-il, que la grande jarre à provisions ou pithos, avec un bord à bourrelet (*collared rim*), n'apparaît pas sur les sites du Négev septentrional, comme Tel Masos, et qu'elle n'est attestée à Tell Beit Mirsim que par quelques tessons, alors qu'elle est très répandue en Cisjordanie centrale, spécialement dans les établissements du Fer I[45]. On pourrait donc considérer ce type de poterie comme typiquement «israélite» au sens propre du terme. On a cependant fait observer que les jarres de ce type apparaissent aussi en Transjordanie, spécialement à Saḥāb, à l'est d'Amman, et dans la vallée du Jourdain[46]. Certes, la rive orientale du Jourdain était occupée par des tribus israélites et la découverte, à Sāḥab même, d'un sarcophage anthropoïde d'un type utilisé par les Philistins à Beth-Shéan[47] indique que ce site avait des relations spéciales avec la Cisjordanie à l'époque du Fer I. Il n'en reste pas moins vrai que Saḥāb n'est pas un site israélite du Fer I et il n'est donc pas possible de considérer cette poterie comme spécifiquement israélite. En revanche, son absence quasi totale dans la partie méridionale du territoire de Juda souligne l'isolation de cette région par rapport à la Cisjordanie centrale. Si le bord à bourrelet ne peut donc servir de critère pour distinguer les pithos d'un site israélite des jarres cananéennes, philistines ou ammonites[48], il pourrait servir à caractériser les sites israélites par opposition à ceux du sud du pays de Juda.

C'est à un *non liquet* que l'on aboutirait en revanche dans le cas des «maisons à quatre compartiments», que le prof. Yigal Shiloh[49] avait considérées comme des innovations architecturales remontant aux dé-

---

[45] A. MAZAR, *art. cit.* (n. 27), p. 27-31. Comparer V. FRITZ-A. KEMPINSKI, *Ergebnisse der Ausgrabungen auf der Ḥirbet el-Mšāš (Tēl Māśōś), 1972-1975*, Wiesbaden 1983, vol. I, p. 74-75. D'après J. BALENSI, *Le rôle de la céramique*, dans *Le Monde de la Bible* 36 (1984), p. 37-42, «il s'avère aujourd'hui que c'est là un type de jarre traditionnel en Samarie depuis le Bronze Moyen» (p. 41). Son *origine* israélite est donc exclue.

[46] M.M. IBRAHIM, *The Collared-Rim Jar of the Early Iron Age*, dans *Archaeology in the Levant. Essays for Kathleen Kenyon*, Warminster 1978, p. 116-126.

[47] W.F. ALBRIGHT, *An Anthropoid Clay Coffin from Saḥāb in Transjordan*, dans *AJA* 36 (1932), p. 292-306.

[48] Il faut toutefois noter que les bords à bourrelet se diversifient typologiquement. Ce sont cependant des différences mineures qui reflètent des ateliers distincts plutôt que des traditions artisanales diverses.

[49] Y. SHILOH, *The Four-Room House — Its Situation and Function in the Israelite City*, dans *IEJ* 20 (1970), p. 180-190; ID., *The Four-Room House — The Israelite Type House?*, dans *I. Dunayevsky Memorial Volume* (Eretz-Israel XI), Jerusalem 1973, p. 277-285 (en hébreu) et 32*.

buts de la période israélite. Pour sa part, G. E. Wright y avait vu une
habitation caractéristique de l'Israël du Nord, empruntée probablement
à la Phénicie[50]. Il se fait pourtant que les plus anciens exemples certains
de ce type d'habitation privée proviennent de la zone d'influence
philistine, de Tell Qasile X[51] et de 'Izbet Ṣarṭah[52], et du Négev
septentrional, de Tel Masos[53], à 15 km environ à l'est de Béershéva,
et de Tel Sera' VIII (Tell eš-Šari'a)[54], à 17 km environ au nord-ouest
de Béershéva. Or, la poterie du niveau VIII de Tel Sera' prouve que la
localité se trouvait alors dans la sphère d'influence philistine[55], tandis
que Tel Masos paraît refléter les us et coutumes d'une communauté
maintenant des contacts suivis avec la population sédentaire depuis une
période relativement longue et vivant dans le prolongement direct de la
culture matérielle du Bronze récent II[56]. Quelle que soit l'origine ultime
de ce type d'habitations privées, qui est peut-être attesté aussi à Tell
Keisan[57], il est désormais clair qu'elles apparaissent aussi bien dans les
régions septentrionales que méridionales de Canaan et ne peuvent donc
servir à différencier la maison nord-israélite de la maison judéenne.

---

[50] G.E. WRIGHT, *A Characteristic North Israelite House*, dans *Archaeology in the
Levant. Essays for Kathleen Kenyon*, Warminster 1978, p. 149-154.

[51] A. MAZAR, *Excavations at Tell Qasile I* (Qedem 12), Jerusalem 1980, p. 74-75; cf.
M. AVI-YONAH - E. STERN (éd.), *op. cit.* (n. 2) IV, Oxford 1978, p. 963-966.

[52] M. KOCHAVI, *An Ostracon of the Period of the Judges from 'Izbet Ṣarṭah*, dans
Tel Aviv 4 (1977), p. 1-13 (voir p. 1-4 et fig. 2).

[53] V. FRITZ-A. KEMPINSKI, *Vorberichte über die Ausgrabungen auf der Ḥirbet el-Mšāš
(Tēl Māśōś). 3. Kampagne 1975*, dans *ZDPV* 92 (1976), p. 83-104 (voir p. 85-94 et 102-
104); V. FRITZ, *The Israelite «Conquest» in the Light of Recent Excavations at Khirbet el
Meshâsh*, dans *BASOR* 241 (1981), p. 61-73 (voir p. 62-69); ID.-A. KEMPINSKI, *op. cit.*
(n. 45), vol. I, p. 11-15, 34; vol. II, pl. 5-10; vol. III, plan 6; poterie philistine, vol. I, p. 75.

[54] E. OREN, *Ziqlag — A Biblical City on the Edge of the Negev*, dans *BA* 45 (1982),
p. 155-166 (voir p. 161-164).

[55] *Ibid.*, p. 163; cf. J.D. SEGER, *The Location of Biblical Ziklag*, dans *BA* 47 (1984),
p. 47-53 (voir p. 48). — Comp. G. W. AHLSTRÖM, *Giloh: A Judahite or Canaanite
Settlement?*, dans *IEJ* 34 (1984), p. 170-172 (voir p. 171).

[56] A. KEMPINSKI-V. FRITZ, *Excavations at Tel Masos (Khirbet el-Meshâsh). Preliminary Report on the Third Season, 1975*, dans *Tel Aviv* 4 (1975), p. 136-158 (voir p. 142-143);
V. FRITZ, *art. cit.* (n. 53), p. 69-70; ID.-A. KEMPINSKI, *op. cit.* (n. 45), vol. I, p. 231-232.

[57] J.-B. HUMBERT, *Récents travaux à Tell Keisan (1979-1980)*, dans *RB* 88 (1981),
p. 373-398 et pl. VIII-X (voir provisoirement p. 394-395). — Malgré ses quatre chambres, la
maison 448 du niveau VI de Tel Batash, datant de la fin du XIIIᵉ siècle, peut difficilement
être considérée comme une maison «à quatre compartiments». Sa forme carrée et l'absence
de piliers ne permettent pas de la rattacher typologiquement à ce genre d'habitations. Cf.
G. L. KELM-A. MAZAR, *Three Seasons of Excavations at Tel Batash — .Biblical Timnah*,
dans *BASOR* 248 (1982), p. 1-36 (voir p. 13-14 et 17, fig. 16). En revanche, les maisons
carrées avec murs internes de séparation en forme de T pourraient être rangées parmi les
prototypes de la maison «à quatre compartiments» de l'âge du Fer. Cf. J. BALENSI,
Revising Tell Abu Hawam, dans *BASOR* 257 (1985), p. 65-74 (voir p. 68 et 72, n. 21-22).

L'architecture monumentale, qui fait malheureusement défaut dans les niveaux israélites et judéens du Fer I, pourrait servir parfois de critère. Le regretté prof. Y. Yadin a posé la question avec acuité à propos du «palais» de Ramat Raḥel, dont les éléments architecturaux et la maçonnerie se rattachent étroitement aux constructions de Samarie[58]. Il a donc proposé d'y reconnaître un bâtiment du temps d'Athalie, l'unique période de l'histoire au cours de laquelle le pays de Juda était gouverné par des gens originaires d'Israël[59]. La présence de cet ensemble «palatial» à 3 km au sud de Jérusalem n'en prouve pas moins qu'il faut aussi tenir compte, à l'époque monarchique, des artisans réfugiés ou transférés d'une région à l'autre et exportant, de la sorte, leurs traditions et leurs techniques. Ce serait peut-être la raison pour laquelle les grandes jarres ovoïdes, répandues dans le Négev et le pays de Juda, sont attestées aussi au niveau V de Megiddo[60]. L'archéométrie permettrait sans doute d'en déterminer l'origine et de répondre indirectement à la question que l'on doit se poser ici, à savoir : sont-ce les jarres qui ont été transportées de Juda en Israël[61] ou sont-ce des potiers judéens qui ont été transférés, au temps de Salomon, dans la forteresse royale de Megiddo?

On voit ainsi que c'est un problème ardu que l'on pose aux archéologues en les invitant à chercher non seulement des éléments matériels qui caractériseraient les sites israélites au sens large du terme, mais aussi les critères qui permettraient de distinguer un site proprement israélite d'un site judéen, qenizzite ou qénite.

Dernière question, enfin : y avait-il une différence entre l'idiome de Juda et celui d'Israël? L'épisode bien connu du *shibbolet*, rapporté au Livre des *Juges* 12,6, laisse entrevoir des variantes dialectales entre la Cisjordanie et la Transjordanie vers la fin de l'âge du Fer I. Ces variantes dépassaient sans nul doute l'alternance de l'interdentale sourde *ṯ*, notée par un «s»[62], et de la palato-alvéolaire sourde *š*, alternance à laquelle le

---

[58] Ceci a déjà été noté par Y. AHARONI, *Excavations at Ramat Raḥel, 1954. Preliminary Report*, dans *IEJ* 6 (1956), p. 102-111 et 137-157 (voir p. 138, 140, 144, 151).

[59] Y. YADIN, *The 'House of Ba'al' of Ahab and Jezebel in Samaria, and that of Athalia in Judah*, dans *Archaeology in the Levant. Essays for Kathleen Kenyon*, Warminster 1978, p. 127-135 (voir p. 130-132). Il faut cependant noter qu'aucune poterie antérieure au VIIIᵉ siècle av.n.è. n'a été retrouvée dans les restes de ce bâtiment : Y. AHARONI, *Ramat Raḥel*, dans *DBS* IX, Paris 1979, col. 1093-1101.

[60] R. COHEN, *art. cit.* (n. 39), p. 75.

[61] Comparer A. MAZAR, *art. cit.* (n. 27), p. 25.

[62] L'explication correcte de *Jug.* 12,6 avait été proposée par E.A. SPEISER, *The Shibboleth Incident (Judes 12 :6)*, dans *BASOR* 85 (1942), p. 10-13 = E.A. SPEISER, *Oriental and Biblical Studies*, Philadelphia 1967, p. 143-150, dont la solution a été reprise

texte fait directement allusion, mais elles ne répondent pas à notre question qui porte sur la différence entre les idiomes du Nord et ceux du Sud. C'est l'épigraphie qui nous livre la preuve indubitable de différences dialectales entre Samarie, la capitale du Royaume du Nord, et Jérusalem, la capitale du Royaume de Juda. Sur les ostraca trouvés dans une annexe du palais royal à Samarie, le mot «vin» est écrit yn[63], ce qui suppose une prononciation $yên$, alors que la tradition jérusalémite, représentée par les ostraca d'Arad[64] et un ostracon de Qumrân, datant du VIIIe-VIIe siècle[65], et suivie par le texte reçu de la Bible, écrit ce mot yyn et le prononce $yāyin$. Cette différence révèle un traitement différent des diphtongues dans l'idiome du Nord, qui les contractait, et dans l'idiome du Sud, plus conservateur, qui les gardait inaltérées dans des cas semblables. Un fragment de Qumrân[66], qui paraît suivre l'orthographe nord-israélite, livre d'autres exemples de monophtongaison. Le mot $\bar{o}y\bar{e}b$, «ennemi», y est écrit $'b$ et se prononçait donc $'\bar{e}b$[67], tandis que $'awl\bar{a}$, «iniquité», y est noté simplement par $'l$[68], ce qui paraît indiquer une prononciation $'\hat{o}l\bar{a}$.

Sur les ostraca de Samarie, le mot «année» est écrit $\check{s}t$, ce qui suppose une prononciation $\check{s}att$[69], avec assimilation du n radical à la consonne t. Par contre, la forme méridionale du même mot était respectivement $\check{s}\bar{a}n\bar{a}(h)$ à l'état absolu et $\check{s}^enat < * \check{s}anat$ à l'état construit[70]. Le nom

par P. SWIGGERS, *The Word Šibbōleṭ in Jud. XII.6*, dans *JSS* 26 (1981), p. 205-207. L'emploi de «s» pour rendre l'interdentale sourde $\underline{t}$ se retrouve dans l'inscription araméenne de Tell Feḥeriye; cf. A. ABOU-ASSAF-P. BORDREUIL-A.R. MILLARD, *La statue de Tell Fekherye et son inscription bilingue assyro-araméenne*, Paris 1982, p. 43-44. C'est ce que vient de remarquer aussi A. LEMAIRE, *L'incident du sibbolet (Jg 12,6) : perspective historique*, dans *Mélanges M. Delcor* (AOAT 215), Kevelaer-Neukirchen-Vluyn 1985, p. 275-281.

[63] G. A. REISNER-C. S. FISCHER-D. G. LYON, *Harvard Excavations at Samaria*, Cambridge Mass. 1924, vol. I, *Text*, p. 227-246; vol. II, *Plans and Plates*, pl. 55c, d, e. Cf. D. DIRINGER, *Le iscrizioni antico-ebraiche palestinesi*, Firenze 1934, p. 21-68; A. LEMAIRE, *Inscriptions hébraïques I. Les ostraca* (LAPO 9), Paris 1977, p. 21-81. Voir les n°s 5,3; 6,3; 10,3; 11,1; 12,3; 13,3; 14,3; 53,1; 54,1; 72,1; 73,2; 101,1.

[64] Y. AHARONI, *Arad Inscriptions*. In cooperation with J. NAVEH, Jerusalem 1981. Voir les n°s 1,3.9; 2,2.5; 3,2; 4,3; 8,5; 10,2; 11,3.

[65] N° d'inventaire KhQ 1236 (campagne de 1954), mentionné dans P. BENOIT-J.T. MILIK-R. DE VAUX, *Les Grottes de Murabba'ât* (Discoveries in the Judaean Desert II), *Texte*, Oxford 1961, p. 93.

[66] 4Q 236, édité par J.T. MILIK, *Fragment d'une source du Psautier (4Q Ps 89)*, dans *RB* 73 (1966), p. 94-106 et pl. I-III (voir p. 94-104 et pl. I).

[67] Ligne 6; cf. E. LIPIŃSKI, *Le Poème royal du Psaume LXXXIX 1-5.20-38* (Cahiers de la Revue biblique 6), Paris 1967, p. 54-55.

[68] Ligne 6; cf. J.T. MILIK, *art. cit.*, p. 102.

[69] Cf. di-dessus n. 63. Voir la ligne 1 de presque tous les ostraca.

[70] C'est la seule forme qui ait été retenue par la tradition biblique.

divin lui-même s'écrivait différemment dans les noms propres israélites et judéens, et devait donc se prononcer de manière diverse[71]. L'élément théophore apparaît sous la forme *yw* au Nord[72] et sous celle de *yhw* au Sud, ce qui permet d'établir la prononciation *yāw* pour Israël et *yāhū* pour Juda[73], avec une tendance à la syncope du *h*[74].

Si de telles différences existaient déjà à l'époque monarchique entre l'idiome d'Israël et celui de Juda, on comprend que la prononciation de l'hébreu ait évolué plus tard d'une manière différente chez les Samaritains et les Juifs.

En conclusion, les analogies indéniables entre les traditions, les coutumes, les institutions, les idiomes et la culture matérielle de Juda et de «tout Israël» ne doivent pas faire perdre de vue les contrastes tout aussi importants qui découlent d'une histoire différente, d'origines partiellement diverses et de contacts culturels variés. Le rôle de l'historien, aussi bien que de l'archéologue, est de mettre en relief ces contrastes que la tendance nivelatrice et panisraélite, qui trouve une base chez les rédacteurs bibliques eux-mêmes, porte trop souvent à négliger au détriment non seulement de la vérité historique, mais aussi de la richesse du patrimoine du peuple ou des peuples de la Bible. Si nous avons insisté

---

[71] Pour ce problème voir H. Torczyner, *The Lachish Letters* (Lachish I), Oxford 1938, p. 24-31; H.L. Ginsberg, *Lachish Notes*, dans *BASOR* 71 (1938), p. 24-27; J.T. Milik, dans *op. cit.* (n. 65), p. 99-100; M. Weippert, *Jahwe*, dans *Reallexikon der Assyriologie* V, Berlin-New York 1976-80, p. 246-253 (voir p. 247-249); H. Ringgren, dans *ThWAT* III, Stuttgart 1982, col. 535, 539-541.

[72] C'est la forme attestée dans les ostraca de Samarie, qui datent de la première moitié du VIIIe siècle av.n.è.; cf. ci-dessus n. 63. Elle apparaît aussi dans les inscriptions de Kuntillet 'Ajrūd qui invoquent Yahvé de Samarie; ce ne peuvent donc être que des noms d'Israélites du Nord. On trouvera la transcription de ces noms, *yw'š* et *'mryw*, chez J. Naveh, *Graffiti and Dedication*, dans *BASOR* 235 (1979), p. 27-30 (voir p. 28).

[73] En position finale, *yhw* est fréquent au VIIIe siècle et apparaît probablement dès le IXe siècle dans la légende sigillaire *lšm'yhw bn 'zryhw*; cf. F. Vattioni, *I sigilli ebraici*, dans *Biblica* 50 (1969), p. 357-388 (voir n° 40); J.C.L. Gibson, *op. cit.* (n. 36), p. 61, n° 6; J.A. Millard, *YW and YWH Names*, dans *VT* 30 (1980), p. 208-212. En position initiale, il n'est attesté qu'à partir du VIIIe/VIIe siècle, notamment dans les noms *yhwmlk* et *yhw'z* de deux légendes sigillaires qui pourraient remonter au VIIIe siècle; cf. F. Vattioni, *art. cit.*, n°s 156 et 162; M. Heltzer-M. Ohana, *The Extra-Biblical Tradition of Hebrew Personal Names* (en hébreu), Haifa 1978, p. 49 et 96, n. 297 et 298. Le palimpseste Mur 17, publié par J.T. Milik, *op. cit.* (n. 65), p. 97 et pl. xxviii, soulève un problème délicat: le texte doit dater du VIIIe siècle et mentionne *šm'yhw* (fils de) *yw'zr* (ligne 4), attestant ainsi l'élément théophore *yhw* en position finale et *yw* en position initiale. Faut-il attribuer ces graphies différentes à deux prononciations distinctes, suivant que le nom divin se trouvait en position initiale ou finale, ou faut-il tenir compte aussi de la vague de réfugiés venus au pays de Juda lors de la conquête de la Samarie par les Assyriens?

[74] C'est ce qui explique l'alternance des forme *yô* < *yāw* et *y°hô/yāhū* dans la Bible, ainsi que les formes en *-ia(-a)-wa$_6$* dans les textes cunéiformes de l'époque perse.

sur les différences, c'est que celles-ci risquent d'être oubliées, alors qu'elles constituent un enrichissement de nos connaissances historiques du passé de la Terre d'Israël.

SUMMARY

The distinction between Judah and Israel is by far more ancient than the political schism which marked the end of David's and Solomon's great kingdom shortly after 930, probably in 929/8 B.C. The so-called Song of Deborah in *Judg.* 5, composed towards the end of the II millennium B.C., shows that, at that time, Judah was neither a part of Israel nor a tribal entity in close contact with the peoples of central and northern Canaan. The events which led to David's accession to the throne of Judah and of Israel, the Israelite revolts against him, and Solomon's political and administrative measures show that Judah and Israel were two separate geopolitical entities even during the reign of those two great kings. The historical background and evolution of these two nations was, in fact, quite different. Judah, which seems to have become a tribal entity only in David's times, originally stemmed from a few Rubenite and Simeonite clans and, above all, from some Kenizzite, Kenite and Ephrataean tribes living in and around «the land full of ravines», *'ereṣ yehūdā*, which gave its name to the tribe of Judah, when the latter came into existence as such and was given an eponym, who was subsequently integrated in the panisraelite framework of the patriarchal traditions.

If we accept the definition of a nation as a community bound together by common traditions, customs, civilization, idiom, and a determined geopolitical situation, it is clear that, in spite of the numerous religious and socio-cultural aspects they had in common, Israel and Judah were, from a historical point of view, two separate nations. In fact, besides the clear geographical boundary which existed between them, there were differences even in the traditions: those related to Abraham and Isaac, for instance, were typical of the Palestinian south, while those concerning Jacob-Israel were peculiar to the tribes of central Canaan. Likewise, the institution of a hereditary monarchy always met with a strong opposition in the traditionalist circles of Israel, whereas the people of Judah was devoted to the dynasty of David, the founder of Judah as a political entity. Furthermore, the Hebrew language spoken in Judah differed from the one spoken in Israel. And lastly, Judah's isolation can be seen also in its material culture, whose regional features would gain in being studied from the new viewpoint of rather radical differences between Judah and Israel.

These various differences, brought out all the more strongly by some undeniable analogies, show that cultural and institutional differences marked the history of the people or peoples of the Bible. Israel, land of contacts, was also a land of contrasts.

E. LIPIŃSKI
Ad. Lacomblélaan 50/11
B-1040 Brussel.

THE MATERIAL CULTURE OF JUDAH AND JERUSALEM IN IRON AGE II: ORIGINS AND INFLUENCES

YIGAL SHILOH

I

Since the dawn of history, Eretz-Israel, due to its geographical position on the map of the Near East, constituted a land-bridge for the passage of tribes, peoples and armies from the desert to the sea and from the north to the south. These movements and the factors involved in them influenced the development of the material culture of the country's population and introduced new cultural and human elements. This process, which had been gaining strength ever since the Bronze Age, reached a peak during the Iron Age, a period for which detailed historical records are available.

A great deal of information concerning the political, cultural and religious factors which shaped the civilization of the Near East and especially of Eretz-Israel during that period is contained in these records. Archaeological research is thus faced with a serious challenge. Not only does it have to present its findings in correlation with these historical processes and to interpret them correctly, but it also must try to illuminate them from fresh view-points. Today, with the introduction of new, more sophisticated methods of archaeological research, important advances have been made, mainly due to the interdisciplinary approach to the study and processing of the material. Some of the results of this approach as applied to the excavations in the City of David will be presented below (fig. 1).

The discussion will be based on the analysis of a number of examples from among the abundant material uncovered in Strata 14-10 in the City of David, dated to the 10th-6th centuries B.C.E. At that time, the city was the capital of Judah and was at the centre of political and social events of the first importance in the history of Eretz-Israel. The discussion will focus on evidence concerning town-planning, architecture and small finds. During seven seasons of excavations, beginning in 1978, more than twenty strata have been excavated, spanning the centuries in the history of the settlement from the late fourth millennium B.C.E. — the

Fig. 1. — The City of David and the Old City of Jerusalem, looking north (Z. Radovan,
         1984).
         (1) The City of David excavations.
         (2) The excavations near the Temple Mount.
         (3) The excavations in the Jewish Quarter.

Chalcolithic period — to our own times[1]. In Jerusalem, like in other
urban centres on the central mountain ridge of Eretz-Israel, the urbani-
zation process started already at the beginning of the Early Bronze Age.
The first houses of the settlement, dating from the Early Bronze Age I,
were founded on bedrock on the east slope, near the Gihon spring and
the cultivated fields along the Kidron (fig. 2) (Stratum 20). During the
Middle Bronze Age II B, in the 18th century B.C.E., the city was
enclosed by a broad wall (figs. 3-4). A considerable section of this wall
and of the structures adjoining it inside the city were exposed in Area E,
on the east slope of the hill (Strata 18-17). A section of the wall, and

_____

[1] Y. SHILOH, *Excavations at the City of David I. 1978-1982. Interim Report of the First
Five Seasons* (Qedem 19), Jerusalem 1984.

Fig. 2. — The eastern slope of the City of David Looking south (Z. Radovan, 1984).
A, B, D, E, J, G : areas of excavations in the City of David.
(1) The Gihon Spring.
(2) The Kenyon excavations.
(3) The excavation near the Temple Mount.

perhaps even the «water-gate» tower uncovered by Kenyon at the bottom of her Section I above the Gihon spring, belong to this period [2].

No archaeological evidence is available concerning the nature of the settlement in Jerusalem during the 16th-15th centuries B.C.E. A few scanty layers containing sherds from the Late Bronze Age II B (Stratum 16) were exposed in Area E 1. These layers were sandwiched between the Middle Bronze Age II B and the Iron Age I (Stratum 15) strata. The important remains of this period were uncovered in Area G, at the northern end of the hill (figs. 2, 5). It is generally accepted that this upper part of the city was the acropolis in the Canaanite period. A complex of retaining walls forming compartments filled with stone were

[2] K. M. KENYON, *Digging up Jerusalem*, London 1974, p. 82-84.

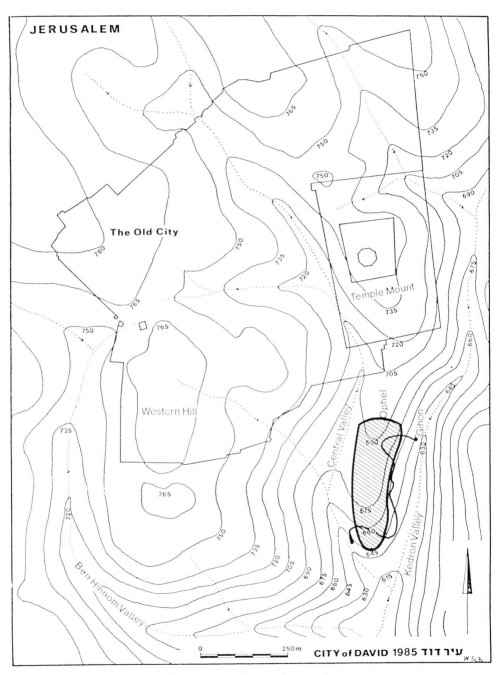

Fig. 3. — Plan of Canaanite Jerusalem.

Fig. 4. — The City of David, Area E, air-photo looking to the west. The city-wall of the
Canaanite and Israelite cities can be seen in the centre of the photo. The
«Ashlar House» is in the upper left corner of the area (Z. Radovan, 1984).

uncovered in Area G, going down steeply, step by step, southwards and
eastwards [3]. This complex of walls and fills created a stone platform
attached to the eastern slope and rising to a height of 6-10 m (figs. 5-7).
The platform provided a man-made addition of some 260 m² to the
very important area on the top of the hill, whose natural dimensions
were very limited. The few sherds found in the fills were not later than
the 14th-13th centuries B.C.E. It can be assumed, therefore, that the
platform carried the Canaanite «stronghold of Zion» which was situated
on this part of the hill.

In the 10th century B.C.E., the City of David became the capital of
the kingdom of Judah and Israel (fig. 8). The Bible, in contrast to its
usual practice, furnishes many details concerning the building activities

[3] Y. SHILOH, op. cit., (n. 1), figs. 16-18 and pls. 27-29:1.

Fig. 5. — The City of David, Area G, air-photo looking west (Z. Radovan, 1983).
   (1) The southern tower and the city wall of the Second Temple
       and the Byzantine Periods.
   (2) The stepped stone structure.
   (3) The substructure of the Late Bronze Age II Citadel.
   (4) The «Ahi'el House».
   (5) The «Burnt Room».

and the edifices erected during that century, especially in Solomon's
reign (*I Kings* 3,1; 9,15.24; 11,27). The correlation of the data provided
by the biblical account with the material accumulated by up-to-date
archaeological research, mainly that of the Kenyon and Shiloh expeditions [4], yields a considerable body of evidence concerning the town-plan
of Jerusalem. The main change occurred in the 10th-9th centuries B.C.E.,
as a result of the expansion of the northern acropolis area and the
construction of the royal complex there, consisting of the Temple, the
royal palaces, and buildings to house the administration, the army and

---

[4] K. M. KENYON, *op. cit.*, (n. 2), p. 98-119; Y. SHILOH, *op. cit.* (n. 1), p. 27.

Fig. 6. — The City of David, Area G, looking west on the remains of the substructure of the Late Bronze Age II Citadel (I. Harari, 1983).

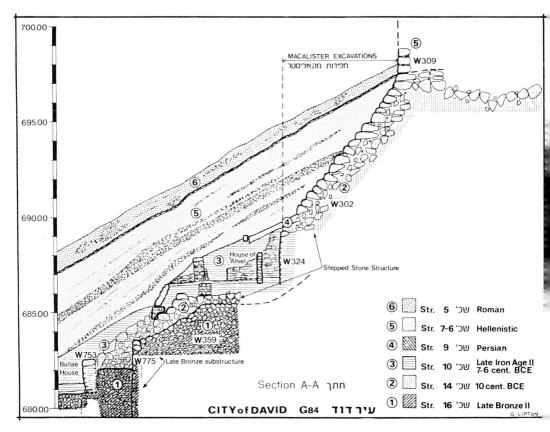

Fig. 7. — The City of David, Area G, general schematic section.

various services. This expansion added an area estimated at about 100 dunams (10 ha) to that of the Canaanite city, which until then had been only 60 dunams (6 ha). At that stage, Jerusalem spread over an area of 160 dunams (16 ha) and thus counted as one of the largest cities in Judah and Israel of that time. No longer was Jerusalem one of several important cities, as it had been in the Bronze Age. Now it was the capital, the foremost city among royal centres such as Hazor, Megiddo and Gezer, which were also built at that time. Kenyon, on the evidence of the pottery in her Areas M, P, H and R, pointed out that in the 10th century B.C.E. the town expanded from the northern end of the City of David in the direction of the Temple Mount [5] (fig. 2).

[5] K. M. KENYON, op. cit. (n. 2), p. 114-116.

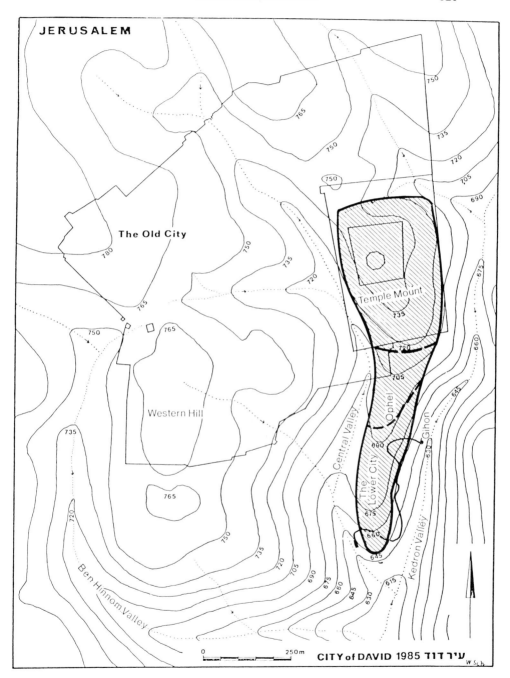

Fig. 8. — Plan of Jerusalem in the 10th-9th centuries B.C.E.

Our excavations yielded a considerable body of information concerning this period. In the area of the Lower City — Areas E 1, E 3,
D 1 and D 2 — the 10th century stratum (Stratum 14) was traced, and
a number of structures, as well as some pottery and cult objects, were
uncovered[6]. The most important archaeological evidence which con-
cerns us here was found in Area G[7]. The stone platform of the Canaanite
«stronghold of Zion», which was conquered by David, served as the
nucleus of the new substructure for the 10th century citadel (figs. 5, 8).
It is for that purpose that the stepped stone structure was erected, which
still stands to a height of about 17 m, though its base has not yet been
exposed (figs. 5-7). Careful tracing of the natural rock topography at
the top of the eastern slope and at the northern end of the hill on which
the City of David is situated led us to the conclusion that our excavations
are touching the southeastern corner of the Upper City and perhaps even
the substructure of David's citadel itself[8]. The citadel, which was erected
at the head of the stepped stone structure, has not been preserved, with
the exception of part of a massive stone wall. This wall fragment was
exposed during the 1984 season under the north tower from the late
Second Temple period[9]. Further evidence uncovered by Kenyon indicates, in our opinion, the proximity of important public buildings.
This evidence includes a tumble of small ashlar blocks[10], a palmette
(Proto-Aeolic) capital[11] and part of a casemate wall found in Kenyon's
Area H, which abuts the northwestern corner of Area G[12].

The evidence outlined above testifies to the changing town-plan of
Jerusalem, both in relation to the Canaanite town-plan and to Israelite
innovations. The Lower City served as a residential quarter from the
Early Bronze Age onwards and until the destruction of the Israelite city
in 586 B.C.E.; during the Middle Bronze Age II the city was surrounded
by a wall which also served as the base of the Iron Age city wall of the
Lower City[13]; the area of the Canaanite acropolis continued to be used

    [6] Y. SHILOH, op. cit. (n. 1), p. 12; ID., Jerusalem, City of David, 1983, in IEJ 34 (1984),
p. 57-58 (see p. 57).

    [7] Y. SHILOH, op. cit., (n. 1), p. 16-17.

    [8] Y. SHILOH, Elements in the City Plan of Jerusalem during the Monarchy, in Proceedings
of the Eighth World Congress of Jewish Studies. Panel Sessions. Bible Studies and Hebrew
Language, Jerusalem 1983, p. 139-144 (see p. 143-144).

    [9] Y. SHILOH, Jerusalem, City of David, 1984, in IEJ 35 (1985), p. 65-67.

    [10] K. M. KENYON, Excavations in Jerusalem, 1962, in PEQ 95 (1963), p. 7-21 (see p. 16).

    [11] Ibid., p. 16; Y. SHILOH, The Proto-Aeolic Capital and Israelite Ashlar Masonry
(Qedem 11), Jerusalem 1979, p. 10-11.

    [12] K. M. KENYON, op. cit., (n. 2), p. 114-115.

    [13] Y. SHILOH, op. cit. (n. 1), p. 26 and 28.

in the early phases of the Israelite acropolis; a larger podium destined
to support the Israelite citadel was built over the Canaanite platform.
At this point a change becomes apparent, due to the new function of
Jerusalem as a capital city, as against the more modest standing of
Canaanite Jerusalem. In the 10th century B.C.E., the need arose for
large-scale urban development, resulting in the considerable extension
of the acropolis area northwards (fig. 8). Quantitatively this extension
added about 100 dunams (10 ha) to the acropolis area, while qualita-
tively it made possible the erection of buildings monumental in conception, plan, size, decoration, and excellence of building materials
(ashlar masonry). «Warren's Shaft», the early water supply system
of Jerusalem which we attribute to this period (fig. 9)[14], provides
additional archaeological evidence, with parallels in other water systems
of large royal cities in Judah and Israel[15]. In conclusion, it should be
noted that the new area added to the city in the 10th century B.C.E.
served mainly royal needs, while the residential quarter remained in the
Lower City, within the same boundaries as the Canaanite city, until the
8th century B.C.E.

II

We suggest, therefore, that Jerusalem can serve as a classical model for
the nature of the contacts and links between the local Cannanite culture
encountered by the Israelites in Canaan in the beginning of the Iron Age
and the independent development of new elements in architecture and
town planning which from now on characterize the Israelite material
culture in Iron II[16]. In the major royal centres of Jerusalem and Samaria
and in royal cities such as Hazor, Dan, Gezer, Megiddo and Lachish,
entire building complexes were erected as part of a comprehensive city
plan. Careful planning is evident in the layout of the various quarters
and in its adaptation to the local topography. In cities like Jerusalem
and Samaria, where the acropolis area was based, first and foremost, on
its commanding topographical position, it was further reinforced by
massive supporting walls providing an even more effective defence. On

[14] *Ibid.*, p. 21-24.
[15] Y. SHILOH, *Underground Water Systems in the Iron Age in the Eretz-Israel*, in
Archaeology and Biblical Interpretation. Glenn Rose Memorial Volume, in press.
[16] K. M. KENYON, *Royal Cities of the Old Testament*, London 1971, p. 36-110;
Y. SHILOH, *op. cit.* (n. 11), p. 50-70.

Fig. 9. — The City of David, the horizontal tunnel in «Warren's Shaft» (A. Fuller, 1984).

other sites, where no elevated location was available, an attempt was made to achieve the same effect by erecting the administrative centre on a raised podium. Instances of this method can be found at the base of the citadel in Area B of Hazor (Stratum VIII) and, at Lachish, in Strata IV-III [17]. Public buildings, which at first may have conformed to the existing layout of the city, for instance in Megiddo Stratum VA-IVB from the 10th century B.C.E., underwent during this period a total reorganization intended to adapt them to their function within the town planning system. Examples can be found at Lachish Stratum IV and especially at Megiddo Stratum IVA, from the time of Ahab. In this respect the comparison between the town plans of Megiddo in Stratum VA-IVB and in Stratum IVA, when the city is rebuilt on a much larger scale and in accordance with a royal centre plan, is most convincing (fig. 10) [18]. In the light of archaeological evidence, the course of events seems clear: in the 9th century B.C.E., especially during Ahab's reign, extensive building activities were carried out in Israel by the state, on a scale larger than those in the 10th century B.C.E. These activities were designed to serve the needs of the Israelite kingdom, which at that time was still a dominant factor in Near Eastern geopolitics. Evidence for this can be found in the rebuilding of Megiddo in Stratum IVA, the extension of the upper tell of Hazor eastward in Stratum VIII, thus doubling the city area [19], and in the construction of new centres in Samaria Stratum I-II and in Dan Stratum III.

The technical elements of the monumental architecture used in these cities appear again and again as a common denominator in all these constructions. They can, therefore, be defined as elements characterizing the material culture of Judah and Israel in the Iron Age. Extensive use is made in the central buildings of ashlar masonry in all its forms [20]. This masonry is accompanied by monumental architectural ornamentation, such as the palmette capital (fig. 11). Up to the present, thirty-five such capitals are known in Western Eretz-Israel [21] and four more were found in Medeibiyeh in Transjordan [22]. A new capital was found by Biran, as

[17] Y. SHILOH, *Iron Age Sanctuaries and Cult Elements in Palestine*, in F. M. CROSS, ed., *Symposia celebrating the Seventy-Fifth Anniversary of the Founding of the American Schools of Oriental Research*, Cambridge Mass. 1979, p. 147-157 (see p. 153).

[18] Y. SHILOH, *op. cit.*, (n. 11), p. 52-53.

[19] Y. YADIN, *Hazor* (The Schweich Lectures of the British Academy), London 1972, p. 165.

[20] Y. SHILOH, *op. cit.* (n. 11), p. 50-70.

[21] *Ibid.*, p. 1-25.

[22] I. NEGUERUELA, *The Proto-Aeolic Capitals from Mudeibi'a, Moab*, in *Annual of the Department of Antiquities of Jordan* 26 (1982), p. 395-401.

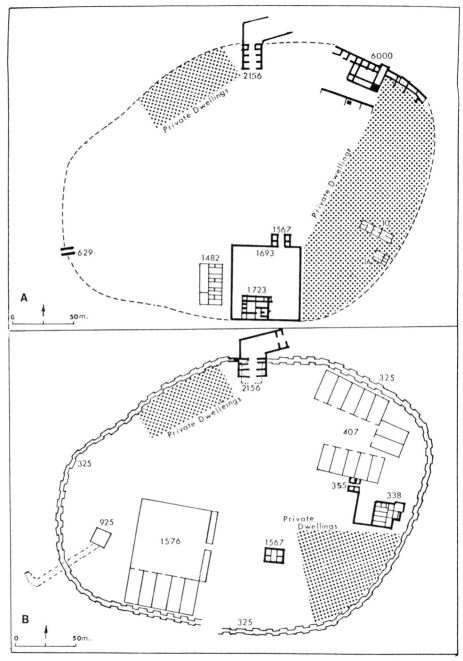

Fig. 10. — Megiddo, general town-plans.
(A) Stratum VA-IVB (10th century B.C.E.).
(B) Stratum IVA (9th-8th centuries B.C.E.).

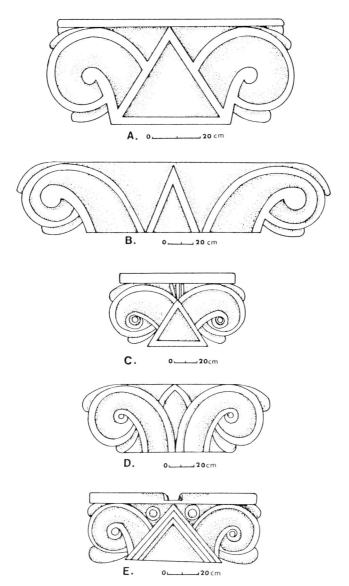

A. 0 ⌞_____⌟ 20 cm

B. 0 ⌞___⌟ 20 cm

C. 0 ⌞___⌟ 20 cm

D. 0 ⌞___⌟ 20 cm

E. 0 ⌞___⌟ 20 cm

Fig. 11. — Typological classification of the palmette (Proto-Aeolic) capital.

expected, in Dan [23]. Buildings such as governors' palaces, storehouses, granaries, stables and service structures, were built in these cities according to identical plans. Furthermore, the components of the

[23] Z. GAL, in I. EPH'AL, ed., *Histôryāh šel ʿEreṣ-Yiśrāʾēl* II, Jerusalem 1984, p. 212.

fortification systems are identical, although there are certain differences in plan and dimensions due to local factors. The monumental gate complexes termed «Solomonic gates» serve as foundations and cores for the succeeding gates built in Iron Age II, supplemented by casemate or massive walls, towers and auxiliary systems [24]. The planners of these centres took care to provide a regular water supply by hewing underground water systems. These ensured the ability of the cities to withstand a siege in times of war and improved the quality of life in times of peace [25].

The same uniformity is evident in the layout of the residential quarters in these cities and in the plan and construction of the houses. The use of the «four-room house» and its sub-types was widespread in Eretz-Israel since Iron Age I. In the great majority of the cases, it charaterizes villages of the settlement period [26] and permanent Israelite settlements [27]. A few examples of this house-plan are also known from sites which ethnically cannot be identified as Israelite, such as for instance Stratum X at Tell Qasile, which is situated in the area occupied by Philistines. It follows that this type of house was also built in the vicinity of areas settled by Israelites. During Iron Age II this type of building came into widespread use in the central cities, as well as in provincial towns and farms throughout Israel and Judah, from Galilee to the Eilat Gulf. During that period, the «four-room house» plan was also used in central public buildings such as the Hazor citadel, in residential quarters of country towns such as Tell el-Far'ah (N), Stratum III-II, and Tell Beit Mirsim, Stratum A, as well as in individual houses [28].

All the components outlined above are in fact more than characteristic features of the material culture of Eretz-Israel in the 10th-9th centuries B.C.E. They appear again and again in the royal centres built during the second part of Iron Age II, such as Ramat Rahel Stratum V or Beersheba Stratum II [29], and can thus be definitely identified with the

[24] Y. YADIN, op. cit. (n. 18), p. 147-178.

[25] Y. SHILOH, art. cit. (n. 15).

[26] V. FRITZ-A. KEMPINSKI, Ergebnisse der Ausgrabungen auf dem Hirbet el-Mšaš (Tēl Māšōš), 1972-1975, Wiesbaden 1983, vol. I, p. 7-113; Z. HERZOG, Beer-Sheba II. The Early Iron Age Settlements, Tel Aviv 1984, p. 78-83.

[27] Y. SHILOH, The Four-Room House — The Israelite Type House?, in I. Dunayevsky Memorial Volume (Eretz-Israel XI), Jerusalem 1973, p. 277-285 (in Hebrew).

[28] Y. SHILOH, The Four-Room House — Its Situation and Function in the Israelite City, in IEJ 20 (1970), p. 180-190.

[29] Y. SHILOH, Elements in the Development of Town Planning in the Israelite City, in IEJ 28 (1978), p. 36-51.

specific material culture of Israel and Judah until the destruction of these kingdoms.

III

Let us now return to the City of David and its place in this context. As we have seen, a few of these characterizing features have also been found on Strata 14-10 of the 10th-6th centuries B.C.E. (figs. 4, 12). In this instance, quantity is not a decisive factor, as the excavation have shown that the strata preceding Stratum 10, the last stratum to be built and destroyed on the eastern slope, are very badly preserved. The people built their houses again and again on the rocky slope, each time destroying whatever remained of previous structures. Some of the remains survived because they continued to be used during several strata before Stratum 10. This is so in the case of the lower city wall and the substructure of the citadel. A palmette, many ashlar stones and a fragment of a decorated stone balustrade which were found in Area G (see below) bear witness to the existence of public buildings in this area.

The complex of the three subterranean water systems in the City of David, all intended to supply water to the city, is one of the most sophisticated systems in the Iron Age (fig. 9). The «Ashlar building» in Area E 1 [30] and the «House of Ahi'el» in Area G (figs. 13-14) [31], both of the 7th century B.C.E., are good examples of buildings constructed on the «four-room house» plan. In the City of David, like on other Judaean sites, monoliths were used in the structures. Jerusalem's Iron Age necropolis encircles the city. The rock-hewn tombs in Silwan, east of the City of David, have been known for a long time [32]. In recent years, tomb complexes have also been discovered north of the city [33] and west of the Temple Mount [34].

---

[30] Y. SHILOH, op. cit. (n. 1), p. 14.

[31] Ibid., p. 18.

[32] N. AVIGDAD, Ancient Monuments in the Kidron Valley (in Hebrew), Jerusalem 1954; D. USSISHKIN, The Necropolis from the Time of the Kingdom of Judah at Silwan, Jerusalem, in BA 33 (1970), p. 34-46.

[33] A. MAZAR, Iron Age Burial Caves North of the Damascus Gate, Jerusalem, in IEJ 26 (1976), p. 1-8; G. BARKAY-A. KLONER, Burial Caves North of Damascus Gate, Jerusalem, in IEJ 26 (1976), p. 55-57.

[34] B. MAZAR, The Excavations in the Old City of Jerusalem near the Temple Mount, in Z. Shazar Volume (Eretz-Israel X), Jerusalem 1971, p. 1-34 (in Hebrew), see p. 24-34. English version available.

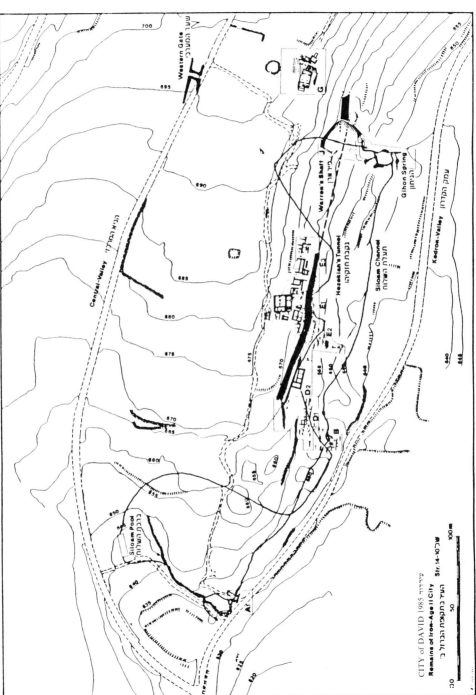

CITY of DAVID 1985 עיר דוד
Remains of Iron-Age II City
מתבני העיר הישראלית ב   Str. 14-10 שכבות

Fig. 12. — The City of David, general plan of Iron Age II remains, Strata 14-10.

Fig. 13. — The City of David, Area G, general plan of Stratum 10B.

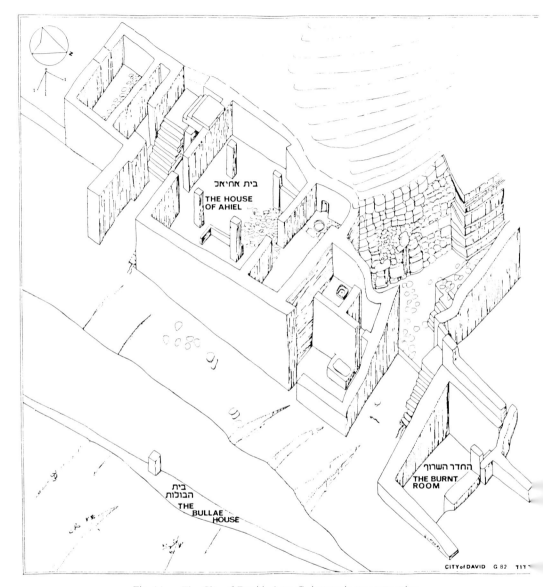

Fig. 14. — The City of David, Area G, isometric reconstruction.

The complex urban planning into which all these elements were integrated, reached its peak in the late 8th century B.C.E., in the reign of Hezekiah. At that time, the western hill was added to the city area and also enclosed in a wall (fig. 15). The Israelite city extended in the 8th-7th

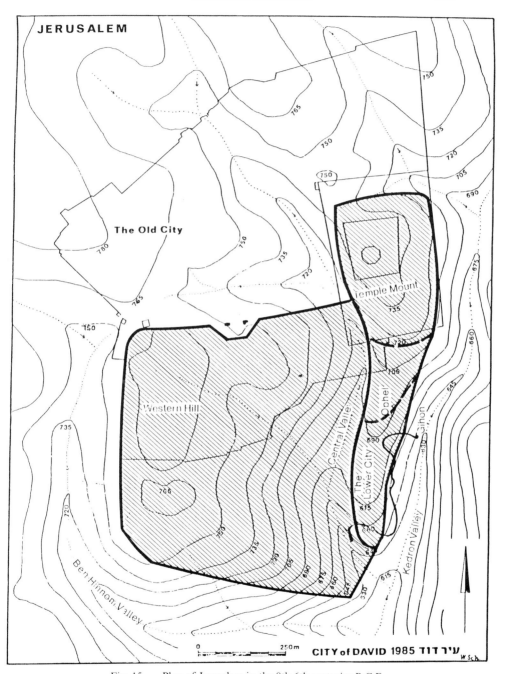

Fig. 15. — Plan of Jerusalem in the 8th-6th centuries B.C.E.

centuries B.C.E. over an area of about 500 dunams (50 ha)[35]. As we
have seen, the Israelite city grew out of the Canaanite city, whose area
did not exceed 60 dunams (6 ha). This expansion testifies to Jerusalem's
leading position as the capital of Judah, both in size and in population,
in comparison with other Israelite cities, whose average size did not
exceed about 100 dunams (10 ha)[36].

IV

We have discussed the town-plan of Israelite Jerusalem, as well as its
buildings and construction methods, and we have compared them with
the scanty archaeological evidence from the Jebusite-Canaanite city.
However, one significant element is missing in this discussion, as we
have no real archaeological evidence concerning the most important
buildings on the Israelite acropolis, the Temple — the House of God,
and the palace — the house of the king[37]. Had their remains survived
they would have furnished valuable information concerning building
methods, architectural ornamentation, interior decoration and artifacts,
as well as connections with neighbouring cultures. This is especially true
of the links with Phoenicia and the cities of North Syria, of which
abundant evidence has been found on sites in the kingdom of Israel,
such as Samaria, Hazor and Dan[38].

The analysis of the numerous small finds from the residential area in
the Lower City demonstrates their local Judahite character. The pottery,
which makes up most of the material, is of predominantly Judahite types.
Only a few fragments of imported Cypro-Phoenician and Assyrian wares
and their local imitations were found in the relevant Iron Age strata.
Local characteristics are also prominent in the Late Bronze Age pottery
and most of the sherds are of local Canaanite manufacture. The range
of pottery types recovered up to the present in the City of David is
unlike the international range of types usually present in the Late Bronze
Age II assemblages in Canaan. However, other items among the small

[35] N. AVIGAD, *Discovering Jerusalem*, Nashville 1983, p. 26-60.

[36] M. BROSHI, *La population de l'ancienne Jérusalem*, in *RB* 82 (1975), p. 5-14; Y. SHILOH, *The Population of Iron Age Palestine in the Light of a Sample Analysis of Urban Plans, Areas, and Population Density*, in *BASOR* 239 (1980), p. 25-35 (see p. 30-33).

[37] K.M. KENYON, *op. cit.* (n. 16), p. 36-52; EAD., *op. cit.*, (n. 2), p. 119-128; D. USSISHKIN, *King Solomon's Palaces*, in *BA* 36 (1973), p. 78-105; B. MAZAR, *The Mountain of the Lord*, Garden City 1975, p. 51-54 and 96-104.

[38] Y. SHILOH, *op. cit.* (n. 11), p. 26-49.

finds of Iron Age II still indicate some contacts with the Canaanite culture prevailing in Jerusalem until the 11th-10th centuries B.C.E. This influence is evident in the great number of female figurines («Astarte» pillar figurines), of which hundreds of fragments were found in the City of David [39]; in special finds, such as the fragment of a decorated cult stand (Reg. No. G. 5689) [40], and a bronze fist, part of an especially large figurine of a Canaanite deity(?) (Reg. No. G.11201) [41], found in Stratum 14 of the 10th century B.C.E.

The strongly local impression gained from the various small finds is further strengthened by the fact that most of the assemblages we are dealing with belong to the period between the second half of the 8th century and the destruction of 586 B.C.E. At that time, Judah was entrenched in the mountains, isolated more than ever from the surrounding cultures in contrast to the situation prevalent in the Second Temple period, especially after contacts between Judah and the Hellenistic civilization. The powerful social, political and religious influence of this civilization is evident in the historical records of the Hellenistic-Hasmonaean and Roman periods, as well as in the material from various excavations carried out in Jerusalem.

In the second part of our discussion we shall examine a number of special Iron Age II finds from the City of David which provide evidence both regarding the local material and the influences and trade relations with neighbouring cultures. These finds have been fully discussed in the publication of the City of David excavations. Here we shall limit ourselves to presenting the main features of each item and the conclusions resulting from its analysis.

1. Decorated Stone Colonnette

The stone colonnette was found in 1983 in Area E 1, Locus 2044 (Reg. No. E 1.16229). Although it is broken, its original form can be reconstructed with certainty (figs. 16-18). It is made of soft white limestone and is 15 cm high, with a diameter of 8-10 cm. After a stone block of suitable size had been carved out, square holes were drilled in the top and bottom of the block in order to provide a hold for the grip of the lathe (fig. 17). After the body and the six ribs of the colonnette

---

[39] T. A. HOLLAND, *A Study of Palestine Iron Age Baked Clay Figurines, with Special Reference to Jerusalem: Cave I*, in *Levant* 9 (1977), p. 121-155.

[40] Y. SHILOH, *op. cit.* (n. 1), p. 17.

[41] *Ibid.*, p. 17.

136   Y. SHILOH

Figs. 16-17. — The City of David, Area E 1, the stone colonnette (Z. Radovan).

had been neatly made on thé lathe, all that remained for the master carver was to shape the eight petals around its middle. The colonnette was found out of context in a layer accumulated during Strata 11-10, from the 7th century B.C.E., on the north side of one of the large buildings erected here in Stratum 11. It is, therefore, reasonable to assume that the colonnette belongs to another building which stood here in Stratum 12 of the 8th century B.C.E.

This object is identical in shape and function with similar colonnettes found in the ruins of the Stratum V A palace at Ramat Rahel (fig. 19). They were correctly reconstructed by Aharoni as parts of a balustrade, which is at present exhibited at the Israel Museum [42]. The small palmette capitals which crowned the colonnettes as separate units have not yet

[42] Y. AHARONI, *Excavations at Ramat Rahel. Seasons 1961 and 1962* (Serie archaeologica 6), Roma 1964, p. 57-58, fig. 78, pl. 48.

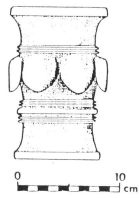

0   10   Fig. 18. — The reconstructed stone colonnette from the
                              City of David.

Fig. 19. — The restored window balustrade from Ramat Rahel (Y. AHARONI, *Excavations
at Ramat Rahel. Seasons 1961 and 1962*, fig. 38:1).

been found in the City of David[43]. The analysis of the finds at Ramat
Rahel indicated that the fragments should be reconstructed as a stone
window balustrade decorated with palmettes and petals. Both these
decorative elements are frequently found in the Syrian-Palestinian-
Mesopotamian area on pottery vessels, cult stands and ivories[44].
Aharoni was right in comparing this balustrade with similar ones

[43] *Ibid.*, fig. 38:3 and pls. 44:1-45.
[44] Y. SHILOH, *op. cit.* (n. 11), p. 26-42.

Fig. 20. — The «lady at the window» ivory from Nimrud.

forming part of windows on reliefs and ivories, especially in the «lady at the window» design (fig. 20)[45].

A fragment of a stone relief representing a similar balustrade was found by Stekelis and Maisler (Mazar) in a cave at Ramat Rahel[46]. Similar windows carved in relief are also known from subterranean stone-built funerary complexes intended to represent the wooden elements in buildings which had existed on the surface. Examples from a period corresponding to ours have been found in Cyprus at Curium, Kouklia and Ktima[47]. Unlike these, the colonnettes from Ramat Rahel and the City of David were used as decorative architectural elements in buildings erected on the surface. They provide additional evidence of the widespread use of stone as the main building material in the royal centres of Judah and Israel. These features were the subject of an

[45] Y. AHARONI, op: cit. (n. 42), p. 58; Y. SHILOH, op. cit. (n. 11), p. 49, n. 129; cf. C. DECAMPS DE MERTZENFELD, Inventaire commenté des ivoires phéniciens et apparentés, Paris 1954, pls. LXXVI-LXXVII et XCIX-CI.

[46] Y. SHILOH, op. cit (n. 11), pl. 14:2.

[47] Ibid., p. 43.

extensive study of ashlar masonry and the associated palmette capitals in these cities[48].

The motif appearing on the palmette capitals and the stone colonnettes is the motif of the palm — the sacred tree — which was in widespread use throughout the ancient East. Wooden architectural elements most likely decorated in similar fashion the superstructure of monumental buildings in neighbouring countries to the north. In Judah and Israel, ashlar masonry and the capitals associated with it, as well as other architectural elements made of stone, such as the window balustrade, took the place of wooden construction. Thus the structure and the form would be identical, though the building materials were different[49].

2. Carved Wooden Fragments

Evidence of destruction in Stratum 10 of the 6th century B.C.E. was found in all the excavation areas, but was especially conspicuous in Area G (figs. 13-14). The «House of Ahi'el», the «Burnt Room» and the «House of the Bullae» were found totally destroyed[50]. Ashes in especially large quantities were found in the «Burnt Room» (Locus 997) and gave the room its name. During the excavations, we conjectured that the fierce conflagration in this room was due to its contents, which included wooden furniture. Small ornamental items, such as ivory buttons and decorated bone fragments, supported this conjecture. A number of pieces of carbonized wood which had not been completely burnt (Reg. No. G.15226) were found in the burnt layer. The pieces do not exceed a few centimeters in length (fig. 21).

After cleaning, it turned out that some of these pieces were carved with motifs well known from the decorated ivory plaques of Iron Age II[51]. The motifs which have survived are mainly parts of the palmette design, such as the tree trunk, the central triangle at the head and the volutes flanking it (fig. 22). The pieces of wood, which were originally painted, probably adorned wooden furniture, like the more costly ivory inlays[52].

Dendro-archaeological tests of the wooden objects from the City of David carried out by Nili Lifschitz and Yoav Weisel of the Department

---

[48] *Ibid.*, passim.

[49] *Ibid.*, p. 82-91.

[50] Y. SHILOH, *op. cit.* (n. 1), p. 18-19 and 29.

[51] Cf. J. W. and G. M. CROWFOOT, *Early Ivories from Samaria*, London 1938, p. 35-39 and pls. XVIII-XX.

[52] Cf. V. KARAGEORGHIS, *Excavations in the Necropolis of Salamis III*, Nicosia 1973, p. 87-94 and pls. A, C.

Fig. 21. — The City of David, Area G, fragments of the carved wood from the «Burnt Room» (Z. Radovan).

of Botany, Tel Aviv University, showed that in Iron Age II a whole range of local trees were used in Jerusalem: olive, almond, vines, terebinth, Thabor oak, evergreen oak, cypress, Jerusalem pine, poplar, acacia raddiana, tamarisk and sycamore. These findings did not present any surprises. The pieces of wood from the «Burnt Room» were examined by A. Fahn and Ella Werker of the Department of Botany in the Hebrew University, Jerusalem, who identified most of the items as made from the local trees listed above. However, it was the carved pieces which provided a surprise, as they were found to be made from boxwood (*buxus sp.*), which does not grow in this country. One species of this tree grows mainly in South Turkey and North Syria. We can assume, therefore, that some time in the 7th century B.C.E. decorated boxwood furniture was imported into Jerusalem from a North Syrian town. These finds demonstrate unequivocally Judah's trade relations with Phoenicia and North Syria in the late Iron Age.

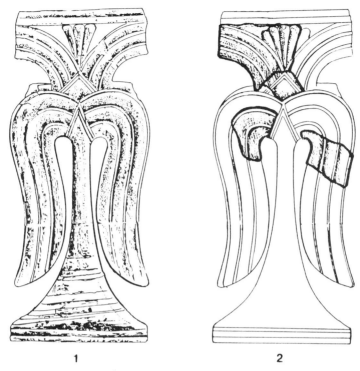

Fig. 22. — The palmette ivory from Samaria according to CROWFOOT, *op. cit.*
(n. 51), fig. 5, pl. XVIII,2 (1) and (2) the location of the fragments of the
carved wood, found in the «Burnt Room» in Area G, in relation
with the palmette motive.

3. *South Arabian Inscriptions on Sherds*

Dozens of ostraca, inscriptions incised on stone or on pottery vessels,
seals, seal-impressions and bullae of the 8th-6th centuries B.C.E. have
been found in the City of David [53]. These inscriptions are written in the
Hebrew language and in the early Hebrew script used in Judah in that
period. The fact that the inscriptions were uncovered in a controlled
stratigraphical excavation and in sealed loci well dated by ceramic finds,
lends added weight and importance to the conclusions reached in the
study of the Hebrew inscriptions and script of Iron Age II from the City
of David.

Three inscriptions incised on Iron Age II sherds are exceptional. Two
were found in Stratum 10, the destruction stratum, and one on the

---

[53] Y. SHILOH, *A Hoard of Israelite Bullae from the City od David*, in *IEJ* 35 (1985),
in press.

surface. When we realized that the script on these ostraca was South Arabian, we sent them to Maria Höfner of Graz University, who specializes in the study of South Arabian script and inscriptions. Her decipherment of these inscriptions will be included in the publication of all the inscribed material from the City of David. According to Höfner, the signs on the ostraca belong to an early South Arabian script and should be read as personal names in monograph form, as is usual in this script. Thus in her opinion the name on one of the ostraca (Reg. No. G.5793) is a monogram (fig. 23): the letter *lamed* ꟽ is combined twice with the letter *ḥet* Ⴤ, creating the monograph Ⴤ. The name should then be read as *ḥll* with the addition of the sign ☉, which can either represent the letter *'ayin* or a magic symbol accompanying such names[54].

Another important feature is the method of executing the signs, which were incised after firing by a chisel, creating an incised zigzag line. Twenty fragments of Hebrew inscriptions incised in this fashion have been found in the City of David (fig. 24), thus increasing the number of such inscriptions known from Judah[55] and especially from Jerusalem[56]. One point is of particular importance in our case: the South Arabian names were inceased on local 7th century B.C.E. pottery vessels by a method practised in Jerusalem. The inference is clear, though surprising: in the 7th century B.C.E. persons bearing South Arabian names lived in Jerusalem and inscribed their names on local vessels by a method used by Jerusalemites.

The study of the nature and extent of the connections between Eretz-Israel and Southern Arabia is still in its initial stages[57]. The early phase of civilization in Southern Arabia is marked by an abundance of inscriptions, but by few remains of any material culture. Two items found in the past in archaeological excavations, the one at Tell el-Kheleifeh and the other in Bethel, have a bearing on this question[58].

[54] G. L. HARDING, *An Index and Concordance of Pre-Islamic Arabian Names and Inscriptions*, Toronto 1971, p. 197.

[55] N. AVIGAD, *Two Hebrew Inscriptions on Wine-Jars*, in *IEJ* 22 (1972), p. 1-9 (see p. 2-3).

[56] J. PRIGNAUD, *Scribes et graveurs à Jérusalem vers 700 av. J.-C.*, in R. MOOREY-P. PARR, ed., *Archaeology in the Levant. Essays for Kathleen Kenyon*, Warminster 1978, p. 136-148.

[57] W. F. ALBRIGHT, *Was the Age of Solomon without Monumental Art?*, in *B. Mazar Volume* (Eretz-Israel V), Jerusalem 1958, p. 1*-9* (see p. 7*-9*).

[58] N. GLUECK, *The First Campaign at Tell el-Kheleifeh (Ezion-Geber)*, in *BASOR* 71 (1938), p. 3-16 (see p. 15-16); ID., *Some Ezion-Geber: Elath Iron Age II Pottery*, in *W.F. Albright Volume* (Eretz-Israel IX), Jerusalem 1969, p. 51*-59* (see p. 53* and pl. VI : 4).

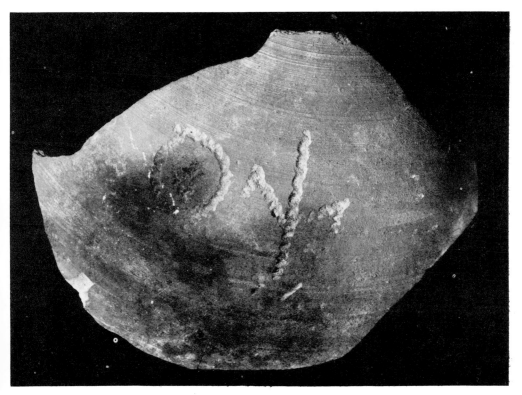

Fig. 23. — The City of David, Area G, South Arabian inscription ḥll (A. Hai).

The story of the stamp from Bethel is fascinating, but the complexities of the evidence are such that it is difficult to reach any historical conclusions[59]. On the other hand, the presence of three South Arabian inscriptions in the City of David appears to indicate that persons who were not Judaeans and who bore South Arabian names were in Jerusalem. They used South Arabian script, but incised the signs in the local manner and on local vessels. These persons may have come to Judah from the distant south through Edom, which at that time included the southern Negev and the Gulf of Eilat. They may have been the

[59] J. L. KELSO, *The Excavation of Bethel (1934-1960)* (AASOR XXXIX), Cambridge Mass. 1968, pl. 118; G. W. VAN BEEK-A. JAMME, *An Inscribed South Arabian Clay Stamp from Bethel*, in *BASOR* 151 (1958), p. 9-16; ID.-ID., *The South Arabian Clay Stamp from Bethel again*, in *BASOR* 163 (1961), p. 15-18; ID.-ID., *The Authenticity of the Bethel Stamp Seal*, in *BASOR* 199 (1970), p. 59-65; Y. YADIN, *An Inscribed South-Arabian Clay Stamp frm Bethel?*, in *BASOR* 196 (1969), p. 37-45; R. L. CLEVELAND, *More on the South Arabian Clay Stamp Found at Beitîn*, in *BASOR* 209 (1973), p. 33-36.

Fig. 24. — The City of David, Area E 2, a jar with the Hebrew inscription *lšm'...* of the
8th century B.C.E. (Z. Radovan).

middle-men in the South Arabian incense trade, which reached Edom,
Judah and places further north[60].

Another possibility concerning the identity of these people are the
Arab tribes transferred from North Arabia by Sargon II to the new
province of Samarina after his conquest of Israelite Samaria in 721
B.C.E. Perhaps it can be suggested that the persons whose names are
inscribed on the sherds from the City of David came from among
Judaea's new neighbours, and that they may also have brought the
South Arabian stamp to Bethel[61].

[60] G. W. VAN BEEK, *Frankincense and Myrrh*, in *BA* 23 (1960), p. 69-95.
[61] I. EPH'AL, *The Ancient Arabs*, Jerusalem 1982, p. 105-107.

V

Conclusions

The discussion in this paper proceeded from the more complex to the simpler issues. We traces the urban development of the City of David from its foundation as a Canaanite city to its establishment as the capital of Israel and Judah in the 10th century B.C.E. This change brought about the development of the city on a new and much larger scale. The nucleus of the Canaanite city was absorbed into the new city, which expanded during the Iron Age and reached a peak of prosperity in the 8th-7th centuries B.C.E. The discussion of the architecture and town-planning underlined planning elements, plans of buildings and local technical methods which characterized this aspect of the material culture of Eretz-Israel during the Iron Age, as it appears in the various royal centres. The use of stone for construction and decoration as well as the typical plans of public buildings, fortifications and houses, indicate first and foremost local solutions of planning and structural problems, using local materials, though some details may well be influenced by neighbouring cultures. Judah's material culture is distinguished by its independent quality and by its well defined local characteristics, even more than the nearby kingdom of Israel, which was more exposed to influences from the north. This quality is attested by the abundance of local finds in contrast to the scarcity of imported objects.

The small finds discussed above also exhibit similar characteristics, though connections are evident with neighbouring cultures, both near and far, such as the cities of Northern Syria and Phoenicia in the north and the culture of Southern Arabia. The main emphasis here is not on the complete isolation of Judah, a view which we cannot support, but rather on the vigour of the Judaean material culture, which could provide satisfactory solutions to the needs of the people and of the developing kingdom[62]. On the other hand, the archaeological evidence indicates commercial and economic relations with neighbouring cultures. In future, the archaeological data available concerning the influences absorbed by the Israelite culture from the Canaanite culture, before its disappearance from the historical scene, should be studied with greater attention.

A comparison of the material from Judaean sites with the contemporaneous material from northern Israel and the coastal plain shows clearly that there is a considerable difference in the range and quality of

---

[62] Y. SHILOH, *op. cit.* (n. 11), p. 82-87.

the artifacts from Judaean sites, such as the City of David, Tell Beit
Mirsim and Lachish, and those from the coastal plain, such as Ashdod,
Tell Jemmeh or Dor. The latter came into much closer physical, cultural
and commercial contact with the neighbouring cultures. Although
Jerusalem was situated at the centre of Palestine, which served as a
landbridge between various civilizations, it lay somewhat off the main
thoroughfare — the coastal plain — where the interaction of the
various was more strongly felt. In the days of the Judaean monarchy,
the city may have lost some of its cosmopolitan image in favour of
its standing as the capital of mountainous Judah, possessing its own
independent culture. Towards the end of the Iron Age, after the fall of
the kingdom of Israel, this tendency became even more pronounced. In
spite of its partial success in preserving its independence, Judah's
isolation continued to grow until it was finally conquered by the
Babylonians.

Yigal SHILOH
Institute of Archaeology
The Hebrew University
Jerusalem, Israel.

LES RELATIONS ENTRE LA PERSE ET L'ÉGYPTE
DU VIe AU IVe SIÈCLE AV. J.-C.

PIERRE SALMON

La période perse est une des plus obscures de l'histoire de la Palestine[1]. Voisine de l'Égypte, cette contrée — en particulier, sa plaine littorale — a été souvent parcourue et exposée aux exactions des armées étrangères au cours des nombreux conflits qui mirent aux prises l'Empire perse et l'Égypte. L'étude des relations entre ces deux puissances du VIe au IVe siècle av.n.è. doit donc permettre de mieux appréhender l'histoire de la Palestine.

Après la prise de Babylone en 539, Cyrus (R. 559-529), en politique avisé, permet aux Juifs captifs de retourner dans leur patrie et de rebâtir un temple à Jahvé à Jérusalem[2]. Durant la période perse, la Palestine est comprise dans le territoire de la satrapie de Transeuphratène[3], ancienne partie de l'Empire babylonien, dont les limites furent remaniées à plusieurs reprises[4]. La Palestine est divisée entre trois types d'entités politiques soumises aux Perses: 1°) au centre, des «États» nationaux ou ethniques comme Juda, Samarie, Megiddo, Ashdod, les Édomites, etc.; 2°) le long de la côté, des cités commerciales phéniciennes; 3°) à l'Est et au Sud, des tribus nomades arabes (d'abord les Qédarites et, plus tard, les Nabatéens). L'ensemble est dirigé par un gouverneur perse. Toutes ces entités politiques conservent le droit de frapper de la monnaie d'argent, mais le Grand Roi se réserve la monnaie d'or[5].

Dans la deuxième moitié du VIe siècle, Cyrus s'empare de Chypre[6] qui commandait les relations commerciales de la Méditerranée orientale.

---

[1] E. STERN, *The Archeology of Persian Palestine*, dans *CHJ* I, Cambridge 1984, p. 88-114 (voir p. 89).

[2] E. STERN, *The Persian Empire and the Political and Social History of Palestine in the Persian Period*, dans *CHJ* I, Cambridge 1984, p. 70-87 (voir p. 70).

[3] *Esdras* 4,10-11.16-17.20; 8,36; *Néhémie* 2,7.9.

[4] E. STERN, *art. cit.*, p. 78.

[5] *Ibid.*, p. 80.

[6] Hdt. III 19. — Cf. H. DE MEULENAERE, *Herodotos over de 26ste Dynastie* (Bibliothèque du Muséon 27), Louvain 1951, p. 99.

Cyrus se dispose à envahir l'Égypte[7] lorsqu'il meurt en 529[8]. Son fils Cambyse (R. 529-522) réalise son projet. Comme il préparait son expédition contre l'Égypte, il fut rejoint par Phanès d'Halicarnasse, général de mercenaires d'Amasis, qui s'offrit à le piloter[9]. Au printemps 525, les troupes perses prennent la route qui mène de Gaza au Delta cependant que des escadres phénicienne, samienne et chypriote longent la côte[10]. Pendant la traversée du désert, les Arabes ravitaillent l'armée de Cambyse en eau[11]. Près de la bouche Pélusienne, Psammétique III (R. 526-525), fils d'Amasis, attendait les Perses à la tête des troupes égyptiennes ainsi que de mercenaires grecs et cariens[12]. Écrasés à Péluse par Cambyse, ils se replièrent sur Memphis[13]. Encerclé dans cette ville par les Perses et abandonné par ses alliés, Psammétique capitula[14]. Il fut d'abord bien traité par Cambyse qui avait l'intention de lui confier le gouvernement du pays. Mais le pharaon, ayant conspiré contre les Perses, reçut l'ordre de s'empoisonner[15]. Quant à Cambyse, après une expédition contre les Éthiopiens[16], il prit le chemin du retour et mourut en Syrie dans des circonstances mystérieuses[17].

Darius Ier (R. 522-486), fils d'Hystaspe, doit, au début de son règne, faire face à de nombreuses difficultés pour s'assurer la possession de l'Empire[18]. En 519, il s'empare de la ville de Babylone qui s'était

[7] Hdt. I 153.

[8] Hdt. I 214. — L'Égypte d'Amasis n'a donc jamais été dans la mouvance perse. Cf. P. SALMON, La politique égyptienne d'Athènes (VIe et Ve siècles avant J.-C.). Réimpression de l'édition princeps (1965) corrigée et mise à jour (Mémoires de la Classe des Lettres et des Sciences morales et politiques de l'Académie royale de Belgique, t. LXV, fasc. 3), Bruxelles 1981, p. 58-60.

[9] Hdt. III 4.

[10] L'invasion de l'Égypte a eu lieu en mai-juin 525. Cf. G. POSENER, La première domination perse en Égypte (Bibliothèque d'étude 11), Le Caire 1936, p. 173.

[11] Hdt. III 9.

[12] Hdt. III 10-11.

[13] Hdt. III 13.

[14] Hdt. III 13. Cf. P. SALMON, op. cit., p. 61 ; A. SPALINGER, Psammetichus III, dans LÄ IV, Wiesbaden 1982, col. 172-173.

[15] Hdt. III 15.

[16] Hdt. III 25.

[17] P. SALMON, op. cit., p. 61 ; R. KRAUSS, Kambyses, dans LÄ III, Wiesbaden 1980, col. 303-304. — E. BRESCIANI, La morte di Cambise ovvero dell'empietà punita: a proposito della «Cronaca demotica», verso, col. c. 7-8, dans Egitto e Vicino Oriente 4 (1981), p. 217-222, souligne que la «Chronique démotique» (P. 215 conservé à la Bibliothèque Nationale de Paris) oppose l'impiété de Cambyse punie de mort violente à la vertu de son successeur Darius. Le destin des souverains égyptiens entre la XXVIIIe et la XXXe Dynastie est déterminé dans cet écrit par leur comportement envers les temples dans le respect ou non de la légalité.

[18] Hdt. III 71-88. — Cf. H. DE MEULENAERE, Darius I, dans LÄ I, Wiesbaden 1975, col. 992.

révoltée. De nouveaux exilés juifs retournent en Palestine. Sheshbassar, puis Zorobabel, deviennent gouverneurs de Juda sous l'autorité du satrape perse. Dans la deuxième année du règne de Darius Ier, Zorobabel commence à reconstruire le Temple de Jérusalem, puis il disparaît soudainement. Selon E. Stern, la région est alors gouvernée par des gouverneurs perses depuis leur siège de Samarie. En 515, la reconstruction du Temple est achevée et Jérusalem redevient la cité sainte[19].

En Égypte, Aryandès, qui avait été nommé gouverneur de ce pays par Cambyse[20], cherchait à se rendre indépendant. L'inscription de Béhistoun (col. II, 5-8) mentionne sans donner de détails un soulèvement de l'Égypte à l'époque où Darius assiégeait Babylone[21]. Selon Polyen[22], des actes de cruauté commis par Aryandès amenèrent une révolte nationale en Égypte[23]. Hérodote[24] confirme ces faits en déclarant que Darius accusa Aryandès de se soulever contre lui.

Entre 521 et 517[25], Darius arriva à Memphis et, habilement, il commença par témoigner de son respect envers les dieux des Égyptiens; ceux-ci louèrent sa piété et firent leur soumission. L'ordre était rétabli[26]. Le Grand Roi instruisit alors le procès d'Aryandès qui fut puni de mort pour crime de rébellion[27]. Par une politique bienveillante, il s'efforce ensuite d'intégrer l'Égypte dans son empire. Cette dernière, avec la Libye, Cyrène et Barcé, forme la sixième satrapie qui doit fournir au total un tribut de 700 talents d'argent babyloniens[28]. Darius nomme Phérendatès satrape en remplacement d'Aryandès[29]. Il installe des

---

[19] E. STERN, art. cit., p. 72. Voir aussi P. ACKROYD, The Jewish Community in the Persian Period, dans CHJ I, Cambridge 1984, p. 135, qui situe la restauration et la reconstruction du Temple approximativement de 538 à 515.

[20] Hdt. IV 166.

[21] L.W. KING et R.C. THOMPSON, The Sculpture and Inscription of Darius the Great on the Rock of Behistun in Persia, Londres 1907, p. 7, lignes 26 sqq. Nouvelle édition de la version akkadienne par E.N. VON VOIGTLANDER, The Bisitun Inscription of Darius the Great : Babylonian Version, Londres 1978, p. 22, lignes 40-41.

[22] Polyen, Strat. VII 11,7.

[23] G.C. CAMERON, Darius, Egypt and the «Lands beyond the Sea», dans JNES 2 (1943), p. 310.

[24] Hdt. IV 166.

[25] La date est incertaine. Cf. P. SALMON, op. cit., p. 63, n. 3.

[26] Polyen, Strat. VII 11,7.

[27] Hdt. IV 166. — Cf. H. DE MEULENAERE, Aryandes, dans LÄ I, Wiesbaden 1975, col. 454.

[28] P. SALMON, op. cit., p. 63-65.

[29] W. SPIEGELBERG, Drei demotische Schreiben aus der Korrespondenz des Pherendates, dans Sitzungsberichte der preussischen Akademie der Wissenschaften, fasc. 28, Berlin 1928, p. 604-614; S.P. VLEEMING, Een lang uitgestelde benoeming, dans Phoenix 27 (1981), p. 82-91.

garnisons perses à Memphis, à Daphnae, à Maréa et à Éléphantine[30].
Il ordonne la réfection du grand canal de Néchao qui reliait la branche
orientale du Nil à la mer Rouge[31]. Enfin, la darique, nouvel étalon offi-
ciel, concurrence les monnaies d'argent diffusées par les cités grecques.

Une colonie militaire juive gardait — vraisemblablement depuis le
VIIe siècle[32] — l'entrée de l'Égypte du côté Sud pour arrêter d'éventuelles incursions éthiopiennes. Elle était installée dans l'île d'Éléphantine en
aval de la première cataracte[33]. Une sorte de sympathie semble avoir uni
les Perses et les Juifs dans leur mépris du polythéisme égyptien[34]. On a
retrouvé à Éléphantine des papyrus rédigés, pour la plupart, en araméen,
échelonnés chronologiquement entre 495 et 399[39]. La correspondance
de Phérendatès et de divers personnages avec les prêtres de Chnum
d'Éléphantine révèle notamment que le satrape nommait divers membres
du clergé égyptien[36].

L'Égypte devient donc une puissance vassale. Son armée et sa flotte
sont à la disposition du Grand Roi et participent aux opérations
militaires entreprises par les Perses. Lors de l'expédition de Scythie, on

[30] Hdt. II 30. Cet auteur ne mentionne pas la présence de soldats juifs.

[31] Hdt. II 158; IV 42; Diodore I 33; Strabon XVII, p. 804. Cf. G. POSENER, *op. cit.*,
p. 48-53. Trois stèles quadrilingues commémorent le percement du canal par Darius. Cf.
G. POSENER, *Le canal du Nil à la mer Rouge avant les Ptolémées*, dans *CdÉ* 13 (1938),
p. 259-273.

[32] Cf. B. PORTEN, *Archives from Elephantine. The Life of an Ancient Jewish Military
Colony*, Berkeley 1968, p. 12, qui situe la construction du temple d'Éléphantine avant la
réforme deutéronomique (622) qui institua l'unité du sanctuaire; P. GRELOT, *La communauté juive d'Éléphantine*, dans *CdÉ* 45 (1970), p. 122, qui estime que «l'arrivée des
mercenaires juifs puis la construction de leur temple pourraient dater des années situées
entre 609 et 587». Voir aussi S.W. BARON, *Histoire d'Israël. Vie sociale et religieuse* I. *Des
origines jusqu'au début de l'ère chrétienne*, Paris 1956, p. 149 et p. 476, qui penche également
pour le VIIe siècle; P. SALMON, *op. cit.*, p. 66 et p. 278; E. BRESCIANI, *Egypt, Persian
Satrapy*, dans *CHJ* I, Cambridge 1984, p. 368, qui suppose que les Juifs d'Éléphantine
seraient venus de Babylonie après 538 sous le règne du pharaon Amasis et qu'ils auraient
construit leur temple peu avant l'arrivée de Cambyse. — On trouvera une abondante
bibliographie sur les papyrus araméens d'Éléphantine dans B. PORTEN, *The Jews in Egypt*,
dans *CHJ* I, Cambridge 1984, p. 376-378. Cet auteur estime que les mercenaires juifs furent
installés à Éléphantine par Psammétique Ier (R. environ 663-609) après sa campagne contre
les Éthiopiens. On trouve des mentions de mercenaires juifs à Éléphantine sous Apriès
(R. environ 588-569) et sous Amasis (en 529). Cf. B. PORTEN, *art. cit.*, p. 379. Le temple
d'Éléphantine daterait du VIIe siècle: *ibid.*, p. 386.

[33] Hdt. II 30.

[34] P. SALMON, *op. cit.*, p. 66.

[35] J.K. FOTHERINGHAM, *Dates in the Elephantine Papyri*, dans *Journal of Theological
Studies* 14 (1912), p. 572 sqq.; E.G. KRAELING, *The Brooklyn Museum Aramaic Papyri.
New Documents of the Fifth Century B.C. from the Jewish Colony at Elephantine*, New
Haven 1953, p. 48 et 113; B. PORTEN, *art. cit.*, p. 378.

[36] W. SPIEGELBERG, *art. cit.*, p. 604-614; S.P. VLEEMING, *art. cit.* à la n. 29.

trouve, dans l'armée de Darius, un contingent égyptien et, au moment de la révolte de l'Ionie, une escadre égyptienne dans la flotte du Grand Roi[37].

Enfin, des textes perses et des trouvailles archéologiques attestent que des ouvriers égyptiens — notamment des sculpteurs de pierre et des décorateurs — travaillent aux nouvelles constructions élevées à Suse et à Persépolis sous Darius I[er][38]. La grande statue de Darius Ier, découverte à Suse en 1972 et datant des dernières années de son règne, est ornée d'inscriptions, notamment hiéroglyphiques. Cette œuvre due à des sculpteurs égyptiens paraît illustrer l'importance prise par l'Égypte dans l'esprit de Darius[39].

L'intervention athénienne dans le conflit ionien (498) provoque le débarquement à Marathon en 490 d'un corps expéditionnaire perse qui est écrasé par Miltiade. L'année suivante, cet échec secondaire est compensé par la défaite de Miltiade à Paros[40].

Cependant, en Égypte, l'augmentation des charges militaires, combinée vraisemblablement avec l'ambition des dynastes remuants du Delta, provoque une recrudescence du nationalisme égyptien. En 487/6, la population indisciplinée du Delta se soulève, mais la Haute Égypte ne bouge pas comme en témoignent des inscriptions du Ouadi Hammamat[41]. Hérodote[42] ne nous indique pas le nom des chefs de la révolte. On a cru jadis que le principal instigateur de l'insurrection était le pharaon Chabbash, mais aujourd'hui cette hypothèse est tout à fait abandonnée[43]. Darius se prépare à entrer en campagne contre les Égyptiens mais il meurt à la fin de l'année 486. Son fils Xerxès Ier (R. 486-465) écrase les révoltés en 485/4 et impose à l'Égypte une servitude beaucoup plus dure qu'elle ne l'était auparavant[44]. Le satrape Phérendatès avait apparemment péri dans la révolte[45] puisque Xerxès

---

[37] Hdt. IV 141 ; VI 6.

[38] G. GOOSSENS, *Artistes et artisans étrangers en Perse sous les Achéménides*, dans *La Nouvelle Clio* 1 (1949-50), p. 32-44 (voir p. 34sqq.). Voir aussi Diodore I 46, 4, qui relate la déportation d'ouvriers égyptiens sous Cambyse pour travailler aux palais perses. Ces derniers furent probablement mis à l'ouvrage sous Darius.

[39] J. YOYOTTE, *Les inscriptions hiéroglyphiques égyptiennes de la statue de Darius*, dans *Comptes rendus de l'Académie des Inscriptions et Belles-Lettres* 1973, p. 256-259.

[40] P. SALMON, *op. cit.*, p. 73-74.

[41] *Ibid.*, p. 76-77, où l'on trouvera les références bibliographiques.

[42] Hdt. VII 1.

[43] P. SALMON, *op. cit.*, p. 77, n. 3.

[44] Hdt. VII 1-7.

[45] A.T. OLMSTEAD, *History of the Persian Empire*, Chicago 1948, p. 235.

confie le gouvernement de l'Égypte à Achaiménès, son propre frère[46].
Vers 483, un autre de ses frères, Arsamès, s'empare par ruse de la ville
libyenne de Barcè[47]. Une révolte a peut-être également éclaté à cette
époque en Judée, où, au témoignage de E. Stern, on constate la
destruction d'un grand nombre de villes[48]. Il n'est pas exclu que les
troupes de Xerxès aient, ici comme ailleurs, pacifié le pays par le fer et
le feu.

Après avoir rétabli l'ordre en Orient, le Grand Roi se tourne vers
l'Occident. Mais les Perses sont battus par les Athéniens à Salamine
(480), à Platées (479) et à l'Eurymédon (468)[49].

En Égypte, le nouvel accroissement des charges fiscales mécontente la
population. La décadence de l'autorité des Achéménides s'y manifeste
comme dans tout l'Empire. En 465, Xerxès est assassiné et Artaxerxès Ier
(R. 465-424) monte sur le trône et pare au plus pressé en écrasant le
satrape de Bactriane qui s'était soulevé contre lui[50]. Entre 463 et 461,
Inaros, fils de Psammétique, vraisemblablement un descendant des
pharaons de la XXVIe Dynastie, soulève la majeure partie du Delta
contre les Perses. Memphis, où se trouvaient les soldats de la garnison
perse du Mur Blanc et des Égyptiens restés fidèles au Grand Roi, ne
bouge pas. La Haute Égypte ne semble pas non plus s'être associée à la
révolte du Delta. Inaros, proclamé pharaon par les insurgés, rassemble
des troupes et requiert l'aide des Athéniens qui répondront à son appel :
une flotte de 200 trières est envoyée de Chypre vers l'Égypte[51].

Artaxerxès, informé de l'ampleur prise par la révolte de l'Égypte,
ordonne la levée de recrues dans toutes les satrapies et fait équiper de
nombreux vaisseaux. Il donne le commandement des troupes à son oncle
paternel, Achaiménès, satrape d'Égypte. En 460, la grande armée perse,
réunie en Phénicie, pénètre en Égypte et est écrasée par les troupes
athéno-égyptiennes à Paprémis, à l'emplacement de l'ancienne Péluse,
c'est-à-dire à l'extrémité orientale du Delta. Achaiménès périt dans la
bataille. Un engagement naval est également fatal à la flotte phénicienne.
Talonnés par les forces d'Inaros et les Athéniens, les débris de l'armée

---

[46] Hdt. VII 7. — Cf. H. DE MEULENAERE, *Achaimenes*, dans *LÄ* I, Wiesbaden 1975, col. 52.

[47] Polyen, *Strat.* VII 28,1-2.

[48] E. STERN, *art. cit.* (n. 1), p. 114.

[49] P. SALMON, *op. cit.*, p. 79-86.

[50] *Ibid.*, p. 91-92. — Cf. H. DE MEULENAERE, *Artaxerxes I*, dans *LÄ* I, Wiesbaden 1975, col. 453.

[51] P. SALMON, *op. cit.*, p. 93-142 ; K.A. KITCHEN, *Inaros*, dans *LÄ* III, Wiesbaden 1980, col. 152.

perse battent en retraite vers Memphis. Les deux tiers de la ville sont occupés par les alliés. Toutefois, le Mur Blanc, citadelle de Memphis, où les Perses se sont retranchés avec les Égyptiens restés fidèles, résiste à tous les assauts. La Haute Égypte, toujours aux mains des Perses, ravitaille les défenseurs du Mur Blanc qui pourront ainsi soutenir un très long siège. Les Athéniens laissent une quarantaine de trières dans le Delta à la disposition d'Inaros. Durant l'année 460, le gros de leur flotte — les 160 trières restantes — opèrent successivement le long des côtes de Phénicie, en Argolide, à Égine et à Mégare. En Égypte, le siège du Mur Blanc se poursuit vainement durant quatre ans[52].

Artaxerxès lève une nouvelle armée dont il donne le commandement à Mégabyze. Les troupes perses sont rassemblées en Phénicie. Elles sont accompagnées par une flotte de trois cents navires chypriotes, phéniciens et ciliciens. Au printemps 456, elles pénètrent dans le Delta et débloquent le Mur Blanc. Submergés par la masse des assaillants, les alliés battent en retraite vers le Nord et se laissent enfermer dans l'île de Prosopitis. Après dix-huit mois de résistance, les Athéniens et les Égyptiens capitulent en avril-mai 454. Inaros est capturé — il sera exécuté cinq ans plus tard. En juin-juillet 454, une escadre athénienne de 50 trières qui venait relever les navires laissés en Égypte depuis 460 est surprise près de la bouche Mendésienne et presque anéantie[53].

Après la victoire perse, Sarsamas devient satrape d'Égypte[54]. Suivant Thucydide, «l'Égypte revint sous l'autorité du Roi, à l'exception d'Amyrtée, qui régnait sur la partie marécageuse; l'étendue des marais empêcha de la réduire, outre qu'il n'y a pas de meilleurs soldats en Égypte que les gens des marais»[55]. Un foyer important de résistance subsistait donc dans le Delta. C'est ce qui encouragea Athènes à envoyer une seconde expédition vers Chypre et l'Égypte. Au printemps 450, deux cent vaisseaux athéniens et alliés dirigés par Cimon partent en expédition contre Chypre. Soixante de ces navires se dirigèrent vers l'Égypte à la demande d'Amyrtée; les autres vaisseaux commencèrent le siège de Kition. À cette époque, Mégabyze ne s'était pas encore soulevé contre le

---

[52] P. SALMON, op. cit., p. 143-158.

[53] Ibid., p. 166-189.

[54] Ctésias, Pers. 35. A.T. OLMSTEAD, op. cit., p. 308, identifie à tort Sarsamas avec Arsamès dont nous parlent les papyrus d'Éléphantine depuis l'an 37 d'Artaxerxès Ier (428) jusqu'à l'an 17 de Darius II (407). Cf. F.K. KIENITZ, Die politische Geschichte Ägyptens vom 7. bis zum 4. Jahrhundert vor der Zeitwende, Berlin 1953, p. 71.

[55] Thuc. I 110, 2. — Traduction de J. DE ROMILLY, Thucydide, La Guerre du Péloponnèse, livre I, Paris 1953, p. 72.

Grand Roi. La mort de Cimon et la famine forcent les Athéniens à lever le siège de Kition. Mais, au retour, ils remportent une brillante victoire à Salamine de Chypre en 450/49. L'escadre athénienne détachée dans le Delta abandonne Amyrtée, dont on ignore la fin, et rentre au Pirée. En 449/8, Callias, beau-frère de Cimon, est envoyé par Périclès à Suse pour y conclure la paix avec le Grand Roi sur la base du *statu quo*. Athènes abandonne toute prétention sur Chypre et renonce désormais à appuyer les rebelles du Delta. En contrepartie, la Perse reconnaît l'autonomie des cités grecques d'Asie Mineure[56].

Sous Artaxerxès Ier, une nouvelle vague de Juifs s'installe avec Esdras, un scribe chargé des affaires juives à la cour de Perse, en Palestine, à Jérusalem, la septième année du règne du Grand Roi, c'est-à-dire en 458[57]. En 449, Mégabyze, retiré dans sa satrapie de Syrie, se révolte contre le Grand Roi. Celui-ci envoie deux expéditions pour réduire le gouverneur rebelle. Mégabyze finit par se soumettre. Après un exil de cinq ans sur les bords de la mer Rouge, il rentrera en grâce[58]. Il est vraisemblable que la Palestine eut à souffrir durant cette guerre. Vers 445, Néhémie, Juif élevé à la cour d'Artaxerxès Ier et échanson de ce souverain, se fait donner par ce dernier la mission d'aller relever les remparts de Jérusalem probablement détruits au cours de la révolte de Mégabyze. Nommé gouverneur de Juda durant douze ans, il retourne en Perse, puis est renvoyé en Palestine une seconde fois pour réprimer certains désordres qui s'étaient introduits dans la communauté[59].

Entre 449 et 430, au moment où Hérodote visite l'Égypte, Thannyras, fils d'Inaros, et Pausiris, fils d'Amyrtée, après avoir reconnu la suzeraineté du Grand Roi, gouvernent leurs petites principautés au Nord du Delta. Il était dans l'intérêt du satrape Sarsamas de laisser subsister dans cette Égypte en pleine fermentation des principautés vassales pour donner une satisfaction apparente aux tendances séparatistes. En outre,

---

[56] P. SALMON, *op. cit.*, p. 195-206.

[57] *Esdras* 7-8. Cf. E. STERN, *art. cit.* (n. 2), p. 73. — Certains exégètes font venir Esdras après Néhémie soit en estimant qu'il s'agit de la septième année d'Artaxerxès II, c'est-à-dire 398, soit en corrigeant le texte d'*Esdras* 7,8 en trente-septième année d'Artaxerxès Ier, c'est-à-dire 428.

[58] Ctésias, *Pers.* 37-40. Cf. W. KROLL, *Megabyzos*, dans PAULY-WISSOWA, *Real-Encyclopädie* XV/1, Stuttgart 1931, col. 122-123.

[59] *Néhémie* 1-13. Cf. E. STERN, *art. cit.*, p. 74. — Les livres d'Esdras et de Néhémie, comme les deux livres des Chroniques, utilisent des documents contemporains des faits rapportés. «Qu'on les date du début du IVe siècle ou de la fin du Ve, remarque S.W. BARON, *op. cit.*, p. 140, ils semblent relater (d'une manière sensiblement sûre et peu de temps après les événements) des développements historiques majeurs».

les troubles provoqués dans l'Empire perse par la révolte de Mégabyze avaient vraisemblablement déterminé le Grand Roi à composer avec les dynastes égyptiens[60].

Artaxerxès Ier, quelques années avant sa mort, a nommé Arsamès satrape d'Égypte. En effet, les papyrus d'Éléphantine mentionnent celui-ci depuis l'an 37 d'Artaxerxès Ier (428) jusqu'à l'an 17 de Darius II (407)[61]. Artaxerxès Ier meurt en 424[62]. Une querelle dynastique éclate en Perse[63]. Après quarante-cinq jours de règne, Xerxès II est assassiné par son frère bâtard Sogdianos. Celui-ci est supprimé six mois plus tard par Darius II (R. 424-404)[64]. Remarquons que le satrape d'Égypte, Arsamès, s'était soulevé contre Sogdianos et avait soutenu le futur Darius II[65]. De nombreux documents araméens nous apprennent que, sous le règne d'Artaxerxès Ier, les Juifs d'Éléphantine connaissent une période de paix et de prospérité[66]. Cependant, en l'an II de Darius (422), le Syncelle[67] signale un soulèvement en Égypte qui a dû être rapidement réprimé[68]. En 419, en effet, l'Égypte est toujours sous le pouvoir perse comme en témoigne un décret de Darius II, pris par l'intermédiaire de son gouverneur Arsamès (Arsham), relatif à l'observation de la Pâque dans la colonie juive d'Éléphantine[69].

Un nouveau soulèvement survient, au témoignage de saint Jérôme, en Égypte en 414/3[70], prélude, selon E. Drioton et J. Vandier, à la grande

---

[60] P. SALMON, op. cit., p. 213-216.

[61] F.K. KIENITZ, op. cit., p. 71; S.W. BARON, op. cit., p. 501.

[62] Thuc. IV 50. Cf. D. MALLET, Les rapports des Grecs avec l'Égypte (de la conquête de Cambyse, 525, à celle d'Alexandre, 331) (MIFAO 48), Le Caire 1922, p. 78; W.W. TARN, Persia, from Xerxes to Alexander, dans The Cambridge Ancient History VI, Cambridge 1927, p. 3.

[63] A. MORET, Histoire de l'Orient II. IIe et Ier millénaires (Histoire générale, éd. G. GLOTZ), Paris 1936, p. 793, qui note avec justesse que chaque succession au trône entraîne des guerres entre prétendants et affaiblit l'Empire perse; E. DRIOTON et J. VANDIER, L'Égypte (Collection «Clio» I/2), 3e éd., Paris 1952, p. 605.

[64] Ctésias, Pers. 44-48. — Darius II monte sur le trône à la fin de l'année 424. Cf. A.T. OLMSTEAD, op. cit., p. 355; E. DRIOTON et J. VANDIER, op. cit., p. 605. — H. DE MEULENAERE, Darius II, dans LÄ I, Wiesbaden 1975, col. 992-993, fait débuter le règne de ce souverain en 423 et rappelle qu'aucun monument, inscription ou objet ne peut lui être attribué avec certitude sur le sol égyptien.

[65] Ctésias, Pers. 37.

[66] E.G. KRAELING, op. cit., p. 31.

[67] Le Syncelle, p. 256 D.

[68] D. MALLET, op. cit., p. 79.

[69] A.E. COWLEY, Aramaic Papyri of the Fifth Century B.C., Oxford 1923, n° 21; S.W. BARON, op. cit., p. 200.

[70] Saint Jérôme, Olymp. 91,3 (414/3) : PL 27, col. 457-458. A. WIEDERMANN, Geschichte Aegyptens von Psammetich I. bis auf Alexander den Grossen, Leipzig 1880, p. 271, se trompe en datant cette révolte (qu'il suppose conduite par Amyrtée) de 415/4.

campagne de libération[71]. Nous ignorons si le chef de la rébellion était Amyrtée[72] ou un autre dynaste du Delta[73]. De 411 à 408, le satrape Arsamès, rappelé par Darius II, combat en Médie, en Anatolie et en Syrie[74]. Son absence a pu favoriser les désordres en Égypte. En 411, selon Diodore, l'alliance du «roi des Égyptiens» et d'un cheikh d'Arabie provoque le transfert d'une importante flotte perso-phénicienne vers la Phénicie menacée par les révoltés[75]. En 410, d'après les papyrus araméens, une persécution éclate en Haute Égypte contre les Juifs d'Éléphantine. Le temple de Jahvé, antérieur à Cambyse, est détruit par les Égyptiens[76]. Waidrang (ou Vidranga), gouverneur perse du district de Syène, participe, avec son fils, le chef de l'armée, au sac du temple[77]. En 408, Bagôhî, le gouverneur perse de Juda, intervient auprès d'Arsamès pour faire reconstruire le sanctuaire[78].

Une fois de plus, les populations belliqueuses et xénophobes du Delta se soulèvent[79]. Le 2 décembre 405, Amyrtée monte sur le trône des pharaons et inaugure la XXVIIIe Dynastie de Manéthon dont il sera le seul représentant. Son règne dure six ans et s'achève à la fin de l'année 399[80]. Amyrtée est vraisemblablement le fils de Pausiris et le petit-fils du dynaste Amyrtée, compagnon d'Inaros[81]. Comme Psammétique Ier, fondateur de la XXVIe Dynastie, dont il est probablement aussi le descendant, il provient de Saïs[82].

---

[71] E. Drioton et J. Vandier, op. cit., p. 605.

[72] Amyrtée a pu se soulever dès 414/3 et ne prendre le titre de pharaon que neuf ans plus tard. Cf. D. Mallet, op. cit., p. 80-81.

[73] D. Mallet, op. cit., p. 79, suppose qu'il y avait toujours dans le Delta plusieurs petits vassaux insoumis rattachés aux anciennes dynasties.

[74] E. Stern, art. cit., p. 74; E. Bresciani, art. cit., p. 363.

[75] Diodore XIII 46,6.

[76] A.T. Olmstead, op. cit., p. 364; E.G. Kraeling, op. cit., p. 31 et 104; F.K. Kienitz, op. cit., p. 74.

[77] E. Bresciani, art. cit., p. 364.

[78] B. Porten, op. cit. (n. 32), p. 130.

[79] P. Cloché, La Grèce et l'Égypte de 405-4 à 342-1 avant J.-C., dans Revue égyptologique n.s. 2/1-2 (1921), p. 83.

[80] Manéthon, chez F. Jacoby, FGH III C, p. 50, fr. 2-3. Cf. E. Bickermann, Notes sur la chronologie de la XXXe Dynastie, dans Mélanges Maspero I (MIFAO 66), Le Caire 1934, p. 77 sqq. Cet érudit, en établissant sur des éléments sûrs les dates du règne de Nectanébo II (359-341), a résolu définitivement le problème de la chronologie des XXVIIIe, XXIXe et XXXe Dynasties. Il est suivi actuellement par la majorité des érudits. Toutefois, plusieurs auteurs s'obstinent, sans motif valable, à faire coïncider le début du règne d'Amyrtée avec la mort de Darius II. Cf. P. Salmon, op. cit., p. 238-239, n. 5; H. De Meulenaere, Amyrtaios, dans LÄ I, Wiesbaden 1975, col. 252-253; J. von Beckerath, Handbuch der ägyptischen Königsnamen, Munich-Berlin 1984, p. 114 et 164.

[81] P. Salmon, op. cit., p. 239, n. 1.

[82] A. Moret, L'Égypte pharaonique (Histoire de la nation égyptienne, éd. G.

Au printemps 404, la mort de Darius II, déjà gravement malade depuis 405, et l'avènement d'Artaxerxès II Memnon (R. 404-358) encouragent encore la sécession de l'Égypte[83]. Les intrigues de la reine-mère Parysatis déclenchent des troubles dans l'Empire perse: Cyrus le Jeune prépare un soulèvement contre son frère Artaxerxès II[84].

Selon Manéthon[85], Amyrtée est alors roi d'Égypte, mais les papyrus d'Éléphantine nous apprennent que la Haute Égypte lui échappe encore et reste aux mains des Perses[86]. On ne trouve, toutefois, aucun cartouche d'Amyrtée ou d'Artaxerxès II sur les monuments égyptiens de cette époque[87]. À la fin de l'année 402, le pouvoir des Perses est toujours reconnu à Éléphantine[88]. Au cours de l'année 401, la Haute Égypte est conquise par Amyrtée. Celui-ci conquiert Éléphantine entre le 18 janvier 401 et le 19 juin 400[89].

Pendant ce temps-là, une armée perse dirigée par Abrocomas se concentre en Syrie pour marcher sur l'Égypte[90]. Mais, en 401, elle se

HANOTAUX, t. II), Paris 1932, p. 586; E.G. KRAELING, *op. cit.* (n. 35), p. 112. — La source historique principale concernant cette période est la «Chronique démotique» (recto du P. 215 de la Bibliothèque Nationale de Paris dont le début et la fin sont perdus) qui est probablement d'origine memphite et qui semble avoir été composée durant la deuxième occupation perse de l'Égypte ou au début de la période ptolémaïque. Cette œuvre de propagande, difficile à lire et à comprendre, n'a pas été écrite contre les Grecs mais contre les Perses. Elle reflète le point de vue des prêtres égyptiens sur la définition du bon souverain qui observe le rituel du couronnement, maintient les rites sacrés, fait don aux temples des dieux et protège l'Égypte des invasions étrangères. La «Chronique démotique» est donc fondée sur une théorie de la royauté solidement ancrée dans la tradition égyptienne. Elle doit être considérée comme un document d'une valeur historique comparable à celle des grandes histoires des auteurs grecs. Cf. J.H. JOHNSON, *The Demotic Chronicle as an Historical Source*, dans *Enchoria* 4 (1974), p. 1-17; ID., *The Demotic Chronicle as a Statement of a Theory of Kingship*, dans *The Journal of the Society for the Study of Egyptian Antiquities* 13 (1983), p. 61-72; ID., *Is the Demotic Chronicle an Anti-Greek Tract?*, dans *Grammata Demotika. Festschrift für Erich Lüddeckens*, Würzburg 1984, p. 107-124.

[83] Ctésias, *Pers.* 57; Xén., *Hell.* II 1, 8; *Anabase* I 1, 3; Diodore XIII 108; Plut., *Artaxerxès* 2-3. Cf. P. SALMON, *op. cit.*, p. 239-240, n. 9; H. DE MEULENAERE, *Artaxerxes II*, dans *LÄ* I, Wiesbaden 1975, col. 454.

[84] Xén., *Anabase* I 1, 1-2. Cf. D. MALLET, *op. cit.*, p. 83; W.W. TARN, *op. cit.*, p. 4; A.T. OLMSTEAD, *op. cit.*, p. 372.

[85] F. JACOBY, *FGH* III C, p. 50, fr. 2-3.

[86] E.G. KRAELING, *op. cit.*, p. 31.

[87] Le dernier cartouche de Darius II se trouve dans une construction du temple d'Amon de l'oasis d'El-Khargeh. Cf. H. GAUTHIER, *Le Livre des Rois d'Égypte* IV, *De la XXVe Dynastie à la fin des Ptolémées* (MIFAO 20), Le Caire 1916, p. 154-155; A. MORET, *op. cit.*, p. 585; J. VON BECKERATH, *op. cit.* (n. 80), p. 164.

[88] E.G. KRAELING, *op. cit.*, p. 31.

[89] Respectivement, A.E. COWLEY, *op. cit.* (n. 69), n°ˢ 7,1 et 35,1. Cf. B. PORTEN, *art. cit.* (n. 32), p. 400.

[90] Xén., *Anabase* I 4,3 et 5. Cf. P. SALMON, *op. cit.*, p. 241.

replie en apprenant que les forces de Cyrus se sont mises en marche pour renverser Artaxerxès II[91]. La rencontre décisive a lieu à Cunaxa, à vingt-cinq kilomètres de Babylone, et la mort de Cyrus met fin à la guerre civile[92]. Après la bataille, ses mercenaires grecs (les «Dix mille») proposent vainement au satrape Tissapherne de se mettre à son service pour l'aider à soumettre l'Égypte révoltée[93].

En 400, l'Égyptien Tamos, auquel Cyrus, avant le départ de son expédition, avait confié le gouvernement de l'Ionie et de l'Éolie ainsi que le commandement d'une flotte de 50 trières[94], se réfugie auprès du roi d'Égypte qui le fait supprimer pour s'emparer de ses biens[95].

«Les monuments égyptiens, comme le constatent E. Drioton et J. Vandier, sont muets sur le règne d'Amyrtée»[96]. Il est possible, toutefois, comme le suppose D. Mallet, que le pharaon Amyrtée ait été renversé par un compétiteur puissant[97]. Le papyrus de Brooklyn n° 13, malheureusement très mutilé mais dernier des textes araméens d'Éléphantine datés à ce jour (1er octobre 399), fait allusion au roi Amyrtée et à l'accession au trône du roi Néphéritès Ier (R. 399-393), dont le règne commence officiellement le 1er décembre 399[98].

Néphéritès Ier est le premier pharaon de la XXIXe Dynastie originaire de Mendès[99]. Il règne sur toute l'Égypte comme en témoignent les monuments qu'il a fait élever dans toutes les régions du pays[100]. Il ordonne la destruction de la colonie militaire juive d'Éléphantine[101]. À cette époque, il existait aussi une colonie militaire arabe à Tell el-

---

[91] Isocrate, *Philippe* 101, confirme que l'Égypte s'était révoltée au moment de l'expédition de Cyrus.

[92] Xén., *Anabase* I 8,1-29; Diod. XIV 22 sqq.

[93] Xén., *Anabase* II 1,14; 5,13. Cf. E.G. KRAELING, *op. cit.*, p. 112.

[94] Diodore XIV 19. Cf. Xénophon, *Anabase* I 2, 21; I 4, 2, qui confirme que cet Égyptien était au service de Cyrus et dirigeait une flotte de vingt-cinq trières au début de la guerre civile.

[95] Diodore XIV 35,3-5. Cf. P. SALMON, *op. cit.*, p. 241-242.

[96] E. DRIOTON et J. VANDIER, *op. cit.*, p. 606.

[97] D. MALLET, *op. cit.*, p. 85; J. YOYOTTE, *Égypte Ancienne*, dans R. GROUSSET et E.G. LÉONARD (éd.), *Histoire Universelle* I. *Des origines à l'Islam* (Encyclopédie de la Pléiade), Paris 1956, p. 257; CL. TRAUNECKER, *Essai sur l'histoire de la XXXe Dynastie*, dans *Bulletin de l'Institut Français d'Archéologie Orientale* 79 (1979), p. 420: «Il semble que ce fut par la force que Néphéritès ravit le pouvoir à la maison d'Amyrtée».

[98] E.G. KRAELING, *op. cit.*, p. 113 et 283 sqq.; B. PORTEN, *art. cit.*, p. 400. — R.S. BIANCHI, *Nepherites I*, dans *LÄ* IV, Wiesbaden 1982, col. 454-455, est d'avis que le nouveau pharaon a écrasé Amyrtée et l'a fait ensuite exécuter.

[99] H. GAUTHIER, *op. cit.*, p. 161; E. DRIOTON et J. VANDIER, *op. cit.*, p. 606.

[100] F.K. KIENITZ, *op. cit.*, p. 79 et 191-193; CL. TRAUNECKER, *art. cit.* (n. 97), p. 408-410 et 419-424.

[101] E.G. KRAELING, *op. cit.*, p. 115; E. STERN, *art. cit.* (n. 2), p. 74.

Maskhouta datant de l'occupation perse (Ve siècle?)[102] qui fut vraisemblablement aussi anéantie.

En 400, les villes grecques d'Asie Mineure, soutenues par Sparte, se soulèvent. Les Égyptiens profitent de cet état de choses pour traverser le désert du Sinaï et la plaine côtière de Palestine. Ils occupent la partie Sud de ce territoire ainsi que le prouve un fragment de stèle en pierre portant le nom du pharaon Néphéritès Ier trouvé à Gézèr[103]. Le pharaon mène également une politique d'alliance avec les Spartiates auxquels il envoie en 396 des troupes de secours, du blé et l'équipement de 100 trières. Cette cargaison tombera, toutefois, aux mains des Perses et de leurs alliés[104].

Les successeurs de Néphéritès Ier furent son fils Mouthis, qui ne régna que quelques mois durant l'année 393, et Psammouthis (R. 393-392)[105]. Achoris (R. 392-380) renverse ce dernier. Il s'intitule «celui qui renouvelle les couronnes» et il ordonne de marteler les cartouches de son prédécesseur[106]. On a retrouvé trente-cinq monuments qui furent édifiés en Égypte au cours de son règne[107].

Vers 389, le pharaon Achoris conclut une alliance avec Évagoras, roi de Salamine de Chypre, en lutte contre la Perse[108], et, par l'entremise de

---

[102] W.J. DUMBRELL, *The Tell el-Maskhuta Bowls and the «Kingdom» of Qedar in the Persian Period*, dans *BASOR* 203 (1971), p. 33-44; J. RABINOWITZ, *Aramaic Inscriptions of the Fifth Century B.C.E. from a North-Arab Shrine in Egypt*, dans *JNES* 15 (1956), p. 1-9; E. STERN, *art. cit.*, p. 74-75.

[103] R.A.S. MACALISTER, *The Excavation of Gezer* II, Londres 1912, p. 313, fig. 452; E. STERN, *art. cit.*, p. 75.

[104] Diodore XV 79; Justin VI 2; Orose III 1,8. Cf. D. MALLET, *op. cit.*, p. 87-90; A. MORET, *op. cit.*, p. 588; F.K. KIENITZ, *op. cit.*, p. 79-80. — On ne peut suivre P. CLOCHÉ, *art. cit.*, p. 84, lorsqu'il affirme que Néphéritès Ier mena contre le Grand Roi «une politique strictement défensive et d'assez médiocre envergure».

[105] F.K. KIENITZ, *op. cit.*, p. 80 et 193-194. CL. TRAUNECKER, *art.cit.* (n. 97), p. 405-406, souligne que nous n'avons aucune trace de Mouthis, fils (?) et successeur malheureux de Néphéritès Ier, dans les monuments et documents égyptiens; le même auteur (*ibid.*, p. 424) situe le règne de Psammouthis entre janvier 393 et janvier 392 et dresse (*ibid.*, p. 410-411 et 424-426) un relevé des monuments édifiés en Égypte au cours de son règne. — E. DRIOTON et J. VANDIER, *op. cit.*, p. 607 et 632, fixent erronément le règne de Mouthis en 393-391 et celui de Psammouthis en 391-390. — Voir aussi J. VON BECKERATH, *Psammuthis*, dans *LÄ* IV, Wiesbaden 1982, col. 1176.

[106] J. YOYOTTE, *op. cit.*, p. 257, qui situe le règne d'Achoris entre 390 et 378; F.K. KIENITZ, *op. cit.*, p. 80, 180 et 194-198; H. DE MEULENAERE, *Hakoris*, dans *LÄ* II, Wiesbaden 1977, col. 931-932, qui date le règne du pharaon de 393-380. CL. TRAUNECKER, *art. cit.* (n. 97), p. 404, 426 et 432, estime qu'Achoris était peut-être un fils illégitime de Néphéritès Ier ou un proche parent de branche illégitime aux yeux de Nectanébo Ier (dont le grand-père pourrait être Néphéritès Ier); le même auteur (*ibid.*, p. 411-419 et 426-435) donne une liste récente des monuments et inscriptions trouvés en Égypte et datés du règne du pharaon Achoris.

[107] F.K. KIENITZ, *op. cit.*, p. 194-198.

[108] Diodore XV 2,2-3. Cf. P. CLOCHÉ, *art. cit.*, p. 85; D. MALLET, *op. cit.*, p. 91; F.K. KIENITZ, *op. cit.*, p. 83.

ce souverain, avec Athènes[109]. Évagoras étend sa domination à l'intérieur de Chypre. Les Perses décident alors de se tourner d'abord contre lui avec le maximum de forces[110]. Évagoras, appuyé par Hécatomnos de Carie, dynaste de Mylasa, les Pisidiens, Achoris, pharaon d'Égypte, et le roi des Arabes[111], rassemble à Chypre une flotte et une armée importantes[112]. En 387, Athènes lui envoie une escadre de 10 trières avec des peltastes et des hoplites commandée par Chabrias[113]. Les alliés remportent des succès à Chypre. Évagoras s'empare d'une partie des côtes de la Cilicie et de la Phénicie avec l'aide des Égyptiens qui contrôlent la partie Nord de la plaine côtière de la Palestine et pendant une brève période Tyr et Sidon[114]. Deux inscriptions portant le cartouche d'Achoris ont été découvertes dans ces régions, l'une à Akko et l'autre à Sidon[115].

En 386, les députés de Sparte, d'Athènes, de Corinthe, d'Argos et de Thèbes signent à Sardes devant le satrape Tiribazos la paix d'Antalcidas qui laisse au Grand Roi toute l'Asie Mineure avec Chypre[116]. Achoris et Évagoras ne pouvaient désormais plus compter que sur leurs propres forces.

Le Grand Roi s'efforce tout d'abord de conquérir l'Égypte et lance sur ce pays en 385 une grande armée perse conduite par Tithraustès, Pharnabazos et Abrocomas, satrape de Syrie[117]. Mais elle se heurte à une solide défense car le pharaon Achoris a pris à son service le stratège athénien Chabrias ainsi qu'une armée de mercenaires grecs[118]. Chabrias organise la défense du Delta aux fins de le rendre inaccessible et inexpugnable[119]. Les travaux ne seront du reste terminés que sous Nectanébo Ier. Quatre siècles plus tard, le nom de Chabrias qui symbolise

---

[109] Aristophane, *Ploutos* 178. — Cette pièce a été représentée au début de l'année 388. Cf. P. CLOCHÉ, *art. cit.*, p. 85; D. MALLET, *op. cit.*, p. 92-93; F.K. KIENITZ, *op. cit.*, p. 83.

[110] Diodore XIV 98.

[111] F. JACOBY, *FGH* II 1 B, p. 558-559, fr. 103.

[112] D. MALLET, *op. cit.*, p. 94.

[113] Xén, *Hell.* V 1,10; Cornelius Nepos, *Chabrias* II. Cf. D. MALLET, *op. cit.*, p. 94; F.K. KIENITZ, *op. cit.*, p. 84; H. DE MEULENAERE, *Chabrias*, dans *LÄ* I, Wiesbaden 1975, col. 896.

[114] D. MALLET, *op. cit.*, p. 94; E. STERN, *art. cit.*, p. 75.

[115] A. ROWE, *A Catalogue of Egyptian Scarabs in the Palestine Archaeological Museum*, Le Caire 1936, p. 295, pl. XXXVIII; W.V. LANDAU, *Die Inschrift von Achoris, König von Ägypten*, dans *MVÄG* 9 (1904), p. 342-347, pl. XII; E. STERN, *art. cit.*, p. 75.

[116] Xén., *Hell.* V 1,31; Diodore XIV 110.

[117] Isocrate, *Panégyrique* 140.

[118] Diodore XV 29; Dém. XX 76.

[119] Diodore XV 42.

la transformation du Delta en un camp retranché ne sera pas oublié. À l'époque de Strabon, on appelait encore une forteresse située en avant de Péluse «le château de Chabrias»[120] et une forteresse située près du lac Maréotis «le bourg de Chabrias»[121]. Près de l'actuelle Alexandrie, une autre série de fortifications portait le nom de «bourg de Nicias», qui était un lieutenant de Chabrias[112]. La grande armée perse parvient à chasser les Égyptiens et les Chypriotes de Phénicie et de Palestine[123]. C'est ce qui explique vraisemblablement, comme le suppose E. Stern[124], la deuxième vague de destruction qui affecte les régions côtières de la Palestine et le Négueb aux alentours de 380 av.n.è. Mais les Perses tentent vainement durant trois ans, de 385 à 383, de pénétrer dans le Delta[125].

Le Grand Roi réunit alors une grande flotte et une armée considérable pour abattre la puissance d'Évagoras. Il en confie le commandement à son gendre Orontès et à Tiribazos. Évagoras réunit une flotte de 200 trières dont 50 envoyées par Achoris avec de l'argent et du blé. Mais il est écrasé par les escadres perses à Kition[126]. Il se rend alors en Égypte auprès du pharaon pour lui demander du secours. Il n'en obtient qu'un peu d'argent, rentre à Chypre et demande la paix aux Perses à la fin de l'été ou au début de l'automne 380. Il règne jusqu'en 374 sur Salamine de Chypre comme vassal du Grand Roi[127].

Achoris s'allie alors avec l'amiral Glos, fils de Tamos et gendre de Tiribazos, révolté contre le Grand Roi, qui sera assassiné peu de temps après[128]. C'est un de ses derniers actes politiques car la fin de son règne est troublée par de graves révoltes[129] et il est remplacé en 380 par Néphéritès II qui régnera quatre mois[130].

---

[120] Strabon XVII, p. 647; Pline, *Hist. Nat.* V 14: *Chabriae castra.*

[121] Strabon XVIII, p. 682.

[122] Strabon XVIII, p. 679; Dém., *De falsa legatione* 287; Aristagoras, dans C. MÜLLER, *FHG*, p. 98, fr. 3.

[123] E. STERN, *art. cit.*, p. 76.

[124] E. STERN, *art. cit.* (n. 1), p. 114.

[125] Isocrate, *Panégyrique* 140. Cf. F.K. KIENITZ, *op. cit.*, p. 85.

[126] Diodore XV 2-3.

[127] Diodore XV 4; 8-9; Isocrate, *Evagoras* 58-67. Cf. D. MALLET, *op. cit.*, p. 94-95; F.K. KIENITZ, *op. cit.*, p. 86-88.

[128] Diodore XV 9; 18.

[129] H. DE MEULENAERE, *La famille royale des Nectanébo*, dans *ZÄS* 90 (1963), p. 90.

[130] A.T. OLMSTEAD, *op. cit.*, p. 402; E. DRIOTON et J. VANDIER, *op. cit.*, p. 608 et 632 (qui situent le règne de Néphéritès II en 378); F.K. KIENITZ, *op. cit.*, p. 88; H. DE MEULENAERE, *art. cit.*, p. 90; CL. TRAUNECKER, *art. cit.* (n. 97), qui situe le règne de Néphéritès II entre juin-juillet et septembre-octobre 380 et qui rappelle que l'on n'a pas retrouvé en Égypte de monument de ce pharaon; R.S. BIANCHI, *Nepherites II*, dans *LÄ* IV, Wiesbaden 1982, col. 455.

En novembre 380, Nectanébo Ier (R. 380-362), fils de Tachos (ou Téôs), petit-fils de Néphéritès Ier, ancien commandant de l'armée du pharaon Achoris, renverse Néphéritès II et inaugure la XXXe Dynastie de Sébennytos[131]. Au début de son règne, il conserve auprès de lui l'athénien Chabrias en tant que conseiller militaire. Mais, en 380/79, des ambassadeurs perses se rendent à Athènes pour demander son rappel. Les Athéniens, désireux de se concilier les faveurs d'Artaxerxès II et de gagner les bonnes grâces de Pharnabazos, rappellent Chabrias à Athènes[132]. Il est d'ailleurs nommé stratège en 379/8[133]. Les Perses, après avoir obtenu le rappel de Chabrias, demandent aux Athéniens de leur envoyer Iphicrate, connu pour sa valeur militaire exceptionnelle. Les Athéniens leur donnent leur accord[134].

Depuis plusieurs années, les Perses concentraient à Akko, dans le Nord de la Palestine, des forces navales et terrestres considérables dont le commandement avait été confié à Pharnabazos, satrape de Cilicie, aidé de Tithraustès et de Datamès. Ils avaient réuni 300 trières, 200 navires à 30 rameurs, de nombreux vaisseaux de transport, 200.000 sujets asiatiques et 12.000 (ou 20.000) mercenaires grecs dirigés par l'Athénien Iphicrate[135]. Au printemps 373, on attend l'ordre d'Artaxerxès II pour se mettre en campagne. Des dissentiments éclatent dans le commandement de l'armée. Au début de mai, l'armée perse se met en marche escortée par la flotte le long des côtes syrienne et palestinienne[136].

Nectanébo Ier, qui a complété le réseau de fortification établi dans le Delta par Chabrias, attend ses adversaires près de la bouche Pélusiaque, qui, outre ses fossés et ses murailles, est protégée par des marais artificiels. Mais Pharnabazos et Iphicrate s'emparent par surprise de la forteresse qui défend la bouche Mendésienne. La route de Memphis est ouverte. Iphicrate veut attaquer tout de suite mais Pharnabazos décide d'attendre des renforts. La crue périodique du Nil et le harcèlement de la tête de pont perse par les troupes égyptiennes contraignent Pharnabazos à évacuer ses positions en juillet-août 373. Iphicrate, craignant une

---

[131] F.K. KIENITZ, op. cit., p. 89; H. DE MEULENAERE, art. cit., p. 90-93; J.H. JOHNSON, art. cit. (n. 82), dans Enchoria 4 (1974), p. 8; H. DE MEULENAERE, Nektanebos I, dans LÄ IV, Wiesbaden 1982, col. 450-451, qui situe le règne de ce pharaon entre 381/0 et 364/3; J. VON BECKERATH, op. cit. (n. 80), p. 115 et 164.

[132] Diodore XV 29. Cf. D. MALLET, op. cit., p. 100; F.K. KÌENITZ, op. cit., p. 89.

[133] Xén., Hell. V 4,14.

[134] Diodore XV 29.

[134] Diodore XV 41; Cornelius Nepos, Datamès 3; Iphicrate 2.

[136] Diodore XV 41; Polyen, Strat. III 9, 63. Cf. P. CLOCHÉ, art. cit., p. 90-91; D. MALLET, op. cit., p. 103-104; F.K. KIENITZ, op. cit., p. 90-91.

vengeance du satrape, regagne Athènes — où il succède à Timothée comme stratège de la flotte qui opère contre Sparte — tandis que les Perses regagnent leur base d'Akko[137].

L'armée perse reprend ses préparatifs pour une nouvelle invasion de l'Égypte. En mai 372, l'Athénien Timothée devient conseiller militaire auprès du Grand Roi[138]. Mais des problèmes logistiques et une épidémie paraissent avoir décimé cette armée qui a vraisemblablement été mise en déroute par les Égyptiens[139].

Artaxerxès II doit bientôt faire face à une grande révolte des satrapes qui va tenir ses armées en haleine de 366 à 360. Datamès de Cappadoce entre le premier en rébellion ouverte. Puis Ariobarzanès étend le mouvement de contestation de la Phrygie à l'Hellespont. Athènes et Sparte, vexées des relations amicales entretenues par le Grand Roi avec Thèbes, envoient à Ariobarzanès Timothée et Agésilas en 365. Orontès, beau-frère du Grand Roi, soulève contre lui en 363 la Lycie, la Pisidie, la Cilicie, la Syrie, la Palestine et la Phénicie ainsi que les cités grecques de la côte. Mausole de Carie favorise les rebelles. Seul Autophradatès de Lydie reste fidèle à Artaxerxès II[140].

Nectanébo Ier profite de la situation pour rétablir la prospérité en Égypte. On connaît une centaine de monuments et d'inscriptions datant de son règne[141]. À la fin de celui-ci, de 365 à 362, il associe vraisemblablement au trône son fils Tachos (ou Téôs)[142]. Ce dernier appuie la révolte des satrapes en Asie Mineure qui prive le Grand Roi de la moitié de ses revenus annuels et l'empêche d'avoir des moyens militaires suffisants pour mater la rébellion. Mais Orontès abandonne la partie et Théomithrès, qui avait obtenu de Tachos 50 vaisseaux et 500 talents d'argent, se soumet[143].

Tachos (R. 362-360), devenu pharaon à la mort de son père, se rend compte qu'il ne peut guère tabler sur une alliance avec les satrapes et s'adresse directement à Athènes et à Sparte. Il envoie deux ambassades à

---

[137] Diodore XV 42-43.

[138] [Dém.], *Contre Timothée* 25,28-29,60.

[139] Isée, *Nicostrat.* 7. Cf. G. STERN, *art. cit.* (n. 2), p. 76.

[140] F.K. KIENITZ, *op. cit.*, p. 92-93.

[141] A. MORET, *op. cit.*, p. 590; E. DRIOTON et J. VANDIER, *op. cit.*, p. 609; F.K. KIENITZ, *op. cit.*, p. 92 («Unter König Nectanebis hat Ägypten den Höhepunkt seiner Macht erreicht») et p. 199-212.

[142] E. DRIOTON et J. VANDIER, *op. cit.*, p. 609 (qui situent cette corégence de 466 à 461); F.K. KIENITZ, *op. cit.*, p. 95; J.H. JOHNSON, *art. cit.* (n. 131), p. 12-16.

[143] Diodore XV 90-92. Cf. D. MALLET, *op. cit.*, p. 109-110; F.K. KIENITZ, *op. cit.*, p. 93-94.

Athènes et à Sparte qui accordent à l'Égypte leur aide et lui dépêchent deux des meilleurs généraux de l'époque : l'Athénien Chabrias et le Spartiate Agésilas[144].

Chabrias devient le conseiller du pharaon en administration financière. Pour renflouer le trésor égyptien, il fait augmenter les impôts des particuliers, prélever les 9/10e des revenus du clergé et créer un emprunt de guerre exceptionnel[145]. Cette politique rend le roi impopulaire et lui aliène le clergé[146]. Avec cet argent, Tachos lève en Égypte 80.000 soldats, rassemble 10.000 mercenaires et équipe 200 trières[147]. Chabrias, nommé navarque de la flotte égyptienne, améliore la mobilité et l'armement des trières[148]. Agésilas reçoit le commandement des mercenaires et non, comme il l'espérait, celui de l'armée que Tachos décide d'assumer personnellement[149]. Il place à la tête des troupes indigènes son neveu Nectanébo et confie la régence à Tcha-hap-imou, père de ce dernier[150].

Au printemps 360, la flotte et l'armée égyptiennes, appuyées par des contingents de mercenaires grecs, occupent la plaine côtière de Palestine et de Phénicie. Tachos envoie Nectanébo assiéger des villes de Syrie où se sont réfugiées des garnisons perses. Mais son frère Tcha-hap-imou, profitant du mécontentement des Égyptiens, soulève le pays en faveur de son fils Nectanébo. L'armée égyptienne de Syrie prend le parti de ce dernier. Agésilas se rallie au nouveau pharaon. Chabrias est rappelé à Athènes. Tachos prend la fuite et se soumet à Artaxerxès II qui lui pardonne et lui promet des troupes pour reconquérir l'Égypte[151].

Nectanébo II (R. 360/359-341) quitte la Syrie et rentre en Égypte où il doit faire face à un autre compétiteur au trône appelé le Mendésien — sans doute un descendant des pharaons de la XXIXe Dynastie — qui est finalement écrasé par les mercenaires grecs d'Agésilas. Comblé d'honneurs, de cadeaux et d'argent, ce dernier meurt sur le chemin du retour à Cyrène[152].

[144] *IG* II² 1, 119; Diodore XV 90-92; Plut., *Agésilas* 36-37; Cornelius Nepos, *Chabrias* 2. Cf. F.K. KIENITZ, *op. cit.*, p. 212-214, qui donne une liste des inscriptions royales en Égypte; J.H. JOHNSON, *art. cit.* (n. 131), p. 10, qui situe le règne de Tachos entre 363/2 et 362/1; J. VON BECKERATH, *op. cit.* (n. 80), p. 116 et 164, qui le place entre 362 et 360.

[145] [Aristote], *Économiques* II 25, 37; Polyen, *Strat.* III 11, 15. Cf. P. CLOCHÉ, *art. cit.*, p. 102-104; D. MALLET, *op. cit.*, p. 111-113.

[146] D. MALLET, *op. cit.*, p. 113.

[147] Diodore XV 90; 92.

[148] Diodore XV 92,3; Plut., *Agésilas* 37; Cornelius Nepos, *Chabrias* III; Polyen, *Strat.* III 11,7,13-14.

[149] Diodore XV 92,3; Plut., *Agésilas* 37.

[150] Diodore XV 92,4. Cf. H. DE MEULENAERE, *art. cit.*, p. 90-93.

[151] Diodore XV 92,4-93; Plut., *Agésilas* 37-38. Cf. E. STERN, *art. cit.*, p. 76.

[152] Diodore XV 93; Plut., *Agésilas* 38-40. Cf. P. CLOCHÉ, *art. cit.*, p. 107-110; D. MALLET, *op. cit.*, p. 593; F.K. KIENITZ, *op. cit.*, p. 97-98.

L'Égypte est prospère sous le règne de Nectanébo II ainsi qu'en témoignent de nombreux monuments[153]. Le pharaon mène une politique fiscale modérée et associe le clergé aux bénéfices du commerce extérieur en lui accordant 1/10ᵉ des droits de douane perçus à Naucratis[154]. Il mène aussi une politique défensive contre les Perses qui, après avoir graduellement rétabli leur pouvoir dans le couloir syro-palestinien[155], tentent vainement, en 360 ou 359, d'attaquer l'Égypte sous la direction du prince héritier Ochos et peut-être même avec la participation de Tachos[156].

En 358, Artaxerxès II Memnon meurt et son fils Artaxerxès III Ochos (R. 358-336) monte sur le trône. Souverain énergique, il cherche à rétablir l'ordre dans l'Empire perse et parvient, après plusieurs années, à écraser la rébellion d'Artabazos, satrape de Phrygie maritime, qui dut se réfugier auprès de Philippe de Macédoine[157].

En 354/3, le Grand Roi se livre à de grands et longs préparatifs pour attaquer l'Égypte[158]. Au cours de l'hiver 351/350, l'armée perse, conduite par le souverain en personne, pénètre dans le Delta, mais ne parvient pas à s'emparer des forteresses qui barrent chaque bras du Nil. Les mercenaires grecs du pharaon, dirigés par Diophantos d'Athènes et Lamias de Sparte, contraignent leurs adversaires à la retraite[159].

Ce grave échec entraîne la révolte des cités chypriotes et phéniciennes conduite par Tennès, roi de Sidon, avec l'aide de Nectanébo II qui lui envoie 4.000 mercenaires grecs commandés par Mentor de Rhodes. Pour le pharaon, en effet, une Phénicie indépendante affaiblirait la menace

[153] D. MALLET, op. cit., p. 123; F.K. KIENITZ, op. cit., p. 99 et 214-230; H. DE MEULENAERE, Nektanebos II, dans LÄ IV, Wiesbaden 1982, col. 451-453, qui date le début du règne de ce souverain de 361/0; J. VON BECKERATH, op. cit. (n. 80), p. 116 et 164, qui le situe en 360.

[154] P. CLOCHÉ, art. cit., p. 112; D. MALLET, op. cit., p. 144-149.

[155] E. STERN, art. cit., p. 76.

[156] F.K. KIENITZ, op. cit., p. 99. Voir aussi Trogue-Pompée, Prol. X («Aegypto bellum ter intulit»); Le Syncelle, p. 487. — D. MALLET, op. cit., p. 154, situe cette campagne en 359.

[157] Diodore XVI 22,34,52. Cf. H. DE MEULENAERE, Artaxerxes III, dans LÄ I, Wiesbaden 1975, col. 454. — Une imitation d'un tétradrachme athénien trouvée en Égypte et datant de l'époque d'Artaxerxès III porte à la place des lettres grecques AΘE une légende en démotique «Artaxerxès Pharaon». Cf. E. LIPIŃSKI, Egyptian Aramaic Coins from the Fifth and Fourth Centuries B.C., dans Studia Paulo Naster oblata I. Numismatica Antiqua (éd. S. SCHEERS; Orientalia Lovaniensia. Analecta 12), Leuven 1982, p. 25 et n. 8.

[158] Dém., Sur les Symmories XIV 4-5,7,25,31.

[159] Isocrate, Phil. 101; Epist. VIII 8; Diodore XVI 40,1-3; 44,1; 48,1-3; Polyen, Strat. II 16; Frontin, Strat. II 3, 13. Cf P. CLOCHÉ, art. cit., p. 112-114; D. MALLET, op. cit., p. 155-156; F.K. KIENITZ, op. cit., p. 100; E. STERN, art. cit., p. 76.

perse sur l'Égypte. Ochos envoie contre la Phénicie Mazaios, satrape de Syrie, et Bélésys, satrape de Chypre, qui sont vaincus par les rebelles[160].

Le Grand Roi rassemble alors une formidable armée de terre de 300.000 fantassins et de 30.000 cavaliers appuyée par une flotte de 300 trières et de 500 vaisseaux de transport[161]. Il marche ensuite sur Sidon. Tennès trahit ses sujets en livrant sa ville qui est incendiée. Mentor et ses mercenaires passent au service d'Ochos[162].

Il semble que Juda ait pris part à la révolte des cités phéniciennes. Suivant Eusèbe[163] et Flavius Josèphe[164], un soulèvement se produisit dans cette province à l'époque de Tennès et, après une action punitive menée par les Perses, l'ordre fut rétabli et de nombreux Juifs furent exilés à Hyrcania sur la côte de la mer Caspienne[165].

À l'automne 343, l'armée perse s'avance sur l'Égypte. Ochos traverse les marécages du lac Sirbonis. Il y perd un corps d'armée, mais le gros de ses troupes passe et arrive devant Péluse. Le Delta, outre le système défensif établi par Chabrias, peut compter sur 20.000 mercenaires grecs, 20.000 Libyens et 60.000 Égyptiens. Mais Péluse est tournée par un canal et la flotte perse pénètre par les bouches du Nil. Nectanébo II, craignant d'être encerclé, se replie sur Memphis. Le satrape Bagoas et Mentor de Rhodes obtiennent la capitulation de Péluse, puis de Bubastis, au confluent de la branche Tanitique et de la branche Pélusiaque, sur la route de Memphis. Nectanébo II abdique à Memphis et s'enfuit en Haute Égypte où il meurt vraisemblablement en 341[166]. Un texte égyptien atteste encore sa présence par des dons au temple d'Edfou la dix-huitième année de son règne[167].

La conquête perse met fin à la reconstruction du temple d'Éléphantine par les Juifs revenus dans cette ville avec l'autorisation de Nectanébo II[168].

[160] Diodore XVI 40-46.

[161] Diodore XVI 40; Théopompe, dans F. JACOBY, *FGH* II 1 B, p. 592-593, fr. 263.

[162] Diodore XVI 45.

[163] Eusèbe, *Chronicon*, ann. Abr. 1657, éd. Schoene, p. 112.

[164] Flavius Josèphe, *Contra Apionem* II 134.

[165] E. STERN, *art. cit.*, p. 77.

[166] Diodore XVI 46-50. Cf. P. CLOCHÉ, *art. cit.*, p. 117-127; D. MALLET, *op. cit.*, p. 157-162; F.K. KIENITZ, *op. cit.*, p. 107 et p. 170-173.

[167] E. DRIOTON et J. VANDIER, *op. cit.*, p. 612.

[168] E.G. KRAELING, *op. cit.*, p. 115. — J'adresse l'expression de ma gratitude à MM. Édouard Lipiński et Jan Quaegebeur, professeurs à la Katholieke Universiteit Leuven, qui eurent la gentillesse de me faire part de diverses suggestions précieuses.

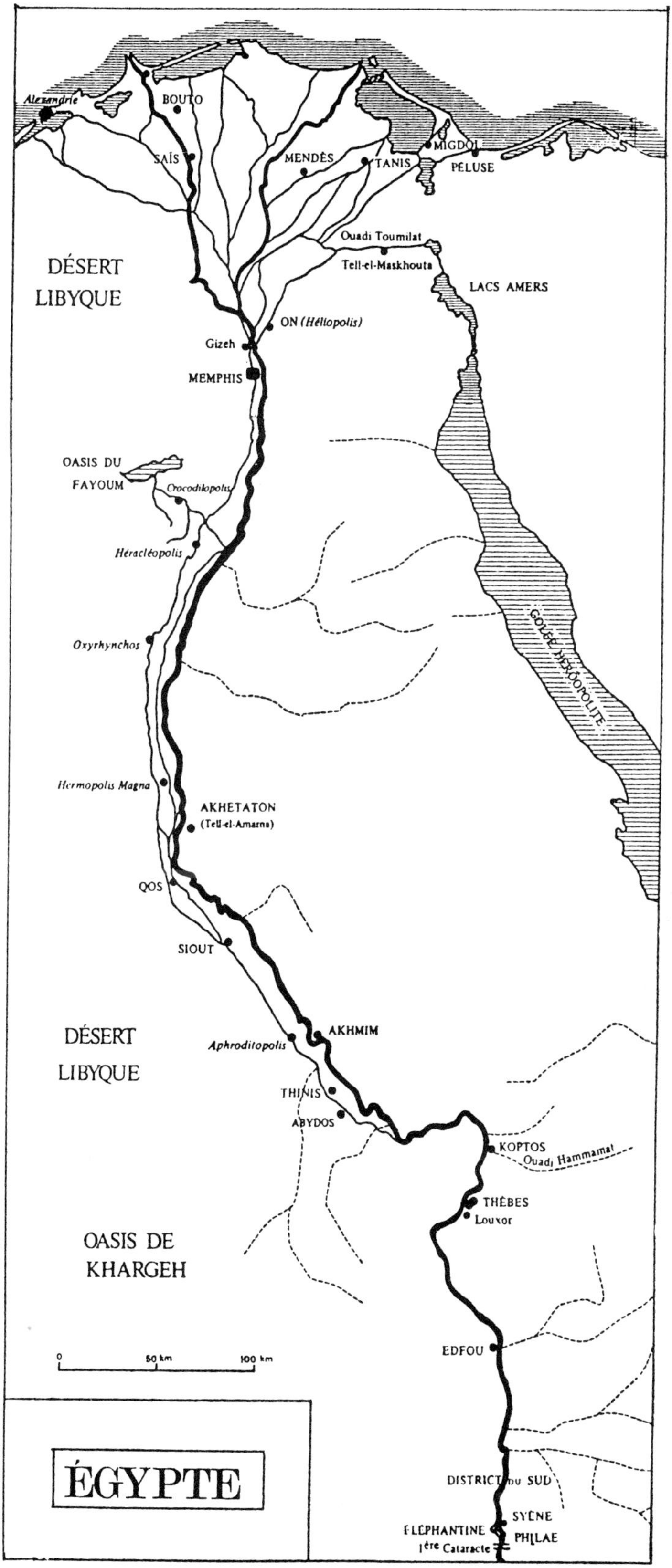
Alexandrie
BOUTO
SAÏS
MENDÈS
TANIS
MIGDOL
PÉLUSE
Ouadi Toumilat
Tell-el-Maskhouta
LACS AMERS
DÉSERT LIBYQUE
ON (Héliopolis)
Gizeh
MEMPHIS
OASIS DU FAYOUM
Crocodilopolis
Héracléopolis
GOLFE HÉROOPOLITE
Oxyrhynchos
Hermopolis Magna
AKHETATON (Tell-el-Amarna)
QOS
SIOUT
AKHMIM
DÉSERT LIBYQUE
Aphroditopolis
THINIS
ABYDOS
KOPTOS
Ouadi Hammamat
THÈBES
Louxor
OASIS DE KHARGEH
0
50 km
100 km
EDFOU
DISTRICT DU SUD
SYÈNE
ÉLÉPHANTINE
PHILAE
1ère Cataracte
ÉGYPTE

SUMMARY

The Persian period is among the most obscure ones in the history of Palestine. Egypt's vicinity caused this region — above all its coastal strip — to suffer from the extortions of the foreign armies passing through it during the numerous wars Egypt and the Persian empire fought. Thus, the study of the relationship existing between these two Near Eastern powers during the period going from the sixth to the fourth centuries B.C. will help us to understand better the history of Palestine.

Cambyses conquered Egypt in 525 and Darius I tried to incorporate this country into his empire after having crushed an Egyptian revolt. Faced with a new rebellion in Egypt, his son Xerxes I succeeded in restoring order in 485/4. During the reign of his successor Artaxerxes I, between 463 and 461, Inaros, son of Psammetichos, roused most of the Delta region against the Persians and obtained Athens' military aid. The Persians crushed the rebels in 454, but a pocket of resistance remained active in the Delta swamps and was supported by the Athenians up to 449/8. From 449 to 430, several Egyptian dynasts, having previously recognized the suzerainty of the Great King, ruled over their small principalities in the north of the Delta. During this period, the Jewish military colony, settled at Elephantine probably since the seventh century B.C., enjoyed a period of peace and prosperity. In 422 and 414/3, however, Egypt was again shaken by rebellion and, in 410, the Egyptians destroyed the temple of Yahweh, in Elephantine. In 405, pharaoh Amyrtaeus founded the Twenty-eighth dynasty, according to Manethon, and conquered Upper Egypt in 401.

At the beginning of the fourth century, pharaoh Nepherites I (Twenty-ninth dynasty) occupied the coastal plain of Palestine. Supported by Evagoras, king of Salamis in Cyprus, Achoris, one of Nepherites I's successors, seized the Cilician and Phoenician coasts, including Tyre and Sidon. The Persians succeeded in driving him out of these territories, but tried in vain, from 385 to 383, to penetrate into the Delta. In 380, Nectanebo I founded the Thirtieth dynasty, at Sebennytos. The Persians renewed their attacks in 373, but failed once again. From 366 to 360, Artaxerxes II was confronted with the widespread revolt of the satraps and Nectanebo took advantage of this circumstance to build up again Egypt's prosperity. His son Tachos, assisted by the Athenian Chabrias and the Spartan Agesilas, occupied the coastal plains of Palestine and of Phoenicia in 360. Domestic quarrels led to his downfall and to the withdrawal of the Egyptian troops. Nectanebo II resisted two Persian attacks led by Artaxerxes III Ochos, but in 343, in the course of a third attack, the latter succeeded, at last, in reconquering Egypt.

Pierre SALMON
Rue du Charme, 17
B-1190 Bruxelles.

THE EXCAVATIONS AT TEL DOR

EPHRAIM STERN

THE SITE AND ITS HISTORY

Biblical Dor, the capital of the Carmel coast, appears for the first time in connection with the Israelite conquest. It was one of the cities that joined the coalition headed by Jabin, king of Hazor, in the war against Joshua (*Joshua* 11,1-2). Its king too, suffered defeat at the hands of the Israelites (*Joshua* 12,23). The Canaanite city of Dor, located in the territory of the tribe of Manasseh, was not conquered until the time of David.

In the account of Wen-Amon's journey to Byblos (circa 1100 B.C.), the port of Dor is mentioned as a town inhabited by the Tjeker, one of the Sea Peoples who invaded the eastern Mediterranean area at that time.

During the reign of Solomon, Dor became the center of his fourth administrative district; it was governed by Abinadab, the king's son-in-law (*II Kings* 4,11). In 732 B.C., Tiglath-Pileser III conquered the city along with that section of the coastal plain which belonged to the kingdom of Israel. He turned it into the capital of the Assyrian province of Duru, extending from the Carmel to Jaffa.

The Eshmunazor inscription suggests that during the Persian period Dor was ruled by the Sidonians, but there was apparently also a Greek colony at Dor at that time.

During the Hellenistic period the city became an important fortress. At the end of the second century B.C. the tyrant Zoilus ruled both Dor and Straton's Tower, until Alexander Jannaeus took both cities from him. Pompey put an end to Hasmonaean rule in Dor and awarded the city autonomy and the right to mint coins. Its coins indicate that Zeus as well as Dorus (a son of Heracles, Dor's mythical founder), and Astarte-Aphrodite were worshipped at Dor.

A Jewish community is known to have existed in Dor at the time of Agrippa I (41-44 A.D.). In the Byzantine period the town declined, but remained a religious center, and bishops are known to have resided there from the fifth till the seventh century A.D. After that time the site was abandoned until the construction of the Crusader fortress of Merle.

According to the Greek and Latin sources, Dor is to be located between the Carmel range and Straton's Tower, later Caesarea. On the basis of these sources it is possible to locate Dor at Tell el-Burj, on the Carmel coast, which is one of the largest mounds in Israel (fig. 1).

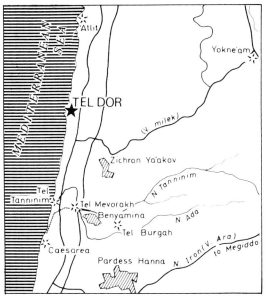

Fig. 1. — Location of Tel Dor.

THE EXCAVATIONS

The Dor project, started in 1980, is conducted on behalf of the Institute of Archaeology of the Hebrew University, Jerusalem, and the Israel Exploration Society, and is affiliated with California State University, Sacramento. The staff members are Prof. Ephraim Stern, of the Institute of Archaeology of the Hebrew University, director; Dr Renate Rosenthal, University of Goettingen; Prof. Lawrence A. Schiffman, New York University; Dr. H. Neil Richardson, professor emeritus, Boston University; Prof. Howard P. Goldfried, California State University, Sacramento. An underwater survey is carried out by the Center for Maritime Studies at Haifa University under Dr A. Raban. The expedition staff also includes: I. Sharon, assistant to the director; J. Berg, architect; B. Guz-Zilberstein and A. Gilboa, registrars.

Up to now five seasons have been concluded (1980-1984). Three areas were opened in 1980 on the eastern edge of the tell, and a fourth area (D) above the southern bay, in 1984. Below, we shall summarize the results of the excavation of these areas, from north to south, in the order C, A, C 1, B, and D (fig. 2).

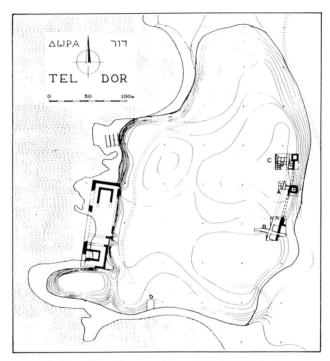

Fig. 2. — Plan of excavated Dor in the Hellenistic Age.

Area C — The Residential Quarter

In this area, almost nothing has survived of the *Byzantine* period. The first remains to be uncovered below the surface were from the *Roman* period, and belong to two phases. The upper phase, only a few centimetres below the surface, includes the scanty remains of a large and elaborate structure (or several structures), almost totally eroded to below floor level. The few sections preserved from the lower phase were mainly uncovered in the south-western corner of Area C and consist of fine masonry walls and cement and mosaic floors.

In the east, too, more walls and sections of cement floors were found which reached the line of the city-wall (see below). These remains are as yet too scanty to permit a comprehensive reconstruction of the stratum's plan; however, there is enough to testify that they were parts of elaborate houses.

Of the *Hellenistic* strata, which also belong to several stages, we have finally cleared the plan of a residential quarter erected in strict accordance with the Hippodamic system, the closest parallel to which may perhaps be found in the city plan of Olynthus in Greece.

Before discussing the residential quarter and its remains, it should be mentioned that in the eastern section of the area, near the mound's eastern edge, an additional part of the Hellenistic city-wall has been uncovered. It proved to be a continuation of that found in Area A (see below). It was built by the same method and here too we found a square tower projecting outside and to the east of the wall. It is about 30 m north of the tower found in Area A and is somewhat smaller and not so well preserved.

The picture emerging from our investigations in Area C to date is that a long row of stores and workshops stood along the entire length of the inner face of the city-wall. In one of these rooms we found a thick layer of crushed murex shells. The doors of the shops opened on a ruler-straight street running parallel to the wall from north to south. On the opposite side of the street, whose width is about 2 m, we found the fine façade of a long, narrow residential block of buildings. The eastern doors of each unit of houses open onto the street, opposite the row of shops. The building is about 20 m wide. We also uncovered its western side, which faces another street, parallel to that on its east. This elongated block of buildings, preserved to a height of over 2 m and traced for a length of dozens of metres, was probably crossed by passages leading from one street to the other, but these seem to fall outside the areas excavated so far. Another, identical building or block of houses existed to the west of this second street. The block was divided by partition walls lengthwise as well as widthwise into smaller units or 'apartments', whose doors opened in each case onto the closest street. It is reasonable to assume that what we have discovered is the ground floor, and that above it was another storey. In one or two places we found traces of basements. It seems also that the easternmost street, between the residence and the stores, was originally roofed to provide shelter for pedestrians (fig. 3).

The structure described above was in use, according to the finds, throughout the Hellenistic period, from the beginning of the third to the first century B.C. It seems not to have been violently destroyed, at least until the days of Alexander Jannaeus, but was rebuilt from time to time.

With each reconstruction the floor was raised, resulting in as many as three Hellenistic floor levels; the openings were blocked and the walls rebuilt on a higher level. In this way, from one phase to the next, the inner divisions of the building and the function of its rooms varied; for example, in one stage, two plastered storage pools for water were added. However, none of the alterations changed the external walls. Many coins were found on the different floors, as well as stamped handles from Greek wine amphorae, especially from Rhodes and Knidos (see below), yielding reliable dates for the different stages.

Some of the floors were of crushed chalk, others of pressed clay. The outer walls of the building were constructed in the usual style of the period, mostly of well-hewn hard sandstone ashlars laid in 'headers' — a sort of small-scale version of the city-wall. The inner walls and divisions, however, were built in the typical Phoenician style of ashlar piers with a fill of rubble. In conclusion, we may state that the plan of this building is Greek, while the structural details are Phoenician.

In several locations we dug below the Hellenistic floors and came upon strata of the Persian period.

Among the large amount of pottery uncovered on the various Hellenistic floors, we found many local vessels, including storage jars, jugs, bowls, juglets, pilgrim flasks, 'frying-pans', etc. Because of the relatively precise dating of the various stages of the buildings and the richness and variety of the finds, it is to be hoped that Dor will serve in future as a valuable key for understanding the ceramic typology and the development of the pottery of this period.

A large number of imported vessels from other Mediterranean countries were also found, notably some fine amphorae from Greece, whose handles were stamped by the producers of the wine. As mentioned above, most of these stamp impressions — already numbering more than a hundred — are from the island of Rhodes, while some are from neighbouring Knidos. We have succeeded in fully reconstructing several amphorae. Many other imported vessels have been recovered, of nearly all the familiar types known throughout the Hellenistic world.

Other noteworthy artifacts found include the dozen or so satyr's heads which originally decorated the rims of the beautiful large clay braziers found in almost every room, some bearing the name of their maker, *e.g.* *EKATAIOY*; clay figurines, mostly depicting naked female figures, or female heads; a beautiful stone incense burner, found close to the surface; many loom weights and stone spindle whorls; and faience and bone amulets executed in the usual Egypto-Phoenician style (fig. 13), amongst them a small bone pendant depicting the god Bes.

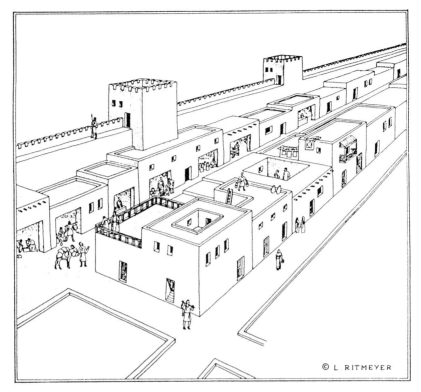

© L RITMEYER

Fig. 3. — Tel Dor. Areas A and C. Isometric reconstruction of the Hellenistic fortifications and of the residential quarter.

On the western side of area C we dug through the Hellenistic levels to reach those of the *Persian* period. It became clear that most of the Hellenistic walls had been robbed and only the floors were preserved; however, in the Persian phase the walls were found standing to a considerable height. Here we were able to confirm that the orthogonal plan of the residential quarter, consisting of long, narrow structures, had its beginnings in this period. During 1983-84 we dug below the street separating the two insulae and below the western insula. It seems that during the Persian period, in contrast to the Hellenistic level, the inner space of the houses was divided into long, narrow rooms. External and internal walls were also built in the Phoenician style, with pillars of masonry and a fill of field stones in between, utilizing the local *kurkar* (hard sandstone).

The excavations *inside* the western insula proved again that the detailed planning of the residential quarter, including the division into adjacent insulae, had started early in the Persian period, perhaps as early as the 6th century B.C., and continued to the early Roman period. During all of this long occupation (some 700 years) the plan of the quarter remains the same, and only the inner partition walls are changed. It was also confirmed that the quality of the builder's craftsmanship, in the classical Phoenician style, is even higher than in the Hellenistic period. Area A (below) presents a similar picture.

In the excavation of the western side of area C we removed several floor levels, and when we reached, in the deepest probe, layers of the *Iron Age*, we stopped working. The preservation of the Persian structures here is excellent. At some points the height of the walls — rebuilt several times during the Persian period and sometimes into the Hellenistic — reaches 3 m.

We intend to leave area C, with its unique preservation of Hellenistic (in the east) and Persian (in the west) structures, for visitors, and shift the excavation of lower strata to other areas.

Many local and imported pottery vessels were found in this area, and especially remarkable is the assemblage of East-Greek wares found in the lower phases.

At the eastern end of Area C, we extended the excavations into the region outside the Hellenistic city-wall. It was soon realized that the entire area is occupied by a brick construction at least 7 m wide. We believe that this is the Iron Age city-wall. Inside the Hellenistic city-wall we reached the Persian period levels in a narrow trench, and a similar picture to that of the western side emerged; the planning of the streets and houses was identical in both periods.

Area A — The Trial Trench

This area, located at the centre of the eastern slope of Tel Dor, was intended to be the main stratigraphic trench.

In the upper stratum, dating from the late Roman period, two sections of acqueducts, constructed of stone and plastered, were uncovered. The first crosses the centre of the eastern slope of the mound and is part of a continuous line which frequently protrudes from the surface. The second appears to extend from it and conveyed water inwards to the city, above the ancient remains. Under this stratum, the area is divided into two sections. The eastern section is completely occupied by a magnificent wall of the Hellenistic period which continued to be in use during the early Roman period; it is perhaps the most impressive fortification of this period discovered so far in Israel. The wall is built entirely of ashlar blocks of local sandstone, and is preserved to a height of more than 2 m. A tower extends outwards for 15 m; it was also constructed of large ashlars, laid so that the end of the blocks face outwards ('headers'). It has become clear that the tower is almost square and made of *kurkar* (hard sandstone) blocks, which are well dressed and of a size similar to the stones used in the city-wall itself. An interesting feature is the central square pier made of large stones, which no doubt served to support a wooden staircase giving access to the roof (fig. 4). As far as the writer is aware, this is the earliest example of this type of staircase ever found in this country, though it is quite common in the architecture of Palestine during the Roman and Byzantine periods. Another section of the city-wall further to the south was also uncovered.

From the coins discovered in the first season and subsequently cleaned and identified, we may conclude that the whole splendid fortification system was not erected at the very beginning of the Hellenistic period, but somewhat later, for the stratum below it contained a coin of Ptolemy II Philadelphos (285-246 B.C.). It is possible, therefore, that the complex was built in the latter part of his reign or shortly afterwards, since a literary source points to the fact that in the year 219 B.C. the well-fortified city withstood the siege of Antiochus III Megas (223-187 B.C.).

The Hellenistic tower was erected above the city-wall of the Persian period which runs below the southern half of the tower. It is made of large square *limestone* blocks.

In front of the tower, towards the east, part of a late Roman waterpipe was found. A large building of the same period was erected above both the Hellenistic city-wall and the tower, after they had gone out of use.

In the western side of the area, within the wall, two strata from the Roman period and two phases from the Hellenistic period were distinguished; below them there are three levels of the Persian period. Because of the narrow area excavated, it was difficult to determine the nature of the Persian period structures, though it seems likely that these were dwelling houses. In most of the levels a row of rooms was built against the wall; beyond this, there was a street, and across it, the façade of a large structure. Especially noteworthy is the continuity in construction from the Persian to the Hellenistic periods. We have excavated further through a stratum of the Persian period into a thick layer dating from the late Iron Age to a depth of about 1.5 m. It proved to be a continuous thick layer composed of ashes, bones of various animals, and local, Phoenician and Cypriote pottery sherds of the late Iron Age. The most significant find is an Egyptian scarab, probably of

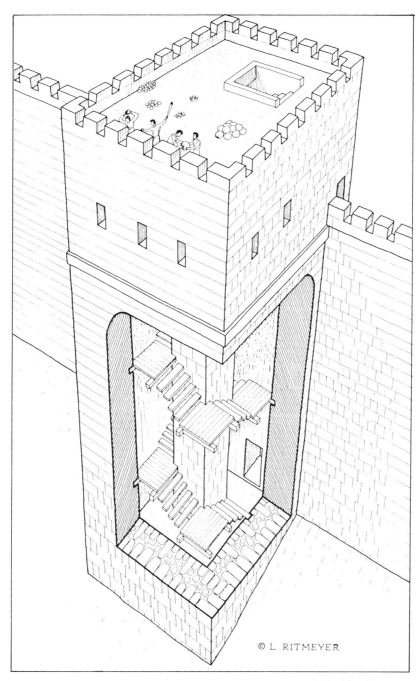

Fig. 4. — Tel Dor, Area A. Isometric reconstruction of the Hellenistic fortification tower.

the 26th Dynasty. No building remains of any kind were found and our provisional conclusion is that, in the late Iron Age, this was an industrial area.

Further west in Area A, the southern continuation of the residential quarter has been excavated in 1983-84. We also reached levels of the Hellenistic and Persian periods. Several superimposed floors were uncovered, as were some of the partition walls which divided the inner space of the house in the same manner as in Area C. Evidently, we found here another part of a residential stucture, including the eastern façade of the easternmost insula, and several rooms adjoining it. Here also the position of the façade remains unchanged in all Persian and Hellenistic phases, while the inner plan of the house changes several times. Fine quality of construction in the earlier periods is observed here too. In this area, we have uncovered local, East-Greek, and Attic pottery. Some remarkable finds are clay figurines, a conical glass stamp decorated with a Phoenician style sphinx, and a complete askos — found in a pit sunk into Iron Age deposits.

Area C 1

During the campaign of 1984, we connected area A to area C along the eastern edge of the tell; this area was labelled C 1 and was entirely dedicated to check the fortification systems, which were well preserved here. So far, five different fortification lines were uncovered. The uppermost is the one built by Ptolemy II, sections of which, including square projecting towers, were found in all areas. At some points, this wall was preserved nearly to the surface. Under this wall and in front of it, a wall constructed in the Phoenician ashlar pier style was exposed. This wall is somewhat thicker than usual in residential houses (nearly 1 m), and served as the outer limit of the town. Adjoining it are several long and narrow rooms (serving as sort of casemates) reaching up to the line of the easternmost street. It is worth remarking that several of the ashlar blocks here are dressed in the typical Israelite-Phoenician irregular marginal drafting. Such masonry is found at Tyre, Dan, Hazor, Megiddo, Samaria, etc., but here it is much later (see below).

The latter structures are built on top of a very wide (2.5-3 m) solid wall, part of which had already been exposed in 1980 under the Hellenistic tower of area A, and it is also known from area B (see below). It was built of large field stones in the offset-inset tradition.

We believe that the chronology of the three upper fortification systems (from bottom upwards) is as follow (fig. 5): the lowermost offset-inset

Fig. 5. — Tel Dor, Area C 1 looking eastwards (season 1984). Three superimposed
fortification systems:
a) Upper wall: Hellenistic city wall.
b) Intermediate Persian/Hellenistic «casemates».
c) Lower wall : Assyrian/Persian city-wall.

wall may have been built as early as the Assyrian period, and was
destroyed late in the Persian period — perhaps in one of the Phoenician
revolts of the first half of the 4th century.

The «casemate» wall above it was built immediately thereafter and
was used until the early Hellenistic period. Being inferior as a fortification, this wall was *replaced* by the massive ashlar city-wall in the days
of Ptolemy II (see below).

The uppermost wall was used at least until the early Roman period.

Two additional fortification lines were found *under* the ones described above, all built of mud brick. Their exact dimensions and
absolute chronology have not yet been determined, though the width of
the uppermost system (which probably includes a wall and a glacis) was

found to be more than 7 m (see below). In the opinion of the writer, the two systems date from the *Iron Age*, but so far the evidence is insufficient. We intend to complete the excavation of this area in the future.

Area B — The Gate Area

This area is located to the south of areas A and C. It is divided into two sub-areas B 1 in the north and B 2 in the south.

Here, in contrast to the other two areas, we came upon many remains of the late Roman period (Stratum 1), mainly of various industrial installations composed of plastered cisterns and water channels covered with large stone slabs.

The late Roman structures were particularly abundant in the southern part of the area, where a whole system of plastered cisterns, one above the other, has been found. In the northern and eastern sections of the area, remains of poorly preserved buildings were uncovered. One of these, in the east, was made of especially fine masonry. On the whole, however, these remains were badly eroded and did not permit us to reconstruct a reasonable plan.

In the following stratum, dating also from the Roman period (Stratum II), several phases could be distinguished. Here the main road leading into town from the eastern city-gate was excavated and a stone-paved monumental causeway and wide court were uncovered. Large stone slabs were found embedded in a thick layer of hard lime cement. We also uncovered a system of small drainage channels leading from the south down into the main drainage channel built of ashlar stones, which leads east-west through and out of the city-gate (fig. 6). On top of the stone slabs of this court, we came upon some sections of black granite pillars which evidently stood along its both sides.

At the western end of Area B, we uncovered the corner of a large house, whose base is made of a solid mix of cement and stones. The width of the walls here is about 1.5-2 m.

Almost nothing has been preserved of the city-gate of the Roman period, and the area had actually been razed down to the level of the paving of the road. At the site of the gate itself, the structures were found destroyed to below the surface of that period. All that remained were two drainage channels which were originally underground. The earlier one came from the south and turned sharply to the east in front of the gate. This system probably went out of use during the Roman period and was replaced by a second system composed of a stone-built channel running

Fig. 6. — Tel Dor, Area B. Main street leading to the gate of the Hellenistic period with the Roman sewer built into its centre.

along and below the main road into the gate area and from there in a straight line to the east.

At the eastern side of Area B and in its north, parts of large buildings from the Roman period have been uncovered. All these were similarly constructed from a solid mix of hard cement and stones. In one of the rooms at the north-eastern corner of Area B, built upon an earlier Hellenistic tower, we found parts of limestone tables, of the type now familiar from the excavations in the Jewish Quarter of Jerusalem, and a complete bronze bowl standing on three decorated feet. Also many vessels and potsherds of the Roman period, both local and imported, were found there. One of the rooms located close to the city-wall and gate served as an arsenal for the defenders, as indicated by a large accumulation of well-worked ballista stones. The stones were of different sizes and two were inscribed with Greek letters apparently giving their weight: IH (18) and KB (22).

During the 1984 season, when we enlarged area B 2 to the south and to the west, we found the continuation of a system of installations of the late Roman period. It includes several plastered pools. To one of these, a re-used sarcophagus was attached as a basin.

In the same season, two massive piers from the early Roman period have been uncovered; they were made of ashlars and cement, with a paved passage in between. It is possible that this was the point at which the Roman aqueduct from the Carmel entered the city. A second possibility is that this is part of a gate structure — later than the one found nearby, on top of the Hellenistic gate.

In the western part of the area we found the continuation of the paved Roman gate court, upon which the base of a statue or a monument was exposed and a water well at the centre of this courtyard. West of the courtyard, more parts of the monumental cement and ashlar building, which formed its façade, were exposed.

Strata III and IV in Area B are of the Hellenistic period and consist of a number of phases. The dominant structure in Stratum III is the city-wall which continues the sections uncovered in Areas A and C. At one location, the scanty remains of a defensive tower projecting to the east of the city-wall could be observed. This tower, unlike the two in Areas A and C, was badly damaged by the intensive Roman structures built above. Another structure found is a beautifully built Phoenician-style long wall with ashlar piers and rubble fill, which runs to the east of the city-wall towards the Hellenistic gate. We may conclude that this wall indicates the location of the main road leading to the gate in this period of which almost nothing has survived.

Inside the city-wall, in the western part of Area B, remains of the street running parallel to it were uncovered. This is the street discussed above in Areas A and C. Sections of residential buildings located to its west are probably also the continuation of those observed in the other areas. Thus, the residential quarter extended along the whole eastern part of the mound as far as the gate.

One of the rooms preserved under the stone pavement of the main Roman road proved to be a store room. It contained about a dozen large pithoi and jars. The building method used here was identical to that observed in Area C; walls were made of well-dressed local *kurkar* stones laid either as headers or alternating masonry piers and field stone fills. The Hellenistic finds in Area B included coins, Rhodian stamped jar handles, pottery vases, both local and imported, loom weights, spindle whorls, etc.

During the 1984 season we uncovered in B 2 the continuation of the structures by the city-gate. These are partly under the monumental building mentioned above. A relatively narrow street leads out from the gate into the town at this stage, where it intersects the first north-south street. Beyond this intersection it leads further west, in the direction of the probable position of the Agora, of the temple, and of the harbor. This street was flanked, no doubt, by shops and workshops, beyond the edge of the excavated area. Some of the constructions of this phase are in the Phoenician ashlar pier and rubble fill style, as was found in other parts of the tell.

The same plan is found also in the lower intermediate Persian/ Hellenistic phase (4th century B.C.), which is associated with the 'casemate' wall (see below). Also in B 2, the gates area, we excavated below the levels of the Hellenistic period. Here we uncovered two super-imposed city-gates (fig. 7). The uppermost one is a two-chambered gate, to which a stone-paved square leads from east to west. Under a layer of hard *kurkar*, we have uncovered the carefully laid stone paving of the entrance and both chambers of the gate, which was partially covered by the Hellenistic city-wall. One socket of the outer door, made of smoothed basalt, was found intact; in the centre of the entrance was found a socket for a bolt which closed the door vertically. The second door socket is still under the Hellenistic city-wall and we hope to discover it next season. We cleared also another stone-paved square which led from the inner entrance of the gate into the town. During the later phases of the Persian period, additional buildings were erected on the square; in the final Persian phase, the entire gate went out of use, leaving only a narrow passage from which a narrow street led into the town. During the 1984

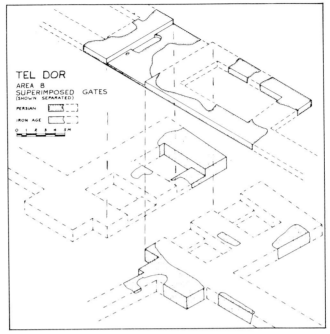

Fig. 7. — Tel Dor, Area B. City gates: Above — Persian period. Below — Iron Age.

season we exposed a long segment of the western wall belonging to the southern two-chambered gate tower and a small part of its eastern wall. We intend to complete its excavation (on both sides) in the future. Parts of a house built against this gate tower on the inside and the first north-south street beyond it were also exposed.

Remains of a four-chambered gate with a tower flanking each side of its façade were discovered below the two-chambered gate. The gate was only partially excavated but its plan, which closely resembles that of the four-chambered gate of Megiddo, is clear. There is, however, a striking difference between the two; the construction of the gate at Dor is much more massive. The width of one of the inner piers, which was entirely uncovered, was 2.5 m; it was built of two huge limestone boulders probably brought from the Carmel range. The western side of the pier, facing the city, was covered by well-dressed orthostats. The chambers were filled with brick material and their openings onto the gate passage were closed by a wide wall, evidently to strengthen the construction. It seems that the entire stone base of the gate was built at one time to carry the heavy superstructure of bricks. The gate is preserved to a

Fig. 8. — Tel Dor, Area B 2. Persian period. Fragment of a figurine of a horse.

Fig. 9. — Tel Dor, Area B 2.
Neo-Assyrian cylinder seal (above) and its impression (below).

height of about 2 m. This is apparently the first known example of
the monumental Phoenician architecture of the Iron Age; other such
structures have not yet come to light in Phoenician centres in the
eastern Mediterranean.

We may assume that the four-chambered gate was in use during the
ninth and eighth centuries B.C. and was destroyed by the Assyrians at
the end of the eighth century. In the two-chambered gate, only material
of the Persian period was found (fig. 8) and there can be no doubt that

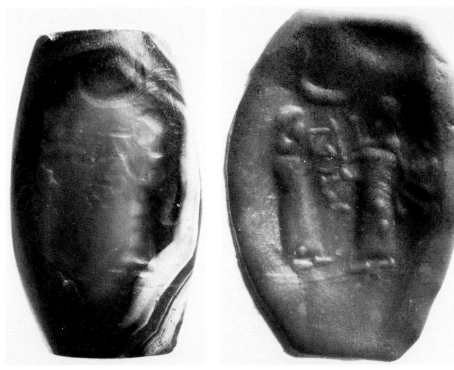

Fig. 10. — Tel Dor, Area B 2.
Neo-Assyrian stamp seal (left), found out of context, and its impression (right).

it was in use at the beginning of that period. It is, however, logical to assume that its construction and first use took place in the Assyrian period (figs. 9-10), and that only material of its last phase is represented. Below the four-chambered gate, we found a layer dating from the tenth century B.C. which we reached only in small sections. During the 1984 season, additional parts of the four-chambered Iron Age gate were reached. Among these are parts of its southern wall and some stones of the central pilaster on its southern half. As mentioned above, the excavation was hampered here by massive later remains.

In the northern part of Area B (B 1) we have worked through four phases of the Iron Age, the earliest of which probably dates from the tenth century B.C. This area, located close to and north of the city-gate, was at that time a residential quarter. In the lower phases, where the building remains are better preserved, one may discern a coherent plan; a line of rooms was probably attached to the city-wall and was flanked on the west by a narrow street, on the other side of which stood additional houses (fig. 11).

In this area, many pottery vessels and sherds were recovered, some local and other imported, and a unique find in the shape of an oval Iron Age stamp seal made of an animal's horn and depicting two stags standing on mountain-tops (fig. 12).

During the 1984 season we dug deeper into strata of the Iron Age in the western side of area B 1, after removing the upper Iron Age phase dating probably from the 7th-6th centuries B.C. Only some pits and installations of this phase were preserved; some of these pits, dug deep into older deposits, were not cleared until this season. In one of these we found, apart from typical pottery, an inscribed «shekel» weight. A lower stratum, to which belong the four-chambered gate (see above) and the mud brick wall, may date to the 9th-8th centuries and has two subphases. Some degree of planning is discerned inside the town. In the east there is a row of rooms, which may have been attached to the city wall. Opposite a narrow alley, running north-south, there is an additional residential unit. More of the town plan will appear, we hope, in the future, when we enlarge the exposure of these lower strata towards the gate.

In 1984 we succeeded in uncovering the town of the 10th and 11th centuries. It seems that the general layout in this phase is similar to the one of the 9th-8th centuries. The houses of both strata are generally built with stone foundations and mud brick superstructure.

Towards the end of the 1984 season, it was determined that there is a deep fill (at this stage deeper than 1 m) made of sand and brick material, with Middle Bronze Age potsherds (and the tooth of an hippopotamus!), in the centre of the excavated area, some 5-6 m inside of the later fortification lines. We may have reached here the top of an MB rampart, but this can only be verified by further excavations.

It is worth noting the existence, in the strata of the 11th-10th centuries, of several fragments of painted Cypriote pottery of types nearly unknown in Israel. We presume that they pertain under the «Proto-White Painted I» and early «Bichrome I» families. This, however, will be examined by experts.

During the same season (1984), we also worked on the eastern side of area B 1. Here we checked again the fortifications and found the same sequence, already described. The uppermost Hellenistic·wall was removed to expose the 'casemate' wall and the full width of the stone socle of the offset-inset wall of the Assyrian, Babylonian, and Persian fortifications. Its width here is over 3 m, that is some 0.5 m more than the

Fig. 11. — Tel Dor, Area B. Iron Age street uses.

width of the Hellenistic wall. Under all of these, the mud brick Iron Age wall was discoverd. Here, as in area C 1, there is a mud brick glacis attached to the outer face of the wall to protect its foundation. As we already know from previous seasons that there are several strata of Iron Age II-III inside the town, it is to be hoped that several stages will be found also in the fortifications to match these strata.

Area D

During 1984 we opened two small areas (D 1 and D 2) on the southern edge of the site, over the southern bay, which is probably the main

Fig. 12. — Tel Dor, Area B 1.
Iron Age : Conial stamp seal, made of horn (above), and its impression (below).

Fig. 13. — Tel Dor, Area C 2. Hellenistic period :
Egyptian faience pendant representing the goddess Toeris.

harbor of the town. The two areas are located on both sides of the section
cut by J. Garstang in the twenties. In the next season we intend to enlarge
this field and connect the two areas.

Area D 1 is the westernmost of the two and is located near the
Crusader fosse. We opened here five units — four in the flat area above
the edge of the tell, and one on the slope. In the upper portion we

discovered mainly structures of the Roman and Hellenistic periods. Of
the Roman period only a system of drainage channels was preserved.
These were used to drain streets which have been completely eroded.

An identical plan emerges from the Hellenistic remains. We have here
an east-west street from which a north-south street emerges perpen-
dicularly. Between these streets there are well-built houses.

Of the Persian strata we have, at this stage, only parts of walls, which
do not as yet form a coherent plan.

In Area D 2, which is located east of the former and closer to the bay,
four units have been excavated on the slope. In the two upper (northern)
units, we found again remains of the Roman, Hellenistic, and Persian
periods. In the upper phases the picture here is similar to that of D 1 — a
well built drainage channel which passed under the continuation of the
east-west street found there. In one of the units, south of the street, we
found part of a spacious Roman residence. The floor of one of the rooms
was decorated with a geometric polychrome mosaic. The preservation of
the Hellenistic stratum here was poor. On the other hand, it seems that
the area was used in the Persian period for store-rooms rather than for
residences. These structures, in which many storage jar fragments were
found, may be connected with harbor activities. Only the northern part
of these structures remains, as the entire southern section collapsed into
the sea.

In the two lower squares we uncovered the edge of a monumental
building recognizable by its thick wall of limestone boulders. According
to a probe excavation made by Avner Raban on the seaward side of the
same structure, the latter was used during the Iron Age and may have
been built even earlier. This area needs to be further enlarged and
deepened in order to explore the nature of this unique structure.

Many artifacts, mainly of the Roman and Hellenistic periods, were
found in Area D. Some of the Roman ones which deserve special
mention are a cup in the shape of a negro's head and a zoomorphic vessel
in the shape of a sheep.

Ephraim STERN
Institute of Archaeology
The Hebrew University
Jerusalem, Israel.

THE CITY OF DAVID
AND THE SELEUCID ACRA IN JERUSALEM

L. DEQUEKER

The history of the Seleucid Acra in Jerusalem illustrates the history of the Maccabean revolt from 167 to 141 B.C. The Acra was the stronghold of the Syrian troops in Jerusalem. It was built in the *City of David*, near the temple (*I Macc.* 1,29ff). At the same time it was the center of Hellenistic reform in Jerusalem, occupied by Greek colonists and Jewish renegades, collaborating with Antiochus IV Epiphanes (175-164 B.C.).

After three years of Jewish national resistance under the leadership of the priest Mattathias, Judas the Maccabee succeeded in conquering and rededicating the Temple, at the end of Antiochus IV Epiphanes' reign. But the Acra remained, as a permanent shame, a witness of foreign domination and apostasy in Jerusalem (*I Macc.* 4,41). Only his brother Simon succeeded in conquering the Acra, completing the liberation of Jerusalem in 141 (*I Macc.* 13, 49-53).

According to Josephus, who is, indeed, 'quite explicit in the matter'[1], the Acra was a huge fortress. Although situated in the Lower City, it was so high that it overlooked the Temple (*Ant.* XII 251-252). And the victory of Simon was so great that he not only conquered the fortress, but razed it to the ground. Simon should even have levelled the hill on which the Acra was built, so that the Temple would be higher than this awful place (*Ant.* XIII 215-217).

Notwithstanding Josephus' explicitness and detailed description (see also *Bellum* V 136 ff.), the location of the fortress is one of the most enigmatic and controversial questions in the topography of Jerusalem in the Second Temple period[2]. During the last century, the opinion prevailed that the Acra was located on the site of the Antonia fortress, that means in the north-western corner of the Temple area[3]. Until recently, scholars followed the opinion of Abel and Vincent, who

---

[1] N. AVIGAD, *Discovering Jerusalem*, Nashville Tennessee 1983, p. 64.
[2] E. SCHÜRER, *The History of the Jewish People in the Age of Jesus Christ (175 B.C.-A.D. 135)*. Revised and edited by G. VERMÈS and F. MILLAR, Vol. I, Edinburgh 1973, p. 154-155; N. AVIGAD, *op. cit.*, p. 64.
[3] F. ex.: C.W. WILSON, *Ancient Jerusalem*, in *PEFQSt* 1893, p. 164-166.

situated the Acra on the southern part of the western hill, on the other side of the *Tyropæon*, opposite the Temple mount[4]. Today, the Acra is situated south of the Temple, on the *Ophel* hill[5]. There is however no direct archaeological evidence. The problem is still mainly historical. Nevertheless, two sites south of the Temple are today shown as the place where the Acra was. First, the 'seam' or 'joint' about 32 meters north of the south-eastern corner of the Temple mount, where the Herodian extension of the wall joins, in a straight line, with the earlier masonry of the *Ḥaram*. According to Yoram Tsafrir, the earlier masonry is to be dated from the Hellenistic period and could be part of an artificial platform upon which the Acra obviously was built, close to the Temple[6]. Secondly, in the excavations of Professor Benjamin Mazar on the *Ophel*, south of the *Ḥaram*, a huge cistern is shown in front of the 'Double Gate', outside the Turkish wall, together with a large house with many rooms in front of the 'Triple Gate'. Meir Ben-Dov refers to both as parts of the Acra[7]. It will appear from the study of the texts that both sites do not correspond to the strict topography of the Acra.

In this paper I would like to analyse the literary and historical sources relating to the Acra, in the light of the recent archaeological researches in the City of David and the Upper City (*Jewish Quarter*). I will investigate the specific character of Josephus' account on the Acra, in comparison with the more historical account in *I Maccabees*. The outcome will be that the location of the Acra in the City of David, i.e. south of the

---

[4] F.M. ABEL, *Topographie des campagnes machabéennes*, in *RB* 30 (1926), p. 518-526; L.H. VINCENT, *Acra*, in *RB* 43 (1934), p. 205-236, reprinted in L.H. VINCENT-M.A. STÈVE, *Jérusalem de l'Ancient Testament*, Paris 1954, p. 175-192; F.M. ABEL-J. STARCKY, *Les Livres des Maccabées*, 3ᵉ éd. rev., Paris 1961, p. 88-89; E.M. LAPERROUSAZ, *Angle Sud-Est du «Temple de Salomon» ou vestiges de l'«Acra des Séleucides»? Un faux problème*, in *Syria* 52 (1975), p. 241-259; M. AVI-YONAH, *Archaeology and Topography of Jerusalem in the Time of the Second Temple*, in *Sepher Yerushalayim* I (Hebrew), Jerusalem-Tel Aviv 1956, p. 317-381. K.M. KENYON, *Jerusalem. Excavating 3000 Years of History*, London 1967, presents a variant of the theory, situating the Acra at the site of the Herodian Citadel, on the northern part of the western hill.

[5] J. SIMONS, *Jerusalem in the Old Testament*, Leiden 1952, p. 131-157; W.A. SHOTWELL, *The Problem of the Syrian Akra*, in *BASOR* 176 (1964), p. 10-19; Y. TSAFRIR, *The Location of the Seleucid Akra in Jerusalem*, in *RB* 82 (1975), p. 501-521. G. VERMÈS, in E. SCHÜRER, *op. cit.*, p. 154, n. 39 : «The site of this Acra is one of the most controversial questions in the topography of Jerusalem. It is probable that it lay on the southern spur of the eastern hill; south, that is to say, of the Temple mount. There can be little doubt that it was built on the site of the ancient Davidic city».

[6] Y. TSAFRIR, *art. cit.*; ID., *The Location of the Seleucid Akra in Jerusalem*, in *Jerusalem Revealed. Archaeology in the Holy City, 1968-1974*, Jerusalem 1975, p. 85-86.

[7] M. BEN-DOV, *The Seleucid Acra South of the Temple Mount* (Hebrew), in *Cathedra for the History of Eretz-Israel and its Yishuv* 1981, p. 22-35.

Temple, is less improbable than was thought by Abel and Vincent, once the epic character of Josephus' account and the exact meaning of the Acra as a Macedonian colony are recognized. Both Abel and Vincent accepted that the texts as they are suggest that the Acra was situated south of the Temple, on the spot of the old Davidic city[8]. In their understanding, however, this location was not possible in view of the fact that neither Judas after his successful campaigns nor Jonathan after his occupation of Jerusalem were able to capture the Acra. The Acra, as it was described by Josephus, was too important to be situated in the Lower City. It was a military fortress, higher than the Temple. From the time of David and Nehemia, one has to accept a shift in tradition. Since the name *Sion* had shifted from the S.E. hill to the Temple area by the time of the Maccabees, as it appears from *I Macc.* 10,10-11, it is legitimate to assume, that the tradition concerning the location of the City of David had also shifted[9].

I. *The Creation of a Greek Stronghold in the City of David: I Macc.* 1, 29-36 — JOSEPHUS, *Ant.* XII 251-252.

The building of a Syrian Acra in Jerusalem is mentioned by the author of *I Macc.* in the context of the plundering of Jerusalem by Antiochus IV, two years after the profanation and plundering of the Temple. Jerusalem was attacked and burnt to the ground, mainly for political reasons: the dubious position adopted by the Jewish leaders in the war between the Seleucids and the Ptolemies[10]. Syrian troops were gar-

---

[8] F.M. ABEL, *art. cit.*, p. 520: «Si l'on opine qu'à l'époque machabéenne le terme *Ville de David* a la même valeur qu'aux temps des Rois et de Néhémie, la question est réglée: la citadelle syrienne se campera sur la croupe de la colline qui s'incline depuis le Ḥaram jusqu'à Siloé, au point dominant les abords de la fontaine d'*Oumm ed-Daradj*»; L.H. VINCENT-M.A. STÈVE, *op. cit.*, p. 179: «La localisation de cette fameuse Acra syrienne serait déterminée dès l'abord s'il était légitime d'accepter comme une équation topographique absolue son identification avec la «Cité de David» au sens primordial, d'après (*I Macc.*) I, 33».

[9] F.M. ABEL, *art. cit.*, p. 525-526: «Nous jugeons suffisant d'avoir mis le lecteur en face de deux conclusions les mieux fondées: la première s'appuyant sur la rigueur des textes et l'invariabilité de l'onomastique, base assez précaire, comme nous l'avons vu; la seconde ressortant de quelques indices documentaires et de la considération du relief du sol; celle-ci plaçant l'Acra à l'extrémité orientale de la ville haute, au quartier juif actuel; celle-là sur le site même de l'antique Ville de David au sud du Temple».

[10] See P. SCHÄFER, *The Hellenistic and Maccabaean Periods*, in J.H. HAYES-J.M. MILLER (ed.), *Israelite and Judaean History*, London 1977, p. 539-604; P. SCHÄFER, *Geschichte der Juden in der Antike. Die Juden Palästinas von Alexander dem Grossen bis zur arabischen Eroberung*, Neukirchen 1983.

risoned in the subjugated city. «The city of David was turned into a citadel, enclosed by a high, stout wall with strong towers, and garrisoned by impious foreigners and renegades» (*I Macc.* 1, 33-34). But the Acra was more than a military garrison. The building of the Acra in the City of David was part of the process of Hellenistic reform, which is described in length by the author before the profanation of the Temple and the plundering of the city. *I Macc.* 1, 1-16 describes the 'Hellenization' of Jerusalem, culminating in the building of a gymnasium, a sports stadium in the gentile style (vv. 14-15). The end of the chapter (vv. 38-64) describes the process of Hellenization in the Temple: Jewish religion was forbidden, and a pagan altar was built on top of the altar of the Lord (v. 59).

In the context of Hellenistic reform one can assume that the Acra was a Macedonian colony, where the Jewish renegades, supporters of the new regime, also lived. The City of David became *their* stronghold: ἐγένετο αὐτοῖς εἰς ἄκραν (v. 33). *For them* refers to the troops, the 'powerful force' mentioned in v. 29, but even more to the 'impious foreigners and renegades' in v. 34, the protagonists of the Hellenistic reform.

The author of *I Macc.* always refers to the people living in the Acra by the general term οἱ ἐκ τῆς ἄκρας[11], or οἱ υἱοὶ τῆς ἄκρας[12]. He never refers to them as a φρουρά, which is the term used by Josephus at the time: a Syrian *garrison* in the Acra[13]. Occasional Syrian troops in the Acra are called δύναμεις, military forces[14]. More important, in the eyes of the author, were the renegade Israelites[15]. Their provocative attitude, in entering into the precincts of the Temple, and thus bringing defilement upon the sanctuary and doing violence to its purity (14,36), constituted a threat to the Temple (1,36). Moreover, their contacts with the king (6,21) made them a perpetual menace to the national movement in Israel (1,36). The Acra was more than a military fortress. It represented the whole Seleucid empire and the Hellenistic world in Jerusalem.

The lamentation on Jerusalem, *I Macc.* 1,37-40, calls the city a κατοικία ἀλλοτρίων, a colony of foreigners. Compare *Dan.* 11,39: «He

---

[11] *I Macc.* 4,41; 6,18; 10,7; 11,41-42; 13,49; comp. 14,36-37.
[12] *I Macc.* 4,2; comp. *Megillat Ta'anit* 5: bᵉnê ḥaqrā' bîrūšalēm.
[13] *Ant.* XII 252.362; XIII 39.182.215-216. Modern translations of *I Maccabees* quite often use 'Josephian' terminology with relation to the people in the Acra. For exemple, the *New English Bible*, Oxford-Cambridge 1970: 'the garrison of the citadel' (4,41; 6,18; 10,7; 11,41-42). However: 'men from the citadel' (4,2 and 13,49).
[14] Only three instances: *I Macc.* 2,31; 7,32; 9,52.
[15] *I Macc.* 1,33; 4,60; 6,21; 14,14.33-37.

(Antiochus IV Epiphanes) will garrison his strongest fortresses with aliens, the people of a foreign god».

With E. Bickermann[16], we understand the Acra as a Macedonian colony, which probably enjoyed the status of a Greek city[17]. From *II Macc.* 4,9 we know that Antiochus IV, in the beginning of his reign, agreed to enrol the men of Jerusalem as citizens of Antioch, or as *Antiochenes*. The existence of a *polis* in Jerusalem by the name of *Antiochia* does not necessarily imply the building of a new city, Hippodamic in plan, as Vincent and Avi-Yonah put it[18]. *Antiochenes* may refer to the status of the City of David as a Greek colony, together with the estates and territories that belonged to it. As recent archaeological excavations have made clear, the intensive re-settlement of the western (upper)-hill after the exile dates only from the Hasmonean period. Hellenistic Jerusalem was limited to the area of the City of David and the Temple[19]. The Acra of Jerusalem, i.e. the fortified Hellenized City of David, enjoyed the same status as the Hellenized city of Gezer (*Gazara*), which, after the victories of Simon the Maccabee, was claimed back, together with Joppe and the Acra, by Antiochus VII Sidetes, as cities belonging to his kingdom (*I Macc.* 15,28).

So much for the status of the Acra and its inhabitants. What about the topographical problem? With J. Simons we agree that the term ἄκρα in *I Macc.* designates the entire fortified city on the south-east hill, rather

[16] E. BICKERMANN, *Der Gott der Makkabäer. Untersuchungen über Sinn und Ursprung der makkabäischen Erhebung*, Berlin 1937, p. 71 : «Die Festung, 'die Akra (d.h. die Burg) in Jerusalem', ... war aber mehr als eine Zitadelle. Sie hatte auch eine zivile Bevölkerung ... Die Bestrafung Jerusalems hatte nämlich auch eine umfassende Konfiskation des Grundbesitzes für Folge, denn das eingezogene Land wurde den fremden Kolonisten zugewiesen. ... Eine derartige Kolonisation war eine beliebte Maßnahme, um eine störrische Provinz zu bestrafen und im Zaune zu halten».

[17] See G.M. COHEN, *The Seleucid Colonies. Studies in Founding, Administration and Organization* (Historia-Einzelschriften 30), Wiesbaden 1978, esp. p. 13-23: «At the colonial site the immediate need was to provide for the security and protection of the settlers. If they were being settled in an urban centre this normally meant handing over the acropolis or fortress of the city» (p. 23). F.M. Abel and L.H. Vincent were right in presenting the population of the Acra as: «Les gens du roi, ramassis de Syriens, de Grecs et de Juifs apostats» (F.M. ABEL, *art. cit.*, p. 518); «Une sorte de caravan-sérail pour les païens (κατάλυμα τοῖς ἔθνεσιν)» (L.H. VINCENT-M.A. STÈVE, *op. cit.*, p. 176).

[18] Y. TSAFRIR, *art. cit.* (n. 5), p. 505. See V. TCHERIKOVER, *Hellenistic Civilization and the Jews*, Philadelphia 1961, p. 165.

[19] N. AVIGAD, *op. cit.*, p. 71-72: «The decisive change in the city's development came about only after Jerusalem had again become the capital of an independent Jewish commonwealth». See M. BROSHI, *La population de l'ancienne Jérusalem*, in *RB* 82 (1975), p. 5-14, fig. 1.

than a fortress within it[20]. *I Macc.* 1,33ff. expressly states that the building of walls and towers turned the City of David into an Acra. 'Syrian Acra' and 'City of David' are considered as synonyms. However, in contrast to J. Simons and in the light of Prof. Y. Shiloh's excavations in the City of David (Area G)[21], we take it for granted that a fortress existed on the acropolis of the City of David, in the north.

In using 'City of David' and 'Acra' as synonyms *I Macc.* is not exceptional. It is traditional biblical terminology. The Greek bible uses the term 'Acra', apart from one or two exceptions[22], only as a synonym for 'City of David', i.e. the fortress, ἡ περιοχὴ Σιων, that David conquered from the Jebusites (*II Sam.* 5,7). The same holds true for the *Targum*, where ḥaqrā' de-Sion is the translation of the Hebrew meṣūdat Sion, which is the *City of David (ibid.)*.

Both terms, 'Acra' and 'City of David', belong to the history of the conquest of Jebus by David, *II Sam.* 5 and *I Chron.* 11. Did both terms have the same meaning in the time of the Maccabean revolt and the beginning of the Hasmonean dynasty, when the First Book of the Maccabees was written[23]? Both archaeology and Josephus, as I will demonstrate, say that they did. As was said before, modern excavations made it clear that Hellenistic Jerusalem did not extend beyond the area of the old City of David and the Temple.

The sports stadium or gymnasium, built by the Hellenists in the beginning of Antiochus' reign, was situated, according to the Second Book of the Maccabees, right under the citadel: ὑπ' αὐτὴν τὴν ἀκρό-πολιν (*II Macc.* 4,12). *II Macc.* 5,5 refers to the same place, when the Hellenized priest Menelaus took refuge in the citadel (εἰς τὴν ἀκρόπολιν) before Jason. This was before the plundering of the city (5,11-27). *II Macc.* does not refer to the construction of the Acra, but it is mentioned in the history of Nicanor: «Judas hung Nicanor's head from the citadel (ἐκ τῆς ἄκρας), a clear proof of the Lord's help, for all to see» (*II Macc.* 15, 31.35).

---

[20] J. SIMONS, *op. cit.* Contrast W.A. SHOTWELL, *art. cit.*

[21] Y. SHILOH, *Excavations at the City of David - I: 1978-1982. Interim Report of the First Five Seasons* (Qedem 19), Jerusalem 1984.

[22] *Deut.* 3,11: the *acropolis* of Amman; *II Sam.* 5,9: *Millo* = Acra!

[23] L.H. VINCENT-M.A. STÈVE, *op. cit.*, p. 187: «Rien ne prouve, en effet, que dans le langage de l'annaliste macchabéen «ville de David» ait conservé mieux son exacte valeur chorographique primitive que «Sion», transposé de la forteresse jébuséenne à la 'montagne du Temple'». Would the problem not be the reverse? «What is required is the positive proof that it ('City of David') did not preserve that meaning. Failing such proof there is no real basis for assuming any change» (J. SIMONS, *op. cit.*, p. 150, n. 1).

It is generally agreed today that the ἀκρόπολις of *II Macc.* was north of the Temple, at the spot of the former *Birāh* or fortress from the days of Nehemia : the fortress of the Temple, *ha-birāh ašer la-bayit* (*Neh.* 2,8 ; 7,2). It was the fortress, it is said, described in the *Letter of Aristeas* as ἄκρα τῆς πόλεως [24].

Scholars in the last century who situated the Acra of the Syrians in the north-western corner of the Temple, where in a later period Herod built the Antonia fortress, identified the ἀκρόπολις of *II Macc.* 4 and 5 with the Syrian Acra. Today it is agreed that after the destruction of Jerusalem, the Syrian garrison moved from the north to a new built Acra in the City of David.

However, if the enrolment of the inhabitants of Jerusalem as citizens of Antioch, *II Macc.* 4,9, refers to the Macedonian colony in the City of David, as pointed out before, then the ἀκρόπολις with the gymnasium is to be sought in the same area. We agree that the ἄκρα or fortress visited by Aristeas about 200 B.C. was north of the Temple; there can be no doubt about it [25]. But the ἀκρόπολις was a different place. By this term was meant the summit of the City of David, the *meṣūdat Ṣion* from the time of David. It was the center of Hellenistic reform, long before the plundering of the city. From the beginning of the Seleucid era in Judaea Syrian soldiers were garrisoned in the Acra fortress north of the Temple. After the sack of Jerusalem they came to the *polis* itself, to the City of David, which became their Acra, an occupied city, a Greek colony [26].

So much for the origin and situation of the Syrian Acra according to *I Macc.* Josephus records the facts in *Ant.* XII, the long history of the Ptolemees and Seleucids from the death of Alexander the Great up to Judas the Maccabee.

The building of the Acra is reported in §§ 251-252. Josephus' record is close to the text of *I Macc.* He refers to the desecration and spoiling of

---

[24] H. VINCENT, *Jérusalem d'après la lettre d'Aristée*, in *RB* 18 (1909), p. 556-575; F.M. ABEL-J. STARCKY, *op. cit.*, p. 243.

[25] A. PELLETIER (ed.), *Lettre d'Aristée à Philocrate* (Sources chrétiennes 89), Paris 1962, p. 155.

[26] Compare the different approach by Y. TSAFRIR, *art. cit.* (n. 5), p. 509-510: «Like a traditional Greek city Jerusalem was surrounded by a wall, including our urban suburb in the relatively lower area, and an acropolis in the upper one. This acropolis was the Temple Mt., i.e. the Temple and the City fortress. When Jerusalem spread to the neighbouring hills during the time of the Second Temple, the Lower City became known as a part of the acropolis hill — the Temple Mt., — due to the fact that it was built on the slopes leading up to it. This is apparently the reason for it also being called the «hill of the citadel», or in short — Akra — ἄκρα. However, in the sources connected with the Hasmonean revolt, the term Akra takes on its minimal meaning — not the whole acropolis, but the fortress only».

the Temple and to the destruction of the city by fire: «He (the king) burnt the finest parts of the city, and pulling down the walls, built the *Acra* in the Lower City, for it was high enough to overlook the Temple, and it was for this reason that he fortified it with high walls and towers, and stationed a Macedonian garrison therein»[27]. In contrast to *I Macc.* the prohibitions against the Jewish religion are mentioned before the burning of the city (§ 251). Moreover, Josephus adds two specifications with relation to the Acra. Firstly, the Acra built by Antiochus IV was the one in the Lower City: τὴν ἐν τῇ κάτω πόλει ᾠκοδόμησαν ἄκραν. Secondly, although situated in the Lower City, the Acra was higher than the Temple: ἦν γὰρ ὑψηλὴ καὶ ὑπερκειμένη τὸ ἱερόν.

Some paragraphs before, in the history of the Seleucid king Antiochus III the Great, Josephus mentioned the Ptolemaic garrison in the citadel of Jerusalem: ἐν τῇ ἄκρᾳ τῶν Ἱεροσολύμων (*Ant.* XII 133). The Jews helped the king to expel the Egyptians from the citadel: τοὺς ἐν τῇ ἄκρᾳ φρουροὺς τῶν Αἰγυπτίων (*Ant.* XII 138). In all probability, this was the Acra visited by Aristeas, north of the Temple, the former *ha-birāh ašer la-bayit*[28]. Dealing with Antiochus IV Epiphanes, Josephus specifies that the king built a new fortress ἐν τῇ κάτω πόλει, in the Lower City. Although built in the Lower City, Josephus adds, the Acra was high enough to overlook the Temple.

Before going on with the topographical question and asking where, in Josephus' understanding, this Lower City was, a word about the inhabitants of the Acra. In the newly built Acra, Josephus says, a Macedonian garrison was stationed: φρουρὰν Μακεδονικὴν ἐγκατέστησεν (*Ant.* XII 252). Nonetheless, there remained in the Acra those of the people who were impious and of bad character: ἔμενον δ᾽ οὐδὲν ἧττον ἐν τῇ ἄκρᾳ καὶ τοῦ πλήθους οἱ ἀσεβεῖς καὶ πονηροὶ τὸν τρόπον (*ibid.*). Although he does not mention the place of the gymnasium (*Ant.* XII 241), Josephus is aware of the fact that the Lower City was the center of the Hellenists in Jerusalem, even before the destruction of the city.

Josephus located the Syrian Acra in the Lower City. Why did he avoid the term 'City of David', which was in his source?

In *Bellum* V 136 ff., in the context of the Jewish revolt against Rome, Josephus gives a detailed description of the topography of Jerusalem. The passage is well known, but one element, as it seems to me, has not yet

---

[27] Transl. R. MARCUS, *Josephus with an English Translation* (The Loeb Classical Library), Vol. VII, Cambridge Mass. - London, repr. 1976.

[28] See R. MARCUS, *op. cit.*, p. 128, n. *d.*

been given a satisfactory explanation: the relation between the 'second hill', which is the Acra, and a 'third hill', claimed by Josephus to be lower than the Acra.

Jerusalem was built, Josephus says, in two portions facing each other on two hills, separated by a central valley, which is called the Valley of the Cheese-makers (τῶν τυροποιῶν). One part is the Upper City, the other part the Lower City. The hill of the Upper City was far higher than that of the Lower City. Owing to its strength it was called by King David the stronghold: φρούριον. We call it, Josephus says, the Upper Agora. The second hill was called the Acra. The Lower City laid around it in the shape of a double crescent (ἀμφίκυρτος).

Opposite the Acra, there was a third hill, by nature lower than the Acra, and once divided from it by another broad ravine. The ravine is no longer there, Josephus explains, since the Hasmoneans, during the period of their reign, filled it up in order to link the city to the Temple. They also reduced the elevation of the Acra by levelling its summit, so that it no longer blocked the view of the Temple.

It is clear from the description that the meṣūdat Ṣion conquered by David from the Jebusites was located by the author in the Upper City, on what still today is called *Mount Sion*. He holds the same view in *Ant.* VII, in the history of David (*Ant.* VII, 62-65). Since by the time of Josephus the City of David was situated in the Upper City, one understands the strange reversal of events that Josephus introduced in his account of the conquest of Jebus. According to the bible, David conquered first the meṣūdat Ṣion, the citadel, then the rest of the Jebusite city: *II Sam.* 5,6-10; *I Chron.* 11, 4-9[29]. In Josephus' presentation David took first the Lower City (τὴν κάτω πόλιν), then the citadel, which he calls ἄκρα according to the terminology of the Septuagint. In *Bellum* V, where ἄκρα refers to the Lower City, the Jebusite citadel taken over by David is called φρούριον.

The transfer of the Davidic tradition to the Upper City, in the west, is probably older than Josephus' time. It may go as far back as the Hasmonean period, when a new citadel was built, which later became Herod's palace. For the new Hasmonean rulers, who were not of Davidic descent, it was important to make the link with David and the ancient Davidic traditions of the bible[30].

---

[29] H.W. HERTZBERG, *Die Samuelbücher* (Das Alte Testament Deutsch 10), 4. Aufl. Göttingen 1968, p. 219: «Zwar hört es sich so an, als sei zwischen der 'Feste Zion' und der übrigen Stadt ein Unterschied gemacht; in der Chronik ist das noch mehr der Fall».

[30] A topic for further study in this respect would be the Tomb of David on Mount Sion. Does the location of the tomb at this place date from the Hasmonean period as well?

From the topographical description in *Bellum* V it is also clear that in Josephus' understanding the Lower City with the Acra was on the other side of the *Tyropœon* valley, i.e. on the eastern hill, south of the Temple[31].

Let me go into the details of this description.

The Acra, Josephus says, was separated from another hill by a broad ravine, which was different from the *Tyropœon*. That third hill was of its nature lower than the Acra: ταπεινότερος τε φύσει τῆς Ἄκρας. 'Of its nature' means the opposite of 'what it looks like'. As it appears to us, the author says, the third hill looks higher than the Acra, or Lower City. But originally, before the demolition of the Acra and the levelling of the summit of the mountain on which it stood, the hill opposite the Acra was lower than it. In the view of Josephus the Acra was even so high, so important, that the remains of it could fill up the broad ravine, separating the Lower City from the third hill.

I will come back to the reliability of those informations about the enormous height and the destruction of the Acra. For the moment it is only important to know where Josephus locates the fortress.

The third hill in the topographical description of *Bellum* V must be the Temple mount, more precisely its southern slopes known as Ὀφλᾶς, the *Ophel*[32]. In Josephus' understanding the Acra was situated in the Lower City, south of a ravine or depression which separated the Acra from the *Ophel* and the Temple mount, in the north[33].

Is there any trace of a ravine or a depression between the Temple mount and the Lower City? F.M. Abel in 1926 was strongly opposed to the 'duality' of the Lower City, as proposed by Josephus[34]. Hermann

---

[31] L.H. VINCENT-M.A. STÈVE, *op. cit.*, p. 185, had to admit : «Prises au pied de la lettre les données de Josèphe ramènent de gré ou de force au S. du sanctuaire».

[32] *Bellum* II 448; V 145-253; VI 355, obviously north of the Acra.

[33] See (!) F.M. ABEL, *art. cit.*, p. 521 : «Par ville basse Josèphe entend le quartier alors situé sur la colline *ed-Ḏehoura*, au sud de l'Ophel proprement dit. Il suppose même qu'entre ce quartier et le Temple existait au temps machabéen un ravin que les Asmonéens auraient comblé pour joindre le sanctuaire à la ville. Ainsi, la colline du Temple faisait face à la colline de l'Acra comme une troisième colline, celle de la ville haute étant cotée première. En conséquence l'historien juif donne une position qui concorde avec le site de l'ancienne ville de David». And further : «Ne nous laissons point, réplique Josèphe, égarer par l'aspect actuel des choses. Là où votre regard ne rencontre plus qu'une colline, il s'en trouvait jadis deux : l'une, celle du Temple, dont l'altitude était par nature (φύσει) moindre que celle de l'Acra, et l'autre celle que nous nommons Acra, autrefois base de la citadelle syrienne et maintenant couverte par la basse ville. L'art a modifié la nature au point de produire l'inverse de l'état originel» (*ibid.*).

[34] «Il n'y a plus à revenir sur la dualité de la colline inférieure. Opinion propre à l'historien juif ou qu'il partage avec ses contemporains, une telle supposition prête le flanc

Guthe (1881) linked his name with a transversal valley, which in his opinion ran from the *Tyropæon* to the Kedron valley, just above the Gihon-spring[35]. Notwithstanding the rejection of the opinion by many[36], there are clear indications of a depression (which is not necessarily a transversal valley) some 100 meters north of the soundings made by Guthe, i.e. immediately north of the area G in the excavations of Prof. Y. Shiloh[37]. Still tempting and scientifically valid is the thesis of Raymond Weill, who identified the biblical *Millo* as the filling ('*remplissage*', '*remblai*') of the depression (*pereṣ* — φραγμὸν: *I Kings* 9,15; 11,27) between the City of David and the Temple[38].

There can thus be no doubt about the place where Josephus situated the Seleucid Acra. It is where it was situated by *I Macc.* in the City of David. Josephus however did not indicate the place as the 'City of David', since in his days the 'City of David' was the Upper City, near the new citadel. The difference between Josephus and *I Macc.* is not in the location of the Acra, but in the enormous shape and military function he gave to it, as it will appear from the next paragraph.

II. *The Acra and the History of the Maccabean Revolt*

What was the position of the Acra in Jerusalem during the Maccabean revolt, especially with relation to the Temple? The chief events of the years 167-141 B.C., the period of the Maccabean opposition against the

à la critique, assez pour n'avoir pas rallié tous les suffrages. De l'avis de plusieurs, la vallée et le resaut rocheux imaginés au sud du Temple constituent un contresens géologique» (F.M. ABEL, *art. cit.*, p. 521-523).

[35] A.H. SAYCE, *The Topography of Prae-Exilic Jerusalem*, in *PEQ* 1883, p. 215-223: «Dr Guthe's recent excavations and researches have brought to light ... (that) a valley or depression formerly ran from the Tyropaeon to the Kedron valley, entering the latter a little above the Virgin's Spring» (p. 216; see the map on p. 214). R.A.S. MACALISTER, *A Century of Excavations in Palestine*, London 1925, referred to the valley as the *Ṣedeq*-valley.

[36] F. ex. C.R. CONDER, *Jerusalem of the Kings*, in *PEQ* 1884, p. 20-29: «We already possess so many observations as to render it impossible to suppose that any valley such as that shown on Professor Sayce's sketch can ever have existed ... It may therefore, I think, be considered proven that no valley dividing the Ophel spur in twain exists, and that any theory founded on this supposition is unsound» (p. 21).

[37] See Y. SHILOH, *op. cit.*, fig. 3. K. KENYON, *Jerusalem*, p. 35, refers to the depression (between the areas H and R) as the northern limit of the Davidic city. Y. TSAFIR, *art. cit.* (n. 5), p. 514-515, n. 35, refers also to the excavations of B. Mazar.

[38] R. WEILL, *La cité de David. 1913-1914*, Paris 1920, p. 17 ff., 24 ff.; *La cité de David. 1923-1925*, Paris 1947, p. 31 ff. (See especially Plate 1, with the indications of *Ravine* and *Escarpe dans le roc*). Compare J. SIMONS, *op. cit.*, p. 137-138, who rejects Weill's basic theory that already in the Jebusite period the later Temple Hill and the *Ophel* were settled. This theory does not invalidate the idea of the *Millo* as a fill between the *Ophel* and the City of David, contrast Simons. See also the LXX-version of *II Sam.*, 5,9: καὶ ᾠκοδόμησεν τὴν πόλιν κύκλῳ ἀπὸ τῆς ἄκρας.

Hellenization of the Holy City and the Seleucid occupation of the land, are the following. First, the purification of the Temple by Judas the Maccabee in 164. Then, the blockade of the Acra by Jonathan, *ca.* 142. Finally, the conquest of the Acra by Simon in 141.

a. During the purification and rededication of the Temple (*I Macc.* 4, 36-62), Jewish troops held back the people in the Acra (τοὺς ἐν τῇ ἄκρᾳ) from intervening, i.e. from going to the Syrian army and informing the king about the uprising in Jerusalem (4, 41). The situation is similar to 6, 21-22, during the siege of the Acra. Josephus greatly amplifies the meaning of the story by saying in *Bellum* I 39, that Judas expelled the Syrian troops from the Upper City and confined them to the Lower City, known as Acra, so that he was master of the Temple. In *Ant.* XII 318 he follows the text of *I Macc.*

After the celebration of the rededication, Judas encircled *Mount Sion*, which, in the terminology of the First Book of the Maccabees, is the Temple mount, with high walls and strong towers (*I Macc.* 4,60). His purpose was not primarily to entrench himself and to transform the Temple into a fortress, but «to prevent the Gentiles from coming and trampling it down as they had done before» (v. 60 b). The main objective was the purity of the Temple. Jewish soldiers prevented the Gentiles and Jewish renegades from defiling the holy precinct (v. 61). Again, Josephus changes the meaning of the passage. Following the location of *Mount Sion* in his time in the Upper City, Josephus says : Judas erected walls around *the city* (*Ant.* XII 326). After the death of Antiochus IV and important military successes in the land, Judas decided to get rid of the inhabitants of the Acra in Jerusalem. As Gentiles and apostates they were a continuous threat to the purity of the Temple (see *I Macc.* 14, 33-37) and a permanent support for the Gentiles in the land. Judas laid siege upon the Acra. This time, however, some of the besieged, Jewish renegades and Greek colonists, escaped and informed the king. The Syrian army reacted by laying siege to the Maccabean fortress Bethsur, and Judas had to withdraw (*I Macc.* 6, 18-32). Josephus' rendering of the episode strengthens once more the meaning of the Acra as a military fortress and its strategic position vis-à-vis the Temple. The Jewish faithful on their way to the Temple for the daily sacrifices, he says, were continuously being attacked and killed by the garrison and the renegades in the Acra, the fortress that overlooked the Temple (*Ant.* XII 362-363)[39]

[39] The same conception of a military fortress, controlling the Temple area and the

b. Under Jonathan, Judas' brother, i.e. in the middle of the second century B.C., the Jewish national movement of the Maccabees benefited greatly from the struggle for power in the Seleucid kingdom. Jonathan was recognized by the Syrians as high priest of the Jews (*I Macc.* 10, 18-20), and took up his quarters in Jerusalem. He began to repair and rebuild the city, and the Temple mount (ὄρος Σιων) was surrounded by a wall of squared stones (*I Macc.* 10, 10-11). Buth the Acra remained under Greek jurisdiction. Taking advantage of the deteriorating situation in Antioch, Jonathan finally decided to lay siege to the Acra by isolating it from its provisions. A high barrier separated the Acra from the city (*I Macc.* 12, 36).

How could Jonathan rebuild the city when the Acra and the City of David were still occupied by the Syrians? Are the big Maccabean towers on top of Area G in the excavations at the City of David (W 310 and W 308) part of the building activities of Jonathan[40]?

It seems much more appropriate to associate the work carried out by Jonathan, except for the Temple wall (10,11), with the resettlement and the fortification of the western hill in the second century B.C. The texts are quite explicit in the matter: «Jonathan *began* to repair and rebuild the city (ἤρξατο οἰκοδομεῖν καί καινίζειν τὴν πόλιν)» (10,10). «Jonathan convened the senate ... They assembled to rebuild the city (συνήχθησαν τοῦ οἰκοδομεῖν τὴν πόλιν)» (12,37). «Simon hurried on *the completion* (τελέσαι) of the walls of Jerusalem until it was fortified on all sides» (13,10)[41]. The western hill is explicitly mentioned in 12,37 as

---

access to it, appears in the post-talmudic *Scholion* of *Megillat Ta'anit*: «For they intimidated the children of Jerusalem and they could not pass during the day — only at night» (M. LICHTENSTEIN, *Die Fastenrolle*, in *HUCA* 8-9 [1931-32], p. 319). *Megillat Ta'anit* fixes the 23rd of Iyyar, the day of the conquest of the Acra by Simon, as a festival, as a day on which it is forbidden to fast and to mourn. Comp.! Y. TSAFRIR, *art. cit.* (n. 5), p. 531: ... *to eulogize*. Y. Tsafrir is influenced by this interpretation, proper to Josephus and later Jewish tradition, saying that «the purpose of the fortress was to control the Temple area, supervising the heathen ritual ... Thus the site of the Seleucid Akra is to the south-east of the temple, within an area later included in the Herodian temenos» (*ibid.*, p. 510). «The continued stress on the fact that the Akra was higher than the temple ... is easier to understand if we remember that two buildings one next to the other are being spoken of, and not a relative comparison of heights» (*ibid.*, p. 514).

[40] Thus K. KENYON, *Excavations in Jerusalem*, in *PEQ* 1962, p. 79; R. DE VAUX, *Jerusalem (Ophel)*, in *RB* 69 (1962), p. 99. Cf. W.A. SHOTWELL, *art. cit.*, p. 13: «It is at once obvious that the existence of a Maccabean tower from the mid-second century B.C. on this site demolishes Simons' theory that the Syrian Akra was the whole fortified area of the S.E. hill. It could not have been fortified by the Maccabees as part of their rebuilding of the city at the same time that it was occupied by a Syrian garrison».

[41] See N. AVIGAD, *op. cit.*, p. 72.

Χαφεναθα, i.e. the *Mishneh*, the 'second' or 'new' city quarter to be restored (ἐπεσκεύασεν)[42]. The 'wall along the ravine to the east', which is mentioned in the same verse, is then the wall of the City of David along the *Tyropœon* valley[43]. Together with the rebuilding and fortification of the new city quarter in the west, the purpose of Jonathan was to isolate the Acra together with the City of David. Would it be possible to associate the 'high barrier' (ὕφος μέγα), erected to separate the Acra from the city, v. 36, with the reconstruction of part of the walls of the City of David along the *Tyropœon* valley[44]?

Again, Josephus has his own reading of the texts. The wall of square stones built by Jonathan around Mount Sion (*I Macc.* 10,11) becomes a city-wall, as in the history of Judas (*Ant.* XIII, 41). Wrong as it may be as an interpretation of *I Macc.* 10,11, it brings to light that Josephus was aware of the fact that the Hasmoneans fortified the Upper City.

Jonathans' Temple wall is mentioned by Josephus further on, in the context of *I Macc.* 12, 36-37. The collapsed wall along the ravine to the east became the wall of the Temple: «Jonathan advised the people to set up again the part of the wall round the Temple which had been thrown down, and to fortify the Temple precincts by high towers» (*Antiq.* XIII 181).

c. Jonathan died before he could carry out his plans. It was his brother Simon who finally conquered the Acra and expelled the Gentiles and Hellenists from the City of David, two years after the people proclaimed him 'the great high-priest, general and leader of the Jews' (*I Macc.* 13, 41-42).

The conquest of the Acra in Jerusalem is preceded by the conquest of Gezer: *I Macc.* 13, 43-48. It is important to notice the parallelism between the two narratives. Gezer was a Greek city, like the Acra in Jerusalem. It was claimed back, together with Joppa and the Acra, by Antiochus VII Sidetes (*I Macc.* 15, 28).

The city of Gezer, which like the Acra in Jerusalem was mainly occupied by Hellenized Jews (v. 46), surrendered after a short siege.

---

[42] L.H. VINCENT-M.A. STÈVE, *op. cit.*, p. 177-179. Compare J. SIMONS, *art. cit.*, p. 155-157.

[43] The wall and the ravine are described as being 'to the east', seen from the 'rebuilt city' in the beginning of the verse.

[44] Compare Y. TSAFRIR, *art. cit.* (n. 5), p. 514, n. 35: «It may be possible to identify the internal wall between the city and the Akra with the line of fortification running from 'the Jebusite Tower' excavated by Duncan-Macalister to the gate dug by Crowfoot-Fitzgerald opposite it, on the western side of the Ophel».

«Simon expelled the renegades from the town, and after purifying the houses in which the idols stood, he made his entry with songs of thanksgiving and praise» (v. 47). Moreover, he strengthened the fortifications of Gezer and built a residence (οἴκησις) there for himself (v. 48)[45].

The conquest of the Acra in the immediately following paragraph (*I Macc.* 13, 49-53) follows the same pattern: siege, surrendering of the besieged, expulsion of the heathen population, cleaning of the place, — a ritual act, as in Gezer, — and solemn entry. Finally: improvement of the fortifications and residence of the conqueror.

Where exactly did Simon take up his residence, in the Acra, or on the Temple hill, i.e. in the City of David, or in a newly built citadel, north of the Temple, as is generally understood by the scholars[46]? The eulogy of Simon, *I Macc.* 14, 36-37, says explicitly that after the expulsion of «those heathen people in the City of David» (v. 36), Simon «settled Jews in it and fortified it for the security of the land and of the city» (v. 37).

The eulogy is conformable to the narrative in ch. 13. The people who took up residence with Simon (οἱ παρ᾽ αὐτοῦ) were not his relatives, who should have lived in the palace (the soldiers remained in the Acra), but his adherents, i.e. the Jews who conquered the Acra, in opposition to the Hellenists, the men in the citadel (οἱ ἐκ τῆς ἄκρας, v. 49). «Simon fortified the Temple hill opposite the citadel, *the Acra, where* he and his men took up residence» (v. 52). The point made is that in the days of Simon the fortress protecting the Temple mount was the Acra. Later on, as we will see, the Hasmonean rulers restored the Temple fortress in the north. The Hasmoneans remained in the Acra, in the City of David, at least until the death of Simon, 135/134 B.C. On the demand of Antiochus VII Sidetes, Simon was willing to negotiate about Joppa and Gezer, but the Acra remained Jewish patrimony (ἡ κληρονομία τῶν πατέρων ἡμῶν) (*I Macc.* 15, 34-35).

Josephus' account of the conquest of the Acra by Simon is very different: *Ant.* XIII 215-217. Simon not only conquered the Acra, Josephus claims, he demolished the fortress to the ground. He even

---

[45] See R.A.S. MACALISTER, *The Excavation of Gezer 1902-1905 and 1907-1909* (Publ. of the PEF), London 1912, and the inscription scratched on a stone of the 'castle': «May fire descend from heaven and devour the house of Simeon». The so-called 'Maccabean Castle' discovered by Macalister appears to be a city-gate from the Solomonic period, probably restored by Simon (Y. Yadin, *Solomon's City Wall and Gate at Gezer*, in *IEJ* 8 [1958], p. 80-86).

[46] L.H. VINCENT-M.A. STÈVE, *op. cit.*, 179.

levelled the hill on which the citadel stood, so that the Temple might be higher, and no foreign ruler should again occupy Jerusalem.

In *Bellum* V 139, as we have seen, the levelling of the Acra is attributed to the Hasmoneans in general. It has been suggested that the work, which in Josephus' account took three years (*Ant.* XIII 217), was done by Hyrcanos I, when a new fortress was built north of the Temple, at the place of the former *birāh* (*Ant* XVIII 91-92)[47].

The new fortress would have led to the complete demolition of the Acra. L.H. Vincent is more stringent, when he proposes that the Acra had to be demolished and the hill upon which it stood levelled, in order to build the prestigious palace of the Hasmonean kings on the same site, upon the western hill. In his opinion, the Hasmonean palace was built by Alexander Jannaios (103-76) or Salome Alexandra (76-67)[48].

A Hasmonean palace in the Upper City certainly existed in the days of Pompey, about 63 B.C., when the partisans of Aristobulos occupied the Temple area, — they entrenched themselves in the Temple fortress, — whereas the faction of Hyrcanos handed over to Pompey's army the city and the palace (τὰ βασίλεια) (*Ant.* XIV 59). But from *Bellum* II 344 it seems clear to me that this palace is to be located, not on the promontory of the south-western hill, in front of the *Tyropœon* valley, but on the site of the Herodian citadel and palace, where indeed important remains from the Hasmonean period have been discovered[49]. Josephus located the Palace of the Hasmoneans πρὸς τὸ πέραν τῆς ἄνω πόλεως, i.e. on the opposite side (= 'aḥarōn-western side) of the Upper City (*Bellum* II 344)[50].

By the construction of a new fortress or βᾶρις north of the Temple, the later *Antonia*[51], or of the Hasmonean palace[52] on the site of the later Herodian citadel[53], the Acra in the Lower City fell out of use. This is history. But its complete demolition, and even the levelling of the hill

---

[47] E. SCHÜRER, *Geschichte des jüdischen Volkes im Zeitalter Jesu Christi*, 3. Aufl., Bd. I, Leipzig 1901, p. 247.

[48] L.H. VINCENT-M.A. STÈVE, *op. cit.*, p. 191-192.

[49] Ruth AMIRAN-A. EITAN, *Excavations in the Courtyard of the Citadel, Jerusalem 1968-1969* (Preliminary Report), in *IEJ* 20 (1970), p. 9-17; EAD.-ID., *Excavations in the Jerusalem Citadel*, in *Jerusalem Revealed. Archaeology in the Holy City 1968-1974*, Jerusalem 1975, p. 52-54.

[50] The Xystus in front of the palace must have been an area between the Citadel and the bridge leading to the Temple (also *Bellum* IV 581).

[51] JOSEPHUS, *Ant.* XIII 307; XV 247-248.292.403-409; XVIII 91-92; *Bellum* I 402.

[52] JOSEPHUS, *Ant.* XIII 411; *Bellum* II 18.344.

[53] JOSEPHUS, *Bellum* I 402; V 161 ff.; *Ant.* XV 247-248.292.318; XX 189-190.

upon which it stood and the filling of the valley between the Acra and the Temple mount, are the scenery of a heroic epic created by Josephus in order to increase the merits of the Maccabean revolt, which in the past had led to a treaty with Rome (*I Macc.* 8,1-32; 12,1; 14,16-19). For Josephus, writing his *Antiquitates* in Rome, it was important to remember the good relations between Rome and Jerusalem in the Maccabean period[54]. The Maccabean revolt in Josephus' presentation is the heroic battle of the Jewish David against a new Goliath, entrenched in the huge fortress, overshadowing even the Temple.

* *
*

The problem of the Syrian Acra in Jerusalem is more than a problem of topography. Next to the topographical problem there is the problem of 'demography' and 'sociology'. Who were the people living in the Acra? Was it a Syrian garrison, or was it primarily a Greek πόλις, a colony? On the main point, which is the topographical problem, there is agreement between *I Macc.* and Josephus. Both locate the Acra south of the Temple, 'in the Lower City, south of the *Ophel*', according to the terminology of Josephus; 'in the City of David', according to the traditional biblical terminology of *I Macc.* On the sociological problem, and the problems of military strategy, Josephus and *Maccabees* differ considerably. In the presentation of *I Macc.* the threat of the Acra was less military than religious and political. The strategic meaning of the Acra lay not so much in its strength as a fortress, than in the fact that it represented the power, the law and order of the Seleucid empire. In the overstated and unrealistic description of Josephus the Acra became an immense fortress, rising high above the Temple, and garrisoned by Syrian troops, outcasts and Jewish renegades.

Is there any chance of discovering archaeological remains of the Acra? In contrast to J. Simons[55], I do believe that especially the *acropolis* of the

---

[54] J. SIMONS, *op. cit.*, p. 151: «Josephus has given free rein to his imagination, perhaps for no other purpose than to accentuate still more the heroic struggle of the Maccabees».

[55] J. SIMONS, *op. cit.*, p. 157: «In the field of archaeology the immediate consequence of this view would be, that all search for the remains or foundations of an individual fortified Syrian building somewhere on the S.E. hill is pointless, and that all city-plans including a neat picture of the Akra in the form of a beautiful octagon or similar figure on a chosen strategic point have no more than artistic value. On the other hand, all building remains revealing vestiges or repairs of a circumvallation of the City of David in the Maccabean period may have belonged to the Syrian Akra».

City of David was fortified by the Syrians and later on improved by Simon. Stratum 8 of Prof. Shiloh's excavations in the City of David is the Early Hellenistic Period, i.e. 4th-2nd centuries B.C., including the period of the Syrian occupation. Stratum 7 is attributed to the Hellenistic-Hasmonean period, from the second half of the 2nd century B.C. onwards. What does the absence of Stratum 8 mean in the *Interim report* of Area G, which is, as I hope to have demonstrated, the site of the Acra[56]?

Although no clear archaeological remains of the Acra have thus far been found in the City of David, the presence of the Hellenists in the area is clearly revealed by the immense number of handles of large wine-jars or amphorae from Rhodes and other Greek islands, bearing seal impressions in Greek. Such handles were discovered in the City of David in much greater number than anywhere else in Jerusalem[57].

L. DEQUEKER
K.U.L. — Fac. Lett. Wijsb.
Blijde Inkomststraat 21
B-3000 Leuven, Belgium.

[56] Y. SHILOH, *op. cit.*, p. 20.

[57] Y. SHILOH, *op. cit.*, p. 29-30: «More than 350 handles of Hellenistic amphorae, bearing Rhodian seal-impressions, were found in our excavations, in addition to the hundreds of similar handles found in earlier excavations in the City of David, by Macalister, Crowfoot and Kenyon. Such a large quantity is especially outstanding in the light of the sparsity of such finds in the widespread excavations adjacent to the Temple Mount and in the 'Upper City' ... This statistical datum provides further evidence for the main concentration of the Hellenistic settlement in Jerusalem in the region of the City of David, at least up to the outbreak of the Hasmonean Revolt». See J. SIMONS, *op. cit.*, p. 91; N. AVIGAD, *op. cit.*, p. 77-79. L.M. VINCENT-M.A. STÈVE, *op. cit.*, p. 192, disapproved the argument haughtily.

GENERAL INDEX

ORIENTALIA LOVANIENSIA ANALECTA